Stafford Library
Columbia College
1001 Rogers Street
Columbia, MO 65216

Fights of Fancy

FIGHTS OF FANCY

ARMED CONFLICT IN

SCIENCE FICTION AND FANTASY

Edited by George Slusser and Eric S. Rabkin

Stafford Library
Columbia College
1001 Rogers Street
Columbia, MO 65216

The University of Georgia Press   Athens and London

© 1993 by the University of Georgia Press
Athens, Georgia 30602
All rights reserved
Designed by Louise OFarrell
Set in 10/13 Sabon by Tseng Information Systems, Inc.
Printed and bound by Thomson-Shore, Inc.
The paper in this book meets the guidelines for
permanence and durability of the Committee on
Production Guidelines for Book Longevity of the
Council on Library Resources.

Printed in the United States of America

97 96 95 94 93   C   5 4 3 2 1
97 96 95 94 93   P   5 4 3 2 1

Library of Congress Cataloging in Publication Data
Fights of fancy : armed conflict in science fiction and
fantasy / edited by George Slusser and Eric S. Rabkin.
p.   cm.
Includes bibliographical references and index.
ISBN 0-8203-1454-4 (alk. paper).—
ISBN 0-8203-1533-8 (pbk. : alk. paper)
1. Science fiction—History and criticism.   2. Fantastic
fiction—History and criticism.   3. Combat in literature.
4. War in literature.   I. Slusser, George Edgar.
II. Rabkin, Eric S.
PN3433.6.F54   1993
809.3′876—dc20   91-40085
                                              CIP

British Library Cataloging in Publication Data available

Contents

Introduction
Wars Old and New: The Changing Nature of Fictional Combat
    George Slusser and Eric S. Rabkin   1

1. Reimagining War
    Eric S. Rabkin   12

2. Science Fiction and the Semantics of Conflict
    Reginald Bretnor   26

3. Wrangling Conversation: Linguistic Patterns in the Dialogue of Heroes and Villains
    Gary Westfahl   35

4. Warfare Celestial and Terrestrial: Osip Senkovsky's 1833 Russian Science Fantasy
    Louis Pedrotti   49

5. "The Evils of a Long Peace": Desiring the Great War
    Laurence Davies   59

6. Armed Conflict in the Science Fiction of H. G. Wells
    Arthur Campbell Turner   70

7. Fights of Fancy: When the "Better Half" Wins
    Rosemarie Arbur   79

8. Vietnam and Other Alien Worlds
    Joe Haldeman   92

9. Evolution and Salvation: The Iconic Origins of Druillet's Monstrous Combatants of the Night
    Paula Rea Radisich   103

10. You're History, Buddy: Postapocalyptic Visions in Recent
Science Fiction Film
        Peter Fitting   114

11. The Apocalyptic Mirage: Violence and Eschatology in *Dhalgren*
        David Clayton   132

12. Demonic Therapy: Reading the Holy Word in the Mushroom Cloud
        Scott Dalrymple   145

13. The Hidden Agenda
        Martha A. Bartter   155

14. Third World Fantasies
        George Slusser   170

15. Solos, Solitons, Info, and Invasion in (and of) Science Fiction Film
        Brooks Landon   194

Contributors   209

Index   211

Fights of Fancy

Introduction

Wars Old and New:
The Changing Nature of Fictional Combat

George Slusser and Eric S. Rabkin

When the casual reader thinks of science fiction and fantasy, the image of warfare comes to mind at once. In their themes and icons, these two genres appear to have kept alive the "epic" strain in literature—feats of arms in the service of great causes. Traditionally, SF has transposed individual deeds of valor and decisive battles to the broader framework of outer space. And traditional fantasy relocates these same deeds in alternate and "other" worlds. Both forms sing of arms and the man in vistas that are not just national or eschatological but cosmic and evolutionary as well. This is our first impression, and in terms of traditional texts, the impression seems true.

Let us go back to the Anglo-Saxon origins of SF—to H. G. Wells. Certainly in the Wellsian tradition we seem destined to reenact *The Iliad*. Wells's *War of the Worlds*, the classic invasion scenario, presents Earth as another Troy. But how easy it is, in this genre, to turn things around. We Earthlings can become the Greeks; we can invade other planets and expand our military conquests across galaxies. Wells gave this paradigm the longest view possible in his seminal *The Time Machine*, though here the "invader" is an observer rather than a combatant (in the 1960 film version, however, he leads a successful insurrection of Eloi against Morlock). In his novel *Star Maker*, Olaf Stapledon sought to fill in the blanks between now and the end of things. In doing so he developed the cosmic epic far beyond our single species and its destiny—but only to multiply panoramas of war and conflict. Subsequent space epics may not have sustained Stapledon's pan-species vision, but they invariably maintained, indeed gleefully augmented, his landscape of intergalactic wars. As Leslie Fiedler puts it, a host of such works, from Doc Smith to *Star Wars*, instead of giving us macrohistory, "end by creating space-time horse operas, intergalactic feudal romances, or pseudo-epics, in which petty earthside heroism is projected upon the empty stretches between stars."[1]

Armed conflict appears to be ubiquitous in SF. Certainly, on the iconic level, along with the spaceship we find the ray gun and the uniform of the interstellar soldier to be common "signs" of the genre. So widespread is their use that, even when a more lyrical book comes along, the first spontaneous reflex is often to bring forth the warlike icons. An example is the first paperback edition of Ray Bradbury's *Martian Chronicles* (Bantam, 1951). Although hardly peaceful (Mars evolves against a backdrop of atomic war on Earth), the book retains an elegiac distance from war throughout. This cover, however, depicts a stream of soldiers, tough and lantern-jawed, pouring out of an invading spaceship, with guns, radios, and binoculars in their hands. All of which, of course, has no relation whatsoever to the actions in the text. It is a knee-jerk reaction within the genre, one that corresponds to the casual reader's automatic association of SF with warfare and armed conquest—and in extreme cases with militaristic jingoism, such as that in Robert Heinlein's notorious *Starship Troopers*. And indeed that reader, to a large degree, is correct in this association. For SF has spawned what seems a virtually inexhaustible stream of janissary and "merc" fictions, leading to such self-fulfilling prophesies as Jerry Pournelle's *There Will Be War*.

Moreover, the "fantasy" commonly referred to in the compound *fantasy and science fiction* is heroic fantasy, which by its popular name, "sword and sorcery," is inexorably linked to warfare. This kind of literature is as old as *Gilgamesh* and focuses on the individual heroic quest within a collective context, a quest marked by prodigious feats, both of arms and of cunning. Cunning and skill because the epic model here is just as much Odysseus as Achilles. In recent heroic fantasy, however, a rival form has come to the fore, which depicts full-scale re-creation of battles or military campaigns in some alternate or "legendary" context. It is as if fantasy since William Morris were reversing the direction of medieval literature, gradually turning away from the novel of chivalry backward toward the embattled world of *The Song of Roland*. Novelists such as David Drake today re-create epic battles with a great precision of detail, discussing tactics like military historians and pondering at length such things as the relative virtues of different types of combat sandals. In a very real sense this heroic fantasy seems connected, through its obsession with martial arts, inextricably with SF. Perhaps this is why the French critic Pierre Versins considers *Gilgamesh* the first SF novel. And is not Jules Verne's archetypal SF hero, Captain Nemo, by virtue of his name an avatar of Odysseus, himself a paradigm for the chivalric knight who turns away from the spectacle of collective war to roam across a landscape of individual feats of arms and cunning, in search of a lost harmony, a personal grail of sorts? Did not Heinlein, the archetypal SF writer, seek to make explicit this link by treating the same chivalric scenario indifferently in an SF novel, *Have Space Suit, Will Travel*, and in a heroic fantasy, *Glory Road*? Finally, what is the difference, in terms of didactic presentation, between David Drake's military science and Robert L. Forward's physics lessons?

Even horror, the most private and intimate of the forms attendant on science fiction and fantasy, is invariably associated with violent, even armed, conflict. To understand horror we must invoke the Hobbesian sense of "war," as Eric Rabkin does in his essay in this volume: the violent anarchy of man against man, which results in nasty and brutish acts and short lives within the community that has fallen prey to it. The result is the manhunt as monster hunt, in which armed bands of citizens hunt down and destroy the rebellious and destructive element in hopes of restoring civil order. Again, the crossover with SF is obvious: from Wells's *Invisible Man*, through the film version(s) of *Frankenstein*, to the skillful miscegenation of SF and horror in Ridley Scott's *Alien*.

Armed conflict appears to be the common denominator of these forms. But at this juncture, nothing is left for readers but to accept or reject. Readers either praise SF and fantasy for depicting warfare as a necessary instrument for change, and mark themselves as technocrats, or, if they see themselves as "humanistic," they damn these forms for the violence they would do to the established (if not preordained) order. Whatever the case, readers seek deeper causes for the sickness—in a national psyche or in some collective unconscious. Such a response, however, tends to force the writers of SF and fantasy themselves into two adversarial categories—hawks and doves. If this division is all there is, then these forms, insofar as they deal with warfare, are propagandistic rather than speculative in nature. Their imaginations of war can only sing the glory of the epic battle, or damn it as irredeemably destructive.

It is perhaps surprising that none of the essays in this volume deals specifically with Doc Smith or Heinlein or sword and sorcery. Nor do they deal, except indirectly, with the opposite "pacifistic" tendency of these genres toward the monitory tale. The critics and authors who responded to the call for essays on the theme of armed conflict in fantasy and science fiction appear to have shifted their focus away from stories of spatial or territorial conquest toward newer, and less obvious, battlefields: the war of temporal logistics, whose model is Vietnam; urban war in the streets; the struggle for the human psyche that is the battle of the sexes; and finally, the war to control technology, from today's nuclear industry to tomorrow's information networks. The responses of the authors in this volume tell us much about the nature of SF and fantasy. For if these are to be speculative genres, they cannot stop at simply imagining war, for that is merely to depict again, in different guises, what has been depicted before—new retellings of the old story. They must rather, to use Eric Rabkin's term, reimagine war, re-create its rules from the ground up in response to new conditions of combat and significant shifts in the very theater of war itself. The topics of the essays that follow reveal that SF and fantasy today are not mired in epic or chivalric models but continue as speculative literatures to meet the challenge of changing modes of combat. In their diverse and complex response to the question of the uses of warfare in fiction, these essays only reinforce the fact that the true function of fantasy and science fiction is neither nostalgia nor play, but analysis. For all treat the texts they examine as a means not of playing war games but of understanding the role of war in the present and the future.

In the opening essay "Reimagining War," Eric S. Rabkin traces a path from Heinlein through Joe Haldeman to Orson Scott Card, noting in their work a definite movement toward "the spatial concentration and psychological involution of war" in SF. This internalization of the zone of combat, Rabkin asserts, may be fortunate in that it offers us a means of confronting warfare not as a necessary condition for humanity but as an idea or concept we ourselves have created and elaborated over the ages. This in turn allows us to challenge the corollary assumption that war is the necessary product of a human nature that cannot change. To challenge this fatalism is, for Rabkin, the urgent task of future SF: "If we can combine the notion of changing human nature with the notion of redefining the zone of combat as the realm within ourselves, then we might be able to direct our 'natural' aggression toward an accommodation with ourselves."

The next two essays focus, respectively, on the semantics and on the lin-

Introduction 5

guistics of warfare in SF. Both show us that these are areas not only where past writers have failed to reimagine war but where untapped possibilities to do so await those who can successfully use the semantic and linguistic range proper to this genre. Reginald Bretnor, addressing the science of war in SF, asks just how scientific it is. If peace is the dream of the wise, war is the history of our species. Thus, to prophesy future wars in SF we must understand the history of war. And we cannot do this without understanding the vocabularies in which the concepts of this history are set forth. If, as Bretnor claims, every theoretical system of warfare, in terms of these semantic factors, is unscientific, or prescientific at best, what about SF? Bretnor uses the term *prediction,* but actually he is describing that process of extrapolation whose function is exactly what he is talking about: the reexamination of basic concepts in the light of changing technological contexts. Instead of analyzing the possible effects of technical change on warfare, then, should SF be merely content, like those who wield the words of war in our press and government today, to recycle old scenarios in the guise of new euphemisms? Before SF can create new terms of war, it must understand those which are so commonly manipulated and misunderstood today. Bretnor offers this challenge to SF.

Gary Westfahl, in his "Wrangling Conversation," says that SF, on the level of the linguistics of combat, has even in its traditional forms already gone further than mainstream literature in opening the rigid patterns of warfare our culture has imposed on us. His focus is on dialogues between hero and villain, both inside and outside SF. Examining such things as the number of commands, questions, and negative expressions used by hero and villain when engaged in verbal strife, he concludes that the latter has the higher level of "readability." The villain is given the voice of the teacher, the parent and scholar, and on this subliminal linguistic level, our culture seems to tell us to distrust that voice. This is the mainstream pattern, and many SF stories follow it. But there are also many SF works that reverse this cultural bias. From Gernsback to Heinlein, heroes are now associated with educated speech. And this, to Westfahl, is a sign that this literature has opted for mind over heart, for reason instead of youthful idealism. If science is changing our world irrevocably, then this changed world requires new attitudes vis-à-vis heroism and villainy, and SF is just the vehicle, turning Bretnor's science of war into what we could call a war of science.

Answering these calls to reimagine war, the next four essays take fresh looks at old wars through the eyes of SF and fantasy. Louis Pedrotti offers a new version of the "celestial assault on our planet." This story, found in the pages of Osip Senkovsky's 1833 Russian science fantasy *The Fantastic Journeys of Baron Brambeus*, represents a genuine "find" in terms of precursors of the genre. The story in question, "Scientific Journey to Bear Island," is a version of the apocalypse-by-comet scenario, replete with internecine warfare, that capitalizes on the predicted appearance of Halley's comet in 1835, some eighty years before Wells wrote *In the Days of the Comet* in anticipation of the next scheduled appearance of Halley's comet in 1910. Fearing the menace from without, society collapses from within in Senkovsky's tale.

Laurence Davies calls the future-war novels that flourished in anticipation of World War I "fantasies of metropolitan collapse." These fictions, though not accurate as prediction, tell of the deep need of an entire generation of Europeans to wish total and terrifying destruction on the urban centers of their culture. To explain the disaster fictions that flourished at this time—fictions that extended Senkovsky's natural disaster to aerial blitzkrieg and political terrorism—Davies evokes the aesthetic of the sublime, terrible, yet pleasurable grandeur transposed to the streets of contemporary London. This particular imagination of disaster may have served its generation as homeopathic magic, Davies concludes, but it is by no means harmless, for, quoting Dürrenmatt, "what once was thought can never be unthought." Even a writer as gifted and sophisticated as H. G. Wells shared this sense of the necessary disaster, of the evils of too much peace. Surveying Wells's entire production of stories and novels devoted to warfare, Arthur Campbell Turner concludes that, despite seemingly radical shifts in belief from pessimism to optimism, and shifts in genre from the scientific romance to the realistic novel, the author "was totally possessed by the curious notion that Utopia could only be achieved on the basis of a tabula rasa. First there had to be nearly universal destruction to shake men free from bad habits of thinking and from the dead hand of existing institutions. Then Wells . . . 'passes a miracle.'"

Rosemarie Arbur discusses a case in which fiction—this time fiction whose direct subject is combat—is used as a weapon in a real-life conflict, in this case the "battle of the sexes." Arbur sees a series of novels, from Joan Slonczewski's *A Door into Ocean* to Suzette Haden Elgin's *Native Tongue*, as narrative shock attacks. Positing total victory by the "better half," these works are designed to "shatter the detachment" of the male reader, forcing him to seek solutions to those unequal gender conflicts he has passively tolerated in previous SF narratives. These radically divisive feminist SF novels actually function, as Arbur sees it, to provoke an angry response from the otherwise complacent male reader. For such anger is the first step on the path to meaningful dialogue, perhaps the only real precondition today. Indeed, as Arbur concludes, "we had better start speaking the same language, lest Mother Eve . . . and the legion of uncanonized housewife saints permit our species to do what none has ever done before: sever one half from the other."

The battle of the sexes is the most intimate yet discussed, and, if we heed Arbur's warning, the most apocalyptic in what has become (symptomatically) the common meaning of the term today: genocide and total destruction. The next set of essays all deal, in various ways, with what we might call the new inverse proportionality of warfare. For as recent battlefields become more intimate and restricted, they become, inversely, more terminally lethal and destructive. Vietnam was perhaps the first terrain war without clear boundaries, a war that isolated the combatant from nation and society, causing him to fall back on self and mind, which in turn became the battlefield. This is the SF battlefield of Joe Haldeman's *The Forever War* as compared with more terrain-oriented SF classics like Heinlein's *Starship Troopers*. And Haldeman, by recounting his own experiences as a veteran, is simply telling us that SF extrapolation must have roots in what we know firsthand, and emphasizing that in the case of armed conflict, the parameters of that experience have changed radically.

Haldeman speaks of returning home to find "land mines between the sidewalk cracks, ambush lurking behind McDonalds." What he is describing is the intimate urban battleground. For Paula Radisich this urban battleground is where evolution and salvation meet and contend. Her essay examines a particularly grim work—Philippe Druillet's *La Nuit*—in which urban warfare and apocalypse have become one and the same. She studies a particularly visionary mode of presentation—the French *bande dessinée*, or "illustrated narrative." Subjecting Druillet's monstrous combatants of the night to iconographic analysis, she finds tension between, on one hand, the author's desire to unleash the destructive force latent in the pure or unbound image, and, on the other hand, the need to place this nihilistic violence within the systematic frame of the traditional Christian icon. Held within this frame, Druillet's images, though they revel in the inevitable evolutionary annihilation of all form, retain at least a suggestion of that order and meaning which traditionally belongs to Christian eschatology.

Peter Fitting sees the same tendency in recent films of urban violence and apocalypse. His first response is to wonder at the pleasure we seem to have in films that indulge in warfare and violence without offering any aesthetic or moral value to redeem this violence. The random destruction in films like *The Terminator* appears to have no political or religious meaning, hence no redeeming quality. There are no overt signs of traditional order like Druillet's Christian icons. But, to Fitting, these are merely another example of the ideological "loop," or mind-forged manacle. These films may constitute an impotent utopian wish, but Fitting sees them, despite their impotence, as operating on a subliminal (that is, material) level to express our repressed hopes for an escape from the ideological loops that have created this deadly association of historical time with the necessity of apocalyptic destruction.

David Clayton's essay places more faith in the individual writer's ability to deconstruct the myths of apocalypse and eschatology. He reads Samuel R. Delany's *Dhalgren* as an "apocalyptic mirage." The city of Bellona, he argues, is a place where war and total destruction are constantly promised and endlessly deferred. The purpose of Delany's attack on the apocalyptic narrative may be similar to Fitting's, but its target is literary, not social, for Delany was challenging the tendency of a particular literary form—science fiction—to effect utopia through the violent means of apocalypse. It was Delany's intention, Clayton argues, to expose a pervasive link in our culture between eschatology—the discourse of ends—and fictional violence as the somehow necessary means of effecting these ends.

Scott Dalrymple makes a similar point about the recent fascination with violence for its own sake in horror literature. Dalrymple argues that behind the current rash of horror lies the specter of the atomic cloud, the symbol of a total destruction wrought not by God on mankind but by mankind on itself. But the purpose of this nuclear-obsessed horror fiction is twofold. It is a symbol of death that we can at the same time read as a new holy writ. It implies that what we have wrought we might also undo. Orthodox religious texts, Dalrymple believes, teach us to sit fatalistically by and accept the coming of apocalypse. But the horror text, as epitomized by Stephen King's *The Dead Zone*, holds out the hope that individuals stirred to action by the terrible sight of the mushroom cloud may yet forestall what appears an unstoppable course toward mass death and destruction.

In the above examples of fictional armed combat, from films of post-urban apocalypse to novels of nuclear apocalypse, the critics all claim to have found a hidden agenda—in each case a desire on the part of both the artist and society to retain some sense of the human will to order in the midst of chaotic violence. Martha Bartter, however, raises this question: What if this hidden agenda is just the opposite? What if the unstated goal is a methodical and total destruction of the human race? Bartter enumerates a series of destructive agendas in fiction, but she focuses on a novel that examines the moral implications of the most destructive hidden agenda of them all: the tale of genetic winnowing and "regeneration" that are in reality (she feels) euphemisms for genocide. The novel in question is M. J. Engh's *Arslan*. This work, which Bartter sees as just as important a "discovery" as Pedrotti's *Baron Brambeus*, offers a woman's critique of the patriarchal agenda of most postapocalyptic narratives. It suggests that by acquiescing in this agenda of "regeneration," we are perhaps just as guilty of genocide as those who, for reasons of "conscience," choose not to act against tyrants such as Hitler. Rather than relying on some subliminal force to save humanity from its own destructive urges, *Arslan* urges direct, conscious ethical action against tyrants who seek to use evolution as an excuse to destroy humanity.

Most of the fights of fancy discussed so far have occurred in SF texts, from Wells to future-war novels to recent feminist dystopian fictions. The recurring function of these SF works has been to redefine the parameters of fictional warfare in response to changing modes of combat in the fields of society and culture. But what of fantasy? Fiction today must deal not with the spatial displacements of Homer and Heinlein but with the temporal dislocations of Vietnam, and with the boundaryless world of an urban, postnuclear landscape. But as we increasingly relocate the battlefield within the mind, we become fixed, skewered, on Clayton's nexus of violence and eschatology. And fantasy, increasingly, becomes the force that seeks to set us free. Perhaps we could even say that, in the context of these fights of fancy, fantasy is itself reimagined. This new fantasy may even offer alternatives to the concept of combat itself, and become the means of challenging its binary logic with a third term. The final two essays offer possible ways in which this new, reimagined fantasy operates, in the context of armed conflict, to do just that.

George Slusser focuses on a set of works that seek to free fictional combat from the logic of binarity: Bruce Lee films, reggae songs, *Rocky*, and the "Third World" SF of Samuel Delany. These are productions whose overt theme may be the battle between haves and have-nots, between poor and rich, yet at the same time they are sophisticated media events. The logic of their production, then, which is the conquest of time rather than the conquest of space, is not only at odds with the logic of their theme but is also the means of introducing a third term into the equation of combat. For the fantasy of the media event operates here as an Ariel in relation to

Prospero and Caliban. Slusser suggests that such fantasies have become the means of freeing combat from the material limits within which political territorialists like the Marxists wish to inscribe it, and thus are a way of returning fantasy to its root sense in *phantazein*. Through the media of film and broadcasting, fantasy recovers its power to body forth images out of nothing—which means, in the context of the most bitter and hopelessly restrictive territorial warfare being fought today, the power to generate real third terms and worlds, and in doing so to break the fatal logic of duality that still today holds our idea of conflict in thrall.

Finally, Brooks Landon describes an even broader shift in the "territory" that underlies the prominent models of conflict not only in fantasy and science fiction but in literature in general. His specific focus is the SF film, because the themes and purpose of this film genre are so closely linked in the popular mind with armed conflict and the "imagination of disaster." And what he sees happening in SF films is the rise of a digital narrative in which (as with the Bruce Lee films Slusser discusses) the depiction of themes is being gradually displaced by *modes* of depicting, by techniques of computerized graphics and animation which have become the true subjects of these films. Looking specifically at cyberpunk films, Landon sees the binary conflict between society and the old "solo" (the individualist hero capable of replacing the human with data-simulated images) gradually being modulated, and perhaps ultimately suspended, by a third, and specifically fantastic, element—the "soliton." This "wrinkle in the medium" functions here as the means not simply of winning a war, which in this case would mean the total displacement of mankind by image and language using electronic display, but of modulating the restrictive concept of warfare into something else, possibly something much better.

The essays in this volume, which were selected from a larger number presented at the Tenth J. Lloyd Eaton Conference, held at the University of California at Riverside in April 1988, are responses to a call to see whether armed conflict remains a central aspect of fantasy and science fiction. And the answer is not only affirmative but positively so. For the essays reveal this literature actively evolving new concepts of warfare in response to the changing conditions of war, leaving behind the old binary logic that still seems to reign in the armed conflicts of traditional literature. Their acute sense of the multivalent nature of the present battlefield is an indication that fantasy and science fiction can continue to speculate fruitfully, not simply on the battlefields of elsewhere but of elsewhen as well.

Note

1. Leslie A. Fiedler, *Olaf Stapledon: A Man Divided* (New York: Oxford University Press, 1983), pp. 128–29.

Chapter 1

Reimagining War

Eric S. Rabkin

Thomas Hobbes believed that "during that time when men live without a common power to keep them all in awe, they are in that condition which is called war; and such a war, as is of every man, against every man." In such a time, he observed, "the life of man [is] solitary, poor, nasty, brutish, and short." To avoid this fate, "men, . . . who naturally love liberty, and dominion over others," put a "restraint upon themselves" in the form of civil organization. Hobbes's particular interest was in establishing the authority of the commonwealth as a form of government, but clearly, from his point of view, government in general had to be formed because, left to their solitary devices, men would simply kill each other. "For as to the strength of body, the weakest has strength enough to kill the strongest, either by secret machination, or by confederacy with others."[1]

The "common power" that binds people together, of course, is typically not so much a matter of brute force as of awesome ideology. Solipsistically—and therefore unarguably—an empowering ideology may rest on honoring the very nation formed by that ideology itself, by the common power. As Horace put it, "Dulce et decorum est pro patria mori" (It is sweet and honorable to die for one's country).[2] Such an imagination of death is far from Hobbes's conception of it. Equally far is the martyrdom of saints and Crusaders that lurks behind the so-called hymn most closely associated with the Salvation Army:

> Onward, Christian soldiers,
> Marching as to war,

> With the Cross of Jesus
> Going on before!³

War itself, or perhaps more properly the idea of war, may supply the common organizing power that motivates people to combine. As Stephen Crane said of his protagonist in *The Red Badge of Courage* (1895), "He had burned . . . to enlist. Tales of great movements shook the land."[4] Like many, Henry Fleming seemed to share Mussolini's sentiment that "war alone brings up to its highest tension all human energy and puts the stamp of nobility upon the peoples who have the courage to face it."[5] In short, although Hobbes may have considered war a possible condition of a single person, he recognized what all others have presumed: war leads to the formation of groups, and groups themselves pursue war, "conflict carried on by force of arms, as between nations . . . as by land, sea, or air."[6] War, then, requiring ideas that combine people and technologies that extend the power of "the weakest," has always represented a stirring and deadly collaboration of the heart and the brain.

But while war of this intermittently glorious kind has characterized all our recorded history, in our own century wars of new types are emerging. When Bernard Baruch first used the term *cold war* in 1947, he already understood that the battle of ideologies in a postnuclear age needed to be conducted in ways that had never previously been imagined. What Baruch did not then recognize, however, but what such popular novelists as John le Carré later made vivid, was that the condition of permanent cold war robbed every ideology of its fundamental promise: the capacity to make the life of the citizen less "solitary, poor, nasty, brutish, and short." War between the so-called superpowers is now fought through proxy; terrorism hangs over our heads "by land, sea, or air." Never knowing whom we might trust, subject to annihilation at the instant whim of foreigners—or even of our compatriots—we often feel ourselves to be adrift in our own country and in every other. No matter that we began with a shining ideology from which we drew our "common power"; like one of le Carré's spies, "we had scruples. . . . We had to overcome them."[7] If we are to live beyond this present, we must not only understand how we have imagined war in the past but reimagine it for the future.

War was a normal state in the ancient world of the Near East; there are few years of record without campaigning. The ancient war was a candid war of conquest or looting. Both of these ends were sanctified by the religious character of war, which was fought on behalf of the gods of the people and under the leadership and protection of the gods. The cruelty and barbarism of ancient war were equally candid; ancient war is shocking only because it involved the primitive means of personal effort, and could not achieve the vast mechanical horrors of modern warfare. Prisoners of war had no rights whatever; the entire population could be enslaved, unless the defeated enemy were regarded as a menace to the victor; if it were, the male population could be exterminated or mutilated. Destruction of conquered towns was a normal act of the victor.[8]

John McKenzie's description of war in biblical times reflects two crucial features of all wars fought before the twentieth century. First, in the context of war, the combatants were not so much individuals as groups: tribes, families, clans, nations. Each of these groups held its own life infinitely worthy and the life of the opposing group virtually worthless. God was on the side of the victors. Second, each group—and indeed each god—had its own distinct geographic domain. Ancient war, then, required either mobilizing the group to cross land or sea (air, of course, came later) to invade the land of another group, or mobilizing the group on its own land to resist the invasion of another group. This is what the Trojans tried to do in *The Iliad*, and what they failed to do when, seeing the Greeks sail off, they accepted Sinon's tale of the wooden horse being a gift to Athena, took it within their own city, and were stabbed in their beds in the night. Odysseus had reimagined war and seen it not so much as a clear confrontation on the plains before the city walls as an invasion of one group by another. His superior imagination gave victory to the invaders.

The very term *invasion* (cognate with the word *wade*)[9] calls to mind marines storming beaches and troops crossing borders from one distinct domain to another. This geographic diffuseness of war is captured in words like *battlefield*. The ideological virtues of the battlefield as a place to display oneself are captured in the phrase *theater of war*. And the separation of the main body of the nation from the actors in these theaters is clear when "Johnny has gone for to soldier" or when Christian soldiers are "marching as to war." Traditional war is never *here* for the group (unless the group is under siege) but there, across the sea or land or, these days, air. The attractive legends of Camelot concern knights-*errant*, that is, noblemen who traveled (from the Old French *errer*, "to travel"),[10] chivalrous (from the French *cheval*, "horse") gentlemen who went on quests and whose successors went on Holy Crusades to the distant Holy Land. Yet in truth, during the Middle Ages,

great battles were, on the whole, infrequent.... The fact would appear to be that the opposing armies, being guided by no very definite aims and invariably neglecting to keep in touch with each other by means of outposts and vedettes, might often miss each other altogether. When they met it was usually from the existence of some topographical necessity, of an old Roman road, or a ford or bridge on which all routes converged. Nothing could show the primitive state of the military art better than the fact that generals solemnly sent and accepted challenges to meet in battle at a given place and on a given day. Without such precautions there was apparently a danger lest the armies should lose sight of each other and stray away in different directions. When maps were nonexistent and geographical knowledge both scanty and inaccurate, this was no inconceivable event.[11]

But these days geographical knowledge is quite exact; the battlefields of Flodden and Flanders have given way to the Battle of Britain and the Siege of Leningrad. Neither the United States in Vietnam nor the Soviet Union in Afghanistan bothered with a declaration of war. Looking for war, Stephen Crane's "men had begun to count the miles,"[12] but today's soldiers, like Joseph Heller's Yossarian,[13] only count missions, eager to fulfill their quota and leave. They worry less about ideology than about keeping their own solitary, nasty, and brutish lives from becoming very short very fast.

When Carl von Clausewitz wrote that "war is not merely a political act, but also a political instrument, a continuation of political relations, a carrying out of the same by other means,"[14] he meant the relations between nations, the politics that leads us to call maps with national borders "political maps." Political maps change, of course, quite rarely as the result of tectonics, but quite often as the result of war. But in the postnuclear age, many feel that von Clausewitz's aphorism is not only wrong but dangerous. Andrei Sakharov said that "a thermonuclear war cannot be considered a continuation of politics by other means. It would be a means to universal suicide."[15] To characterize war today, we need not even use words like *battle* or *siege;* city names, and perhaps a date or two, are quite enough: Beirut, Belfast, Detroit 1967, the Prague Spring, Munich 1972, Tian'anmen Square. Where once wars crossed the landscape and battles were fought in fields or around cities, modern warfare has obliterated the classic city-country distinction. There is no safe city, and the notion of buffer zone is outmoded. In so-called cyberpunk science fiction novels like William Gibson's *Neuromancer,*[16] the groups armed against each other frequently walk the same streets, always depend on the same economy, and virtually never find any open countryside as an alternative to the city-as-theater-of-war.

Science fiction, of course, has always been motivated at least in part by the fear and fascination of scientific and technological development.

A Frankenstein monster (from the Latin *monere,* "to warn")[17] symbolizes the awesome, terrific changes the brain may work. The whole system of medieval chivalry fell largely because of technological change, when it became clear that "masses of pikemen could solidly withstand cavalry charges, . . . [and] longbowmen and crossbowmen, since their arrows would easily penetrate ordinary mail, could be used to good effect for defense or for offense."[18] Rather than supporting expensive knights through vassalage, the monarch could now assemble a superior mercenary army almost at will. When the longbow pierced mail, it also destroyed armed knighthood.

Mark Twain imagined just how vulnerable knights would be to modern technology in his "Battle of the Sand-Belt," the dark penultimate chapter of *A Connecticut Yankee in King Arthur's Court*[19] in which Hank Morgan, his assistant, Clarence, and fifty-two loyal adolescents prepare for the onslaught of all the knights of the realm. This almost Carrollian deck of cards and two jokers occupy a secure position, ring it with twelve concentric circles of wire, and plant dynamite charges in a yet more distant ring underlying the factories Hank had built over the course of his years in old England. As the attack begins, "I touched a button. . . . In that explosion all our noble civilization-factories went up in the air and disappeared from the earth. It was a pity, but it was necessary. We could not afford to let the enemy turn our own weapons against us." When the moat these explosions create is bridged, Hank lets the first wave of knights enter his territory through three rings. Then he electrifies the fences before and behind them. Thousands are killed in a moment, "and of course there was a smell of burning flesh." Soon his "camp was enclosed with a solid wall of the dead." He lets in more when they attack en masse and then "pushed a button and set fifty electric suns aflame . . . what a sight! We were enclosed in three walls of dead men! All the other fences were pretty nearly filled with the living. . . . I shot the current through all the fences and struck the whole host dead in their tracks. *There* was a groan you could *hear*! It voiced the death-pang of eleven thousand men. It swelled out on the night with awful pathos. . . . Within ten short minutes [from the first attack of the knights] [t]wenty-five thousand men lay dead around us."[20] Here, even before The Great War, is the imagination of modern warfare: a handful of men against thousands, murder at a distance, military superiority reliant on technological superiority, the willful destruction of the civilian economy, and walls of dead. Powerfully, prophetically, Twain gives Hank a victory that wins him nothing and costs him the love of his wife, Alisande (known as "Sandy"). Perhaps one covert message is that the belt of sand may be not only a ringed arena for combat (*arena* means "sand" in Spanish) but also the girdle (in the medieval sense) of Hank's lover—which should be approached not with weapons but with tenderness. There are, after all, other "common powers" than war that cause people to combine. Equally prophetic, unlike the conquerors of classic wars, Hank cannot withdraw to enjoy his victory; he is immured by the corpses he has created. Only through Merlin's envious magic is Hank able to leave, by sleeping his way back to the nineteenth century and a permanent separation from the family for which he forever after yearns.

Like Mark Twain, Jules Verne too saw that modern technology would affect war, but Verne was almost always the more hopeful of the two. In *20,000 Leagues under the Sea*, for example, one mysterious night Captain Nemo surfaces to give gold in support of a popular revolution in Greece.[21] The gold, we later learn, comes from a mine accessible only via his submarine technology. Seventy years or so later, in his famous Weapon Shop stories, A. E. van Vogt tried to effect revolution by putting superior firepower directly in the hands of well-intentioned citizens.[22] Just as Nemo is able to sail away from the zone of conflict, the weapon makers themselves live in a location inaccessible to the evil government. In giving their heroes a geographic escape, neither Verne before him nor van Vogt after were as prescient as Twain in seeing how war needed to be reimagined. Edward Bulwer Lytton at least saw that there was no escaping the range of whatever new weapons the brain turned loose, although by putting a "vril staff" in everyone's hands in *The Coming Race* (1871) he supposed that what amounted to a personal policy of "mutually assured destruction" would make everyone polite and cooperative, with vril truly supplying the place of an awesome Hobbesian common power. And in *We* (1920), Yevgeny Zamiatin knew that the spaceship *Integral* could be used both for evil (to impose the ideology of the United State on yet undiscovered peoples) or for good (to break out of the United State). In short, science fiction has sometimes reimagined war well enough to warn us of one aspect or another of our modern reality. But in one of its most accurate reimaginings—Twain's—science fiction turned to a magical fantasy more concerned with nostalgia than politics. Indeed, despite the necessary connection between science (brain), fiction (heart), and war, the reimaginings of science fiction have all too often been more specious than real.

Most science fictions, for example, have continued to presume the geographic diffuseness of war. The great opening paragraph of Wells's *War of the Worlds* has us look "across the gulf of space [where] minds that are to our minds as ours are to those of the beasts that perish, intellects vast and cool and unsympathetic, regarded this earth with envious eyes, and slowly and surely drew their plans against us."[23] Edgar Rice Burroughs's wildly popular science fictions are often spatially expansive westerns re-costumed. Indeed, *A Princess of Mars* opens with "Captain Jack Carter of Virginia"[24] being chased by Indians across the Arizona desert into the cave where a mysterious miasma overcomes him and inexplicably transports him to Mars.

Even when science fiction writers have looked to new "common powers," new awe-inspiring ideologies, to combine people into groups, the resulting groups have typically indulged in geographically diffuse wars. This is the case, for example, under the flag of individuality-in-community in Olaf Stapledon's *Star Maker* (1937), under the flag of ecumenical communication in Ursula K. Le Guin's *The Left Hand of Darkness* (1969), under the flag of ecology in Lloyd Biggle's *Monument* (1974), and under the flag of cultural relativism in virtually all the "Star Trek" episodes. The persistent appeal of battles among the stars is indicated by Brian Aldiss's two-volume *Galactic Empires* anthology (1976) and the recent Hugo and Nebula awards given to David Brin's *Startide Rising* (1983), which in many ways pleasingly resembles the sort of World War II film in which a racially mixed group of "our guys," cut off and under attack, must come together to break out of the clutches of "the enemy." In Brin's novel, the military breakout from the planet's surface resonates with the "Uplift" by which one species at a time (porpoises and chimpanzees among earth species) is brought to a level fitting it for interstellar commerce. But enjoyable as these works are, they still reflect the old imagination of biblical warfare, the army of one tribe transporting itself through space to invade the territory of another. This is simply inadequate to modern reality.

Nobel laureate Konrad Lorenz has made clear the crucial connection between territory and combat in maintaining the lives of species. In *On Aggression* he explains that "even in the case of animals whose territory is governed by space alone, the hunting ground must not be imagined as a property determined by geographical confines; it is determined by the fact that in every individual the readiness to fight is greatest in the most familiar place, that is, in the middle of its territory. . . . As the distance from this 'headquarters' increases, the readiness to fight decreases proportionately."[25] In perhaps the most famous modern wartime exhortation, Winston Churchill moves from an exposition of territorial withdrawal after the defeat at Dunkirk to an imagination of territorial invasion in order to rally his countrymen. "We shall not flag or fail. We shall go on to the end. We shall fight in France, we shall fight on the seas and oceans, we shall fight with growing confidence and growing strength in the air, we shall defend our island, whatever the cost may be, we shall fight on the beaches, we shall fight on the landing grounds, we shall fight in the fields, and in the streets, we shall fight in the hills, we shall never surrender" (June 4, 1940). Churchill here pumps up the rhetoric as he imagines the enemy moving into the heart of British territory. He knows that the closer the enemy is to the nation's "headquarters," the greater will be the will to resist, the will he stokes by this very speech precisely so as to forestall that invasion.

Science fiction offers us three Hugo-winning novels that demonstrate this domestication of warfare as applied to what is essentially the same story. In Robert A. Heinlein's *Starship Troopers* (1959), Joe Haldeman's *The Forever War* (1974), and Orson Scott Card's *Ender's Game* (1985), the first section concerns the training of the protagonist in a military academy and the second the combat in which that protagonist engages. In Heinlein's novel, which came essentially on the heels of the Korean War, the protagonist does his fighting in superior body armor on a distant planet. In Haldeman's novel, which grew out of his Vietnam experiences, the combat takes place not so much across space as across time, and thus permanently removes the protagonist from those he is supposed to protect. In Card's novel, the protagonist spends the second half of the tale isolated in the academy playing hyperrealistic electronic combat games, only to discover that the games were real and he has been duped into becoming the sole coordinator of a near genocide—the war brought right into his school and overwhelming guilt brought right into his soul. We easily see two movements in this sequence: a progressive dissociation of the individual from the group of which he is a putative part, and a domestication of combat as it moves ever closer to the interior of the defended territory and the interior of the defender's psyche.

Like Hobbes, Lorenz believed that war is part of human nature, and in that sense is as concentrated in the individual as one can imagine. Unlike Haldeman and Card, however, instead of trying to imagine the warfare of the present or future, Lorenz imagined the warfare of the past:

Now let us suppose that our assumption is correct and that the men of such a paleolithic tribe did indeed have the same natural inclinations, the same endowment with social instincts as we have ourselves; let us imagine a life, lived dangerously in the exclusive company of a dozen or so close friends and their wives and children. There would be some friction, some jealousy about girls, or rank order, but on the whole I think that this kind of rivalry would come second to the continuous necessity for mutual defense against hostile neighboring tribes. The men would have fought side by side from earliest memory; they would have saved each other's lives many times; all would have ample opportunity to discharge intra-specific aggression against their enemies, none would feel the urge to injure a member of his own community. In short, the sociological situation must have been, in a great many respects, comparable to that of the soldiers of a small fighting unit on a particularly dangerous and independent assignment. We know to what heights of heroism and utter self-abnegation average, unromantic modern men have risen under these circumstances. Incidentally, it is quite typical of man that his most noble and admirable qualities are brought to the fore in situations involving the killing of other men, just as noble as they are. However cruel and savage such a community may be to another, within its bonds natural inclination alone is very nearly sufficient to make men obey the Ten Commandments—perhaps with the exception of the third. One does not steal another man's rations or weapons, and it seems rather despicable to covet the wife of a man who has saved one's life a number of times. One would certainly not kill him, and one would, from natural inclination, honor not only father and mother, but the aged and experienced in general, just as deer and baboons do.[26]

Lorenz, then, like Card after him, saw the deepest consequences of human war not between groups but within the individuals in groups. Unlike Card, however, Lorenz hearkened back to a romantic other time when obedience to the supposedly desirable Ten Commandments flowed spontaneously from the breasts of a race of generally happy warriors. But Card is not alone in seeing the warfare within as corrosive. Indeed, a modern—and perhaps not illegitimate—reading of the story of the Trojan Horse might suggest that the Trojans were defeated precisely because they brought war within their walls, because they concentrated it geographically, because they tried to domesticate it, because they allowed it to be a part of them.

Whether or not the spatial concentration and psychological involution of war that Card explored is unique to our century, certainly in our century we are most likely to find writers who not only view war this way but see this sort of war as fundamentally different from earlier war. In *A Farewell to Arms*, a novel about two people who try to remove themselves physically from World War I but find that in wartime death sunders them even in neutral territory, Ernest Hemingway's narrator wonders early on if "perhaps wars weren't won any more. Maybe they went on forever."[27] Perhaps so; after all, the relative peace that the United States has sustained since 1945 has required us constantly to roil our dreams with images of Armageddon. Philip K. Dick understood that our reliance on ever more sophisticated technology would wipe out the obvious verities—such as group identification—that made it possible for someone like Lorenz—or his paleolithic forebears—to view war positively. In "Second Variety," for example, little children holding teddy bears befriend soldiers and follow them home, only to explode. Not only are the teddy bears robots, but so are the little children.[28] Inhuman we may think them; and what did we think of the Vietnamese children, mines strapped to their bellies, who befriended American soldiers? We may not have thought them robots, but we must acknowledge that the mines they carried made it possible for them, "the weakest," to kill the strongest in ways never before imagined.

In this sort of world, war doesn't liberate, or at least it doesn't liberate the child suicide; rather, it controls. War is no longer an instrument of politics but a horrible condition. Heller's Yossarian, of course, wants to get away (as if geographical displacement can end one's involvement in war in this century):

> "I'm nuts. Cuckoo. Don't you understand? I'm off my rocker. They sent someone else home in my place by mistake. They've got a licensed psychiatrist up at the hospital who examined me, and that was his verdict. I'm really insane."
> "So?"
> "So?" Yossarian was puzzled by Doc Daneeka's inability to comprehend. "Don't you see what that means? Now you can take me off combat duty and send me home. They're not going to send a crazy man out to be killed, are they?"
> "Who else will go?"[29]

If not during World War II, then certainly now, as Sakharov said, thermonuclear war at least is an instrument for universal suicide.

What, then, are the alternatives? Can we reimagine war so that even with our ever-evolving technology we may survive? Some writers seem to have taken the grim view. In *The Genocides* (1965), Thomas M. Disch's aliens decide to farm our planet—all of it. To these incomparably advanced agriculturalists, we are merely vermin reducing their yield. Although the novel is narrated primarily from the human point of view, readers know that the aliens are aware of our "war" against them only in the way that a human farmer might be aware of the bellicosity of, say, rabbits. In a bitter comment on our human faith in struggle, on that marvelous collaboration of heart and brain, the book ends with these words: "Nature is prodigal. Of a hundred seedlings only one or two would survive; of a hundred species, only one or two. Not, however, man."[30] At the end of *Neuromancer*, that purest of all cyberpunk novels, Case has managed to survive, but, like Hank Morgan, he must enter a world bereft of the one reason outside himself that his experience had given him for living. The last words: "He never saw Molly again."[31]

While such pessimism certainly offers an alternative to the romanticism of Heinlein, Brin, and even Lorenz, it offers us few constructive options, given what these authors believe about human nature. Another set of authors, ever more common in the last decade or so, seem to have simply thrown up their hands at the fact of human nature and decided to let God get us out of our troubles. These authors resort to dei ex machina revealed improbably at their narratives' ends. While most critics disparage this device, the popular acclaim for these novels suggests that in the post-Vietnam era any solution, be it merely aesthetic or highly fantastic, is desired. In Asimov's *The Gods Themselves*, a Hugo and Nebula winner from 1972, the heat death of two universes is avoided when one of the characters discovers a new fundamental law of physics to make everything right. In John Varley's *Millennium* (1983), the heroine's robot lover snatches humanity at the last moment from inevitable ecocatastrophe by revealing himself as a god. And in Greg Bear's *Blood Music* (1985), the utter and excruciating biomorphosis of humanity into dripping protoplasm magically gives us a new viewpoint in which "nothing is lost. Nothing is forgotten. It was in the blood, the flesh. And now it is forever."[32]

If war does come from within us, then one alternative we might usefully imagine is the proverbial "safety valve." The frontier, with its licit armed conflict, according to Frederick Jackson Turner served that purpose in America. "What the Mediterranean Sea was to the Greeks, breaking the bond of custom, offering new experiences, calling out new institutions and activities, that, and more, the ever retreating frontier has been to the United States directly, and to the nations of Europe more remotely."[33] Huckleberry Finn understands that his rough ways must suffer Hobbesian "restraint" in any civilized locale, and so, rather than go to war against all, he uses the safety valve. Huck's narration ends with a turn toward the future based on a glimpse of the past:

Tom's most well now, and got his bullet around his neck on a watch-guard for a watch, and is always seeing what time it is, and so there ain't nothing more to write about, and I am rotten glad of it, because if I'd 'a' knowed what a trouble it was to make a book I wouldn't 'a' tackled it, and ain't a-going to no more. But I reckon I got to light out for the Territory ahead of the rest, because Aunt Sally she's going to adopt me and sivilize me, and I can't stand it. I been there before.[34]

In *The Moon Is a Harsh Mistress*, Heinlein too, once the revolt of the moon (read America) against the earth (read England) is won, needs to get his violent heroes off-stage, or at least to other theaters of war. The computer Mike, who has really run the revolution, conveniently and enigmatically goes silent; the human Manny, who supposedly has run the revolution, ends his narration much as Huck did:

Too many changes—May go to that talk-talk tonight and toss in some random numbers.
Or not. Since Boom started quite a few young cobbers have gone out to Asteroids. Hear about some nice places out there, not too crowded.
My word, I'm not even a hundred yet.[35]

In other words, one alternative is to reimagine war not as intraspecific conflict but as the conflict of humanity against the environment. Unfortunately, it is precisely that attitude—that the environment is our adversary—that has so successfully led us to the brink of ecocatastrophe.

In one sense, the reimagination Orson Scott Card provides in *Ender's Game* suggests that, just as for Ender, our real zone of conflict is internal. The alternatives we have been offered have been disappointing because we have presumed human nature will not change. If we expect ourselves to be changed by a deus ex or qua machina, of course, change is unlikely ever to come; and if we expect to reimagine war as a safety valve only in geographically diffuse terms, then, confined as most of us are to the surface of this ever less spacious planet, we are in trouble. But if we can combine the notion of changing human nature with the notion of redefining the zone of conflict as the realm within ourselves, then we might be able to direct our "natural" aggression toward an accommodation with ourselves. Indeed, if we can reimagine "conflict" not as two parties aiming to destroy each other but as, say, two adversaries trying to hammer out truth (as in English law) or as two opposing principles struggling to create a total world between them, as in the Tao, then the way may open for us yet. At the end of Bruce Sterling's *Schismatrix* (1985), a cyberpunk novel in which another narratively unprepared-for god figure at the end joins with the hero to allow him to go off to "somewhere wonderful,"[36] we not only have Huckleberry's escape but an implicit suggestion that fiction in general, and science fiction in particular, with its vaunted "sense of wonder,"[37] offers us a new instrument, a continuation of politics by radically different means. The question before us now, then, is whether we can use this instrument to reimagine yet more boldly the collaboration between heart and brain. All that hangs on the answer is our survival.

Notes

1. Thomas Hobbes, *Leviathan* (1651), quoted in *Main Currents in Western Thought*, ed. Franklin Le Van Baumer (New York: Alfred A. Knopf, 1952), pp. 338–39.
2. Horace, *Odes* (23 B.C.E.), III.ii.13.
3. Sabine Garing-Gould, "Onward Christian Soldiers," 1864, stanza 1.
4. Stephen Crane, *The Red Badge of Courage* (1895), in *The Portable Stephen Crane*, ed. Joseph Katz (New York: Viking Press, 1969), p. 193.
5. Benito Mussolini, in a passage written for *The Italian Encyclopedia*, quoted in Bartlett's *Familiar Quotations* (Boston: Little, Brown, 1980).
6. Jess Stein, ed., *Random House Dictionary of the English Language*, unabr. ed. (New York: Random House, 1966).
7. John le Carré, *The Looking-Glass War* (London: Pan, 1965), p. 102.
8. John L. McKenzie, *Dictionary of the Bible* (New York: Macmillan, 1965), p. 919.
9. Stein, *Random House Dictionary of the English Language*.
10. Ibid.
11. C. W. C. Oman, *The Art of War in the Middle Ages* (1885; Ithaca; N.Y.: Cornell University Press, 1976), pp. 62–63.
12. Crane, *Red Badge of Courage*, p. 209.
13. Joseph Heller, *Catch-22* (1955; New York: Dell, 1967).
14. Carl von Clausewitz, *On War* (1833), quoted in Bartlett's *Familiar Quotations*.
15. Andrei D. Sakharov, *Progress, Coexistence, and Intellectual Freedom* (1966), quoted in Bartlett's *Familiar Quotations*, p. 448, n. 4.
16. William Gibson, *Neuromancer* (New York: Ace Books, 1984).
17. Stein, *Random House Dictionary of the English Language*.
18. Carl Stephenson, *Mediaeval Feudalism* (1942; Ithaca, N.Y.: Cornell University Press, 1961), p. 102.
19. Mark Twain, *A Connecticut Yankee in King Arthur's Court* (1889; San Francisco: Chandler, 1963).

20. Ibid., pp. 554–64.
21. Jules Verne, *20,000 Leagues under the Sea* (1869; New York: Bantam Books, 1962), chap. 30.
22. See, for example, A. E. van Vogt, "The Weapon Shop" (1942), in *Science Fiction Hall of Fame*, ed. Robert Silverberg (New York: Avon Books, 1970), pp. 183–225.
23. H. G. Wells, *The War of the Worlds* (1898), in *The Time Machine & The War of the Worlds* (Greenwich, Conn.: Fawcett, 1968), p. 107.
24. Edgar Rice Burroughs, *A Princess of Mars* (1912; New York: Ballantine Books, 1974), p. 11.
25. Konrad Lorenz, *On Aggression* (1963; New York: Bantam Books, 1971), p. 32.
26. Ibid., pp. 242–43.
27. Ernest Hemingway, *A Farewell to Arms* (New York: Scribners, 1929), p. 118.
28. Philip K. Dick, "Second Variety" (1953), in *Robots, Androids, and Mechanical Oddities: The Science Fiction of Philip K. Dick*, ed. Patricia S. Warrick and Martin H. Greenberg (Carbondale: Southern Illinois University Press, 1984).
29. Heller, *Catch-22*, p. 314.
30. Thomas M. Disch, *The Genocides* (1965; New York: Pocket Books, 1979), p. 208.
31. Gibson, *Neuromancer*, p. 271.
32. Greg Bear, *Blood Music* (New York: Ace Books, 1985), p. 247.
33. Frederick Jackson Turner, *The Significance of the Frontier in American History* (1893; New York: Ungar, 1963), p. 58.
34. Mark Twain, *The Adventures of Huckleberry Finn* (1884), in *The Portable Mark Twain*, ed. Bernard De Voto (New York: Viking Press, 1946), p. 539.
35. Robert A. Heinlein, *The Moon Is a Harsh Mistress* (New York: Berkley, 1966), p. 302.
36. Bruce Sterling, *Schismatrix* (New York: Ace Books, 1985), p. 288.
37. See, for example, Sam J. Lundwall, *Science Fiction: What It's All About* (New York: Ace Books, 1971), p. 24.

Chapter 2

Science Fiction and the Semantics of Conflict

Reginald Bretnor

Those of us in the science fiction field who write of war in the future cast ourselves, willy-nilly, in the role of prophets. Though this may not please those who would leach the science out of science fiction and who deny it any valid prophetic function, it is still the truth, for not only do we take it upon ourselves to prophesy, we take as our field of interest an area of human activity immediately critical to our survival.

We are not always true prophets—not by any means. But we are widely accepted as prophets, not only by people whose view of conflict in the future begins and ends with *Star Wars* but by a great many others better qualified to judge, including many in professions closely associated with determining the nature of future wars. Much of this acceptance is subconscious, a spin-off from the general cultural influence of science fiction, but its existence is undebatable, and its influence is increasing. Therefore we should accept some responsibility and at least try to prophesy as accurately as possible.

This means that we should seek to understand the history of war, and also those maps of cause and effect generally referred to as "the science of war," "the art of war," and, less frequently, "the theory of war." We cannot do this without examining the vocabularies in which they are set forth, any more than we can understand the physical sciences without understanding the symbols that express their values and relationships. Because they lack the rigor of scientific terminologies, however, we should not hesitate to reevaluate and, when necessary, to discard them.

These vocabularies can be separated into two classes: those which deal with the purely physical values of destructive force and of humankind's vulnerability to its expression, and those which involve human minds and wills in the realization of these physical values.

Where the first class is concerned, we are dealing with terms largely measurable through the various phases of expression of destructive force and the realization of vulnerability: production and supply, and the physical facts governing the performance limits of weapons and enabling devices.

It is the second class that will give us the most trouble, for its values are infinitely harder to measure, and thus to evaluate accurately: intelligence, determination, mental flexibility or rigidity, erroneous doctrine, and misplaced faith. All these factors enter into the vocabularies from which are constructed our "arts," "sciences," and "principles" of war. Every existing theoretical system I know of is unscientific and prescientific when dealing with these factors on the level, let us say, of the medieval protosciences.

I am not denigrating the intellectual brilliance or, indeed, the value of many of these systems. While some have been little more than sets of more or less useful maxims, others have exhibited profound perceptions of the processes of war, and—like the work of Sun Tzu—have withstood the test of the centuries. Yet every one confuses the two vocabularies by not treating them separately.

In the days prior to the industrial and scientific revolutions there was little harm in this, for the known values of destructive force changed, when they changed at all, very slowly. A common soldier or commander would not have felt out of place on battlefields a century after his time. One of Tilly's veterans would not have been totally lost on the field of Malplaguet, nor Marlborough's at Waterloo, nor Wellington's at Gettysburg—though now we begin to stretch it just a bit. But even during medieval times, on the rare occasions when the physical values of destructive force did change abruptly and completely, the wisdom of the past could fail utterly. Thus when the Mongols with their totally mobile, totally self-supporting armies swept over China, the fact that many of the generals opposing them knew Sun Tzu by heart did them no good whatsoever. (Had they been given the leisure to study Sun Tzu's dicta afresh and apply them to the situation, the outcome might have been different, but they would have needed years, together with extraordinary resources, to profit by them.)

At any rate, when the old sets of rules—never too precise and never too clearly applicable—began to lose their practical applicability, the curve of scientific-technological progress, in its effect on the tools of war, started steepening sharply. This stimulated efforts to formulate new theoretical schemes, new sets of principles, verbal maps of cause and effect intended to approximate reality more closely and so to be more generally applicable to actual warfare.

Probably most important among these principles were those set forth by Major General J. F. C. Fuller, chief of staff of the British Tank Corps in the last year of World War I and generally recognized as the father of mechanized warfare. In *The Reformation of War* (1923) and *Foundations of the Science of War* (1926), he published two sets of principles, the latter somewhat more profound (and rather more difficult) than the former. These in turn gave rise to other principles, such as the set taught at the United States Army Command and General Staff College, which can serve as an example:

1. Objective
2. Offensive
3. Simplicity
4. Unity of command
5. Mass
6. Economy of force
7. Surprise
8. Security

By no stretch of the imagination can "principles" such as these be said to constitute a science of war. They share the imprecision characteristic of the terminologies of most of our social studies and so are capable of any number of individual interpretations. Taken too literally they can very easily, depending on the situation, conflict with each other.

Their first central fault is that they concern themselves directly only with the forces of the side employing them and include those of the enemy only by implication—and the equations of war cannot be written that way. Their second fault is that they do not deal separately with the physical and the mental-morale factors present in every military equation.

This sort of thinking resulted in such dangerous axioms as "The moral is to the physical as three to one," implying that high morale can always compensate for a lack of physical force or negate a perilous intrinsic or situational vulnerability. It has been responsible for an almost mystical faith in "cold steel," which persists today against more than a century of hard evidence showing that edged weapons are useless except when used in very special situations by very special troops (e.g., "Argentino meet Gurkha"). This thinking was largely responsible for the defeat of the Japanese in World War II and continues to bear responsibility for the enormous amount of time wasted by eager young men perfecting themselves in the so-called Oriental killing arts. In science fiction, its influence is still exhibited by the persistence of the sword even in interstellar warfare and by such utter idiocies as the novel in which hordes of barbarian horsemen triumph over visitors capable of space travel and armed with appropriate weaponry. (There are exceptions, like Poul Anderson's *High Crusade*, in which the cards are so carefully and logically stacked that the victory of the primitives follows quite believably, but these are few and far between.)

What, then, is the true role of mental and morale factors in the military equation? Simply, they ensure that destructive force is expressed to the maximum of its capacity, and that applies equally to the physical endurance of the soldier or the spaceman and to the designed maximum performance limit of his weapons and enabling devices. The maximum multiplier value of the mental-morale factors in every military equation, therefore, is exactly *one*. Even the kamikaze pilot or the Shiite fanatic driving an explosives-laden truck into a hotel or hospital cannot change that.

Similarly, the role of these mental-morale factors with regard to one's own vulnerability is to *prevent* its maximum realization, to act as a divisor. Neither martial ardor nor the gratifying sense of power nor such false practicalities as permitting large concentrations of vulnerability in order to save money should be allowed to interfere—advocates of resurrected battleships, giant carriers, and enormous tankers to the contrary.

Now, what has all this to do with the semantics of war? That should be obvious. The terms in which we think about a process, the symbols we employ to describe its relationships, must correspond to reality if we are to control the process successfully, and this applies equally to the planning of a war, a campaign, an isolated engagement, or the invasion of the Squidge System with its eighteen planets inhabited by bloodthirsty super-insectoid female warrior-scientists. Science fiction writers, of all people, should avoid transferring past wars and the techniques of past wars into the future and into galaxies as yet unvisited. Therefore we should do our utmost to achieve an understanding of war's processes and values—the all-important processes and values of destructive force and vulnerability. I cannot emphasize too strongly that in order to do this we must get down to the bedrock of war's realities by examining and evaluating the terms we use to describe and measure them.

The terms of military theory are critically important, but there are others, not always directly involved in the military equation, that are equally important, and their habitual use holds risks—especially the risk of self-delusion—quite as perilous. These are terms that have entered the languages of diplomacy, of preparation for war, of attempts to prevent war, and of public thinking in these areas, and which have been adopted uncritically by people in authority and the common person on the street.

First, and perhaps most important, among these are the *words of promise,* words that carry an inescapable freight of emotional connotations not generally acknowledged. Consider the word *disarmament.* Its explicit promise is simple: if all nations agree to scrap their weaponry, we will have peace. This promise has been repeated ad nauseam for nearly a century, ever since the czar convened the first disarmament conference at The Hague in 1899. Since then, innumerable other conferences have been held and many a solemn treaty signed; the number of editorials and thumping speeches in the League of Nations, the United Nations, and assorted parliaments, plus doctoral dissertations and hopeful popular books, must have reached many tens of thousands—and what has been accomplished? We have outlawed the dumdum bullet and (more or less) poison gas!

What has gone wrong? Why has the idiocy persisted in defiance of the obvious: *that you cannot disarm any technological society even if it wants to be disarmed?* Too many of the tools of peace can be converted with little trouble into effective tools of war. We do not fight wars because we have weapons, or because unscrupulous arms dealers make money out of weapons, or because wicked kings and charismatic madmen drive us to it. I very much doubt that, fundamentally, the Russians really fought to conquer the world for Marxism, or that Khomeini's followers or those of the Irish Republican Army wage terrorist campaigns for their alleged ideals. We fight wars for the same reason that heroin addicts jab themselves with loaded needles—because too many of us have the habit, and these addicts make it difficult or impossible for nonaddicts not to go along. Remember, *peace is the dream of the wise; war is the history of mankind.* That is why, throughout history, sane people have done their best not to end war overnight but rather to ameliorate it by elaborating rules of conduct, of honor and humanity.

Words of promise like *disarmament* provide a magnificent excuse for us not to kick the habit. How long will it take us to understand that our new needles are infected, that the drug we are using is far more deadly than ever before? Not as long as we view the enormous energies and the incredible destructive powers of the space age reduced to World War I dogfights and the absurd laser swords and other silly toys of *Star Wars.* Not as long as totalitarian systems, by institutionalizing their own paranoias, force the rest of us into paranoia. Not as long our world anarchy permits people who are clinically insane to govern countries and preach holy wars for Marx or for Mohammed as a deliberate policy. Certainly not as long as we are silly enough to sell such people modern weapons and equipment.

Another word of promise that has assumed unprecedented importance in a world already dangerously paranoid is *security*. Until relatively recently, at least in the West, the word had a restricted and quite sane military meaning. It is not mentioned in Duane's *Military Dictionary* (1810), or in Scott's of 1862, or in the two editions of Farrow's *Military Encyclopedia* published in 1885 and 1895. Even after the turn of the century, the eleventh edition of the *Britannica* says nothing of security's military or political aspects. Yet the word was in common military use during that time. Farrow's 1918 *Dictionary of Military Terms* defines security simply as "the term embracing all those measures taken by a command to protect itself from observation, annoyance, or surprise by the enemy."

Today's military dictionaries, however, define it in almost the same terms as do general and psychiatric dictionaries, with the emphasis on assured safety, protection, and freedom from fear. The inevitable psychological implication is that all measures taken under its umbrella guarantee that we will be able to sleep cozily without a worry in the world.

I am not arguing against military secrecy, which is sane and necessary, or against measures taken to ensure the integrity of personnel or the safety of establishments; but it should be clearly understood that in a military world, *there is only one way to be secure: to be strong and to be invulnerable*. Otherwise we risk a situation encouraging abuse of power and the protection of incompetence. A good example of this is prewar Japan, where security measures were so strict that tourists did not even dare to photograph the emperor's horse—and where any criticism of military policy was considered subversive, sometimes punishable by death.

A third important word of promise, but one that touches less on our fears than on our sense of right and wrong, is *defense*. Not too many years ago, a Union general—was it Benjamin Butler?—could say, "I love war, wine, and women!" and nobody thought the less of him for it. In those days, too, we had a forthright War Department. Then, not too long ago, suddenly our generals began proclaiming that they hated war, and what had been our forthright War Department transmuted into the Department of the Army, and over that the Department of Defense—a fine Orwellian term telling us and the world that war is bad, it is wrong to make war—

but it is good and right to defend ourselves. Just about every other nation adopted some similar terminology, which really did nothing to relax world tensions or change the world situation. Perhaps this was a reaction to the media-relished horrors of much-touted "total war" and its assorted holocausts, but might we not have been better off had we openly and honestly kept the older terms? And with them, perhaps, those civilized—the term is relative—rules of war that pertained in Napoleon's day?

There have also been subtle changes in the accepted meanings of some of the "everybody knows what that means" words of war. Take *strategy* and *tactics,* for example. Carl von Clausewitz provided a clear and precise definition: "Tactics teaches the use of armed force in engagements, and strategy the use of engagements to attain the object of the war." Let us compare this definition with the words as they are used today, notably in such terms as *strategic bombardment.* Were this practice confined to the selective elimination of targets on which the enemy's war effort depends, it would be justified, but when it is applied to deliberate terror bombing or used as a pretext for the murder of entire cities, like Dresden, that contain no such targets, it in no way fits the Clausewitzian definition. Here we have a splendid example of a term employed to give a false picture of the military reality. It was General Giulio Douhet who formulated the doctrine, motivated by his apparent belief that civilians and the professional military were different species and that civilian morale would collapse almost immediately under mass bombing. In how many countries has this doctrine been proved false? But it has not been renounced; indeed, it has been used as an excuse for the rebarbarization of warfare. It is much easier to talk of strategic bombardment than to admit that those who carry it out are committing what Canadian General E. L. M. Burns termed *megamurder.*

As a matter of fact, the definitions of *strategy* and *tactics* have become so fuzzy that it is now easier to go along with our mass media and simply use them as though *tactics* means something done by lower ranks and *strategy* that which is done by the top brass.

Another term that has an immense and unhealthy influence on our thinking about warfare is *total war.* Though its origin is political rather than military, it is a lineal descendant of Germany's World War I doctrine of *Schrecklichkeit,* or frightfulness. During World War II it was used to stimulate fear in the enemy and martial ardor at home, and it certainly succeeded in making many noncombatants feel ferocious. Actually, it probably was never meant to be taken literally, certainly not by major Western leaders. (Had it been, we would have destroyed Japan's hydroelectric capacity and railroad network as soon as we had the air superiority to do so. Instead, we left them intact to make the world safe for Hondas.) However, the slogan provided one more excuse for breaking with the Western tradition of moral restraint in warfare.

One more slogan, probably adopted for its psychological value, is *unconditional surrender*. Again, it sounds great to home radio audiences, but it violates one of the main psychological precepts of warfare: if you want the enemy to turn tail and run, you have to leave him a bolt-hole to run to. As a matter of fact, there can be little doubt—as J. F. C. Fuller pointed out in *The Conduct of War*—that its persistent use almost certainly prevented the surrender of Japan during the spring of 1945, when we were not ready to give the Japanese the one assurance we finally did give them after Hiroshima and Nagasaki—that the institution of the emperor would be retained. Not only did it delay the surrender, but it helped to ensure that the Russians would move into Manchuria and North Korea, something they were not in a position to do a few months previously.

Our everyday languages are primitive and inaccurate maps of structure and process, accumulations to which more or less accurate concepts have been occasionally added, but from which the inaccuracies are seldom purged. As one example, we still say that the sun rises and sets, though we know very well that it does nothing of the sort and that as the earth turns we observe a stationary sun. Vocabularies that purport to describe human interactions are usually no more accurate, to the point that critical words such as *democracy* can have almost as many meanings and connotations as there are people to employ them. I have tried to show that the words of war, with the exception of those technical terms which describe measurable processes accurately, are quite as imprecise, frequently conveying meanings that their users do not intend. Obviously, systems erected with such building blocks must share their faults and weaknesses. Therefore, when they are used, they should be used only with a constant awareness of their imprecision. Many of them should probably be discarded and replaced by new, more accurate terms.

In my opinion, what this means to science fiction writers is that we should study military history with the awareness that it is a record of the past, and *only* of the past, and that unless it illustrates principles in no way dependent on changing technologies we should hesitate to adduce lessons from it. We should study military theory from the same perspective. (As an analogy, it is interesting and rewarding to read Michael Faraday's *Experimental Re-*

searches, for the elegant clarity of his procedures and discussions if for no other reason, but they do not constitute a course in modern electronics.)

We should especially avoid accepting trendy innovations as any basis for extrapolation: those which go along with the changing fashions of behavior, and particularly those urged by mass-media noise making. There *are* innovations from which we can extrapolate with safety—those, for example, from which laser and particle beam weapons are being developed—but we should ignore those that are superficial. Examples? Well, after the Franco-Prussian War, some armies adopted the Prussian *Pickelhaube,* the spike helmet, presumably in the (I trust subconscious) hope that it would make them comparably victorious; and in the past, of course, many military uniforms followed civilian fashions and traditions with no thought of practicality. On a more serious level, consider the eagerness with which we, with many a shove from women's lib, are busily integrating women into our armed forces, completely ignoring the probability that if this were militarily practical we might have some record of victorious armies containing a high percentage of women—as well as the only too obvious fact that once we accept women as legitimate targets in combat we take another long step backward into absolute barbarism.

Most important, we should never forget that the semantics of conflict as we know it is a curious hodgepodge inherited from the antique and the medieval, the Renaissance and the nineteenth century's New Iron Age, and the earlier decades of our own century. By not allowing ourselves to forget this, we can avoid many absurd anachronisms and improbabilities and—even more important—foresee probable realities.

Chapter 3

Wrangling Conversation: Linguistic Patterns in the Dialogue of Heroes and Villains

Gary Westfahl

Eric Frank Russell's "And Then There Were None" depicts a conflict between would-be invaders and planetary colonists that is exclusively verbal in nature: the colonists succeed by refusing to obey orders and by persuading many invaders to convert to their side. The novella explicitly refers to the fact that there are fundamental differences in the languages of the two forces: one colonist asks an invader, "Are we talking the same language?" Another invader later comments that the conflict involves "a problem in semantics."[1] Although the variations described here are generally minor—basically, a few unusual neologisms developed by the colonists—the story does raise the questions of whether there are indeed significant and quantitative differences in the language of heroes and villains in science fiction works, and whether there are parallel differences in works outside the genre.

To explore these issues I employed two methods. First, I adapted Edward Fry's method for establishing the "readability" of texts by estimating the number of words per sentence and the average number of syllables per word and applied it to the dialogue of heroes and villains in ten science fiction works and ten general works.[2] Second, I subjected four works in each category to more detailed analyses by counting the number of sentences in dialogue that featured at least one use of these surface structures: commands; first-person pronouns, both singular and plural; negative con-

Table 1. Readability of Dialogue of Heroes and Villains in Science Fiction Works

Work	Character (role)	Average number of sentences per 100 words	Average number of syllables per 100 words	Grade of readability
Cherryh, *Downbelow Station*	Damon (hero)	11.0	142	5th grade
	J. Lukas (villain)	8.1	153	8th grade
Fontenay, *The Day the Oceans Overflowed*	Brand (hero)	5.3	135	7th grade
	Ashley (villain)	4.8	144	9th grade
Heinlein, *Between Planets*	Sir Isaac (hero)	9.0	139	6th grade
	Phipps (villain)	5.5	143	8th grade
Le Guin, "The Word for World Is Forest"	Selver (hero)	7.3	122	4th grade
	Davidson (villain)	9.7	128	4th grade
Lewis, *Perelandra*	Ransom (hero)	5.7	132	7th grade
	Weston (villain)	5.4	143	8th grade
Rocklynne, "The Men and the Mirror"	Colbie (hero)	8.5	134	5th grade
	Deverel (villain)	6.4	139	7th grade
Russell, "And Then There Were None"	Baines (hero)	9.6	128	4th grade
	Ambassador (villain)	7.6	150	8th grade
Smith, *Galactic Patrol*	Kinnison (hero)	5.9	140	7th grade
	Helmuth (villain)	5.1	146	9th grade
Spinrad, *Bug Jack Barron*	Barron (hero)	8.2	138	6th grade
	Howards (villain)	5.1	150	9th grade
Verne, *20,000 Leagues under the Sea*	Aronnax (hero)	5.8	138	7th grade
	Nemo (villain)	5.0	145	9th grade

structions; passive voice; and questions. The Appendix describes my methods in greater detail. Regarding as significant those patterns seen in at least three-fourths of the cases in each category and overall, I can construct and explain a "profile" of villainous speech, which differs from that of heroes in these six ways:

1. *Higher level of readability.* As shown in tables 1 and 2, the dialogue of villains emerges as about two grade levels higher than that of heroes in sixteen out of twenty cases, suggesting that villains have more intelligence and education by the criteria of Fry's formula. That is, villains used longer sentences and longer words than did heroes. This difference reflects a widespread and age-old attitude of anti-intellectualism, a belief in admirable youth and evil elders, virtuous innocence and corrupt experience.

2. *More commands.* As shown in the first columns of tables 3 and 4,

Table 2. Readability of Dialogue of Heroes and Villains in General Works

Work	Character (role)	Average number of sentences per 100 words	Average number of syllables per 100 words	Grade of readability
Achebe, *A Man of the People*	Odili (hero)	11.0	133	4th grade
	Nanga (villain)	7.4	143	7th grade
Alger, *Cast upon the Breakers*	Rodney (hero)	10.6	125	3rd grade
	Wheeler (villain)	8.8	131	5th grade
Chandler, "Red Wind"	Marlowe (hero)	10.9	125	3rd grade
	Copernik (villain)	7.6	120	4th grade
Dickens, *Hard Times*	Blackpool (hero)	5.5	127	7th grade
	Gradgrind (villain)	3.4	145	10th grade
Fleming, *Doctor No*	Bond (hero)	8.6	124	4th grade
	Doctor No (villain)	10.0	148	7th grade
Grey, *The Last Trail*	Jonathan (hero)	8.0	128	5th grade
	Brandt (villain)	7.0	132	6th grade
Steinbeck, *In Dubious Battle*	Nolan (hero)	11.5	119	2nd grade
	Bolter (villain)	8.1	138	6th grade
Stevenson, *The Master of Ballantrae*	Henry (hero)	7.1	123	5th grade
	James (villain)	4.3	142	9th grade
Wallace, *Ben-Hur*	Ben-Hur (hero)	6.4	122	6th grade
	Messala (villain)	4.8	136	8th grade
West, *Miss Lonelyhearts*	Miss L. (hero)	11.0	137	4th grade
	Shrike (villain)	5.6	137	7th grade

villains employed commands more frequently than heroes in seven out of eight cases, revealing their desire to dominate others and a natural dislike toward those who do so.

3. *More use of first-person plural pronouns.* As shown in the fourth columns of tables 3 and 4, villains made greater use of the first-person plural in seven out of eight cases, suggesting an arrogant and obnoxious willingness to speak for a group and not just for themselves.

4. *Fewer negative constructions.* As shown in the fifth columns of tables 3 and 4, villains tended to use fewer negative constructions than did heroes in seven out of eight cases. I am not sure why this should be the case; perhaps it is because a typical narrative structure involves a villain with some nefarious plan which the hero must oppose, so that the hero emerges as a negator, both in action and in speech.

Table 3. Selected Surface Structure in the Dialogue of Heroes and Villains in Science Fiction Works

Work, character, (role)	Commands	First-person pronouns total	singular	plural	Negatives	Passive voice	Questions
Fontenay, *The Day the Oceans Overflowed*							
Brand	3	61	63	46	28	6	18
(hero)	(3/109)	(67/109)	(42/67)	(31/67)	(30/109)	(6/109)	(20/109)
Ashley	5	62	51	54	24	8	14
(villain)	(7/152)	(94/152)	(48/94)	(51/94)	(36/152)	(12/152)	(21/152)
Villain fits profile (2–6) in 5 out of 5 cases.							
Russell, "And Then There Were None"							
Baines	8	36	73	29	30	5	21
(hero)	(10/124)	(45/124)	(33/45)	(13/45)	(37/124)	(6/124)	(26/124)
Ambassador	12	33	56	47	19	7	19
(villain)	(43/355)	(118/355)	(66/118)	(55/118)	(69/355)	(24/355)	(66/355)
Villain fits profile in 5 out of 5 cases.							
Smith, *Galactic Patrol* (chapters 11–14)							
Kinnison	7	54	72	32	28	7	10
(hero)	(9/121)	(65/121)	(47/65)	(21/65)	(34/121)	(8/121)	(12/121)
Helmuth	24	35	76	28	26	10	18
(villain)	(34/139)	(46/130)	(35/46)	(13/46)	(34/130)	(13/130)	(24/130)
Villain fits profile in 3 out of 5 cases.							
Spinrad, *Bug Jack Barron* (chapter 9)							
Barron	14	52	92	12	31	2	21
(hero)	(25/177)	(92/177)	(85/92)	(11/92)	(55/177)	(4/177)	(37/177)
Howards	9	42	86	16	24	3	20
(villain)	(11/117)	(49/117)	(42/49)	(8/49)	(28/117)	(4/117)	(23/117)
Villain fits profile in 4 out of 5 cases.							

In tables 3 and 4, the top figure is the percentage of sentences with the structure; below is the numerical breakdown (number of sentences with structure/total number of sentences). In the breakdown of first-person pronouns, percentages are more than 100 percent because some sentences contained both types of pronouns.

5. *More passive constructions.* As shown in the sixth columns of tables 3 and 4, villains made more use of the passive voice in seven out of eight cases, another sign of educated and scholarly speech. Also, the passive voice can be employed to obfuscate issues of personal responsibility—for example, "You will be punished" instead of "I will punish you."

6. *Fewer questions.* As shown in the seventh columns of tables 3 and 4,

Table 4. Selected Surface Structure in the Dialogue of Heroes and Villains in General Works

Work, character, (role)	Commands	First-person pronouns total	First-person pronouns singular	First-person pronouns plural	Negatives	Passive voice	Questions
Chandler, "Red Wind"							
Marlowe (hero)	7 (30/444)	32 (142/444)	94 (133/142)	6 (9/142)	21 (95/444)	1 (6/444)	14 (63/444)
Copernik (villain)	16 (30/189)	28 (53/189)	72 (38/53)	30 (16/53)	17 (32/189)	0 (0/189)	20 (38/189)
Villain fits profile in 3 out of 5 cases.							
Grey, *The Last Trail* (chapters 4–13)							
Jonathan (hero)	9 (18/206)	33 (67/206)	79 (53/67)	25 (17/67)	24 (50/206)	4 (8/206)	17 (36/206)
Brandt (villain)	11 (12/110)	44 (48/110)	67 (32/48)	35 (17/48)	23 (25/110)	5 (6/110)	11 (12/110)
Villain fits profile in 5 out of 5 cases.							
Wallace, *Ben-Hur* (Book 2, chapters 2 and 3)							
Ben-Hur (hero)	10 (10/98)	67 (66/98)	92 (61/66)	11 (7/66)	35 (34/98)	4 (4/98)	21 (21/98)
Messala (villain)	21 (26/126)	46 (58/126)	86 (50/58)	17 (10/58)	17 (21/126)	6 (8/126)	18 (23/126)
Villain fits profile in 5 out of 5 cases.							
West, *Miss Lonelyhearts*							
Miss L. (hero)	13 (18/142)	32 (46/142)	89 (41/46)	13 (6/46)	15 (21/142)	4 (6/142)	18 (25/142)
Shrike (villain)	17 (46/274)	35 (96/274)	77 (74/96)	28 (27/96)	19 (51/274)	5 (15/274)	8 (22/274)
Villain fits profile in 4 out of 5 cases.							

villains asked fewer questions than heroes in six out of eight cases, which may indicate that heroes tend to be open-minded and curious, while villains are set in their evil ways. In addition, a question functions as an invitation to the listener to participate in the conversation; asking fewer questions makes it easier for one to dominate the discussion.

Overall, this profile of villainous dialogue can be characterized as the voice of a parent, a ruler, a teacher, a scholar—a voice culture and literature have conditioned readers to mistrust and dislike. Since I found no notable differences in this profile in science fiction works and general works, my results seem to suggest that science fiction is not, after all, different from other types of literature, and it can correctly be viewed as an outgrowth

Table 5. Readability of Dialogue of Heroes and Villains in Two Exceptional Science Fiction Works

Work	Character (role)	Average number of sentences per 100 words	Average number of syllables per 100 words	Grade of readability
Gernsback, *Ralph 124C 41+*	Ralph (hero)	3.8	154	11th grade
	Fernand (villain)	6.5	127	6th grade
Heinlein, "Solution Unsatisfactory"	Manning (hero)	5.0	147	9th grade
	3 opponents (villains: Kaust, Labor Secretary, new President)	12.3	143	5th grade

and continuation of older forms such as the pastoral, the romance, the satire, the utopia, and the Gothic novel. The results seem to discredit the ideas of men like Hugo Gernsback and John W. Campbell, Jr., who argued that science fiction was a new and distinct form of writing, one that championed discarding old values and celebrated the virtues of scholarship and knowledge.[3]

Before I reached this conclusion, however, I decided to examine two works that I have always regarded as especially fascinating and close to the heart of science fiction: Gernsback's *Ralph 124C 41+: A Romance of the Year 2660* and Robert A. Heinlein's "Solution Unsatisfactory," and here I found dramatic differences. Tables 5 and 6 show that the readability levels of heroes Ralph and Manning are vastly higher than those of their opponents, and in three of the other five cases their dialogue fit the profile of villainous speech. Thus, in at least these two science fiction works, the heroes speak in a manner traditionally associated with villains.

Based on the admittedly scanty evidence of these two examples, I suggest that while science fiction on the whole conforms to conventional patterns in language and attitudes, the genre encompasses two possible tendencies that can change or distort those patterns.

The first tendency, seen in Gernsback's novel, is a deliberate attempt to create a new and different kind of hero in the belief that science has irrevocably changed the world and that this changed world requires new opinions regarding heroism and villainy. Such a belief in a fundamentally altered society is evidenced in Ralph's comment, "Today it is not brute force that counts, but scientific knowledge."[4] Gernsback was aware that he was defying readers' expectations in presenting a professorial hero given

Table 6. Selected Surface Structure in the Dialogue of Heroes and Villains in Two Exceptional Science Fiction Works

Work, character, (role)	Commands	First-person pronouns total	First-person pronouns singular	First-person pronouns plural	Negatives	Passive voice	Questions
Gernsback, *Ralph 124C 41+* (chapters 8–13)							
Ralph	7	31	75	30	25	25	9
(hero)	(10/140)	(44/140)	(33/44)	(13/44)	(35/140)	(35/140)	(12/140)
Fernand	6	77	96	9	24	10	2
(villain)	(5/90)	(69/90)	(66/69)	(6/69)	(22/90)	(9/90)	(2/90)
Hero fits villain profile in 3 out of 5 cases.							
Heinlein, "Solution Unsatisfactory"							
Manning	10	46	74	39	23	7	10
(hero)	(21/210)	(96/210)	(71/96)	(37/96)	(49/210)	(14/210)	(21/210)
opponents	5	46	76	24	26	7	5
(villain)	(4/81)	(37/81)	(28/37)	(9/37)	(21/81)	(6/81)	(4/81)
Hero fits villain profile in 3 out of 5 cases.							

to long-winded, condescending explanations and a villain who was a man of passion and action; but he was committed to changing conventional attitudes, not catering to them. Ralph is the kind of person we *should* admire, even though we have traditionally despised his type. Similar reversals in language patterns might be found in the works of other scientifically inclined authors like George O. Smith and Hal Clement.

The second tendency, seen in "Solution Unsatisfactory," reflects Campbell's belief that science fiction is "the freest, least formalized of any literary medium."[5] In his view, scientific ideas are the engines that drive science fiction stories, and if the author properly understands and follows those ideas, the story can veer off in unexpected and unprecedented directions. That is exactly what happens in "Solution Unsatisfactory." While Heinlein sometimes seems to lose control of his narratives, he usually manages to reassert his authority, tie up the loose ends, and resolve the story in a satisfying manner. But in this case, the inexorable force of Heinlein's scientific logic—the idea that radioactive dust would be an unstoppable weapon—leads to a situation in which his hero is obliged to speak and act like a villain by overthrowing the United States government, destroying democracy, and establishing a worldwide military dictatorship. Since this "solution" is clearly unstable and temporary, the story essentially has no ending—a structure rarely found in fiction except in deliberate puzzles like Frank

Stockton's "The Lady or the Tiger." Such erratic variations from conventional patterns might also be found in the works of writers like A. E. van Vogt and Philip K. Dick, whose unbridled imaginations have often resulted in stories that fail to cohere or resolve themselves according to normal expectations.

Although science fiction contains these potentials for variety, it is not surprising that the genre generally adheres to traditional attitudes. After all, writers face economic pressures to produce palatable—and therefore predictable—products, and editors and publishers often have their own preconceived opinions. Campbell, for example, despite his espousal of authorial freedom, was well known for insisting that in all stories involving conflict between humans and aliens, the humans must invariably triumph. And literary critics must shoulder some of the blame. Trained in and responsive to other types of literature, they frequently praise or criticize science fiction according to how well it conforms to age-old beliefs and patterns. Brian Aldiss is an excellent example: in his celebrated short definition of science fiction—"hubris clobbered by nemesis"—he essentially argues that the genre is obliged to reflect an attitude toward human behavior developed in ancient Greece.[6] For that reason he found fault with Robert A. Heinlein's *Job: A Comedy of Justice*:

> This is the beginning of a whole series of switches between universes which are meant to test Hergensheimer/Graham in the same way that God tested Job in the biblical book of that name. It is an excellent idea.... Unfortunately, Heinlein's use of the idea betrays an imaginative and creative failing.
>
> In the place of real suffering is material inconvenience.... he and his woman ... are taught nothing of the real cruelty of the world.[7]

According to Aldiss, choosing Job as a model was "an excellent idea," no doubt because that story is a classic illustration of "hubris clobbered by nemesis." But Heinlein dared to change the pattern, to conform to his belief that any man who is sufficiently resourceful and energetic can effectively avoid suffering. It is simply outrageous, and deeply inimical to true creativity, that Heinlein's *originality* in this matter should be condemned as "an imaginative and creative failing."

I argue that Gernsback was right: modern science has fundamentally altered the human condition, and many of our problems stem from our stubborn refusal to abandon old ways of thinking: "DESPITE THE TREMENDOUS ADVANCE OF SCIENCE," he proclaimed, "THE WORLD IS MENTALLY STILL IN THE MIDDLE AGES."[8] To refer specifically to the attitudes studied in this paper, we persist in dressing eloquent and educated people in masks and black capes when they may in fact represent our only means of salvation. Science fiction should be cherished, then, as a type of literature that can, if only sporadically, challenge and undermine ancient beliefs and opinions. It wages a fight *against* fancy—that is, against the fancies that continue to permeate our narratives: that hubris is inevitably evil, that youthful idealism is superior to learned reason, that the country bumpkin always outwits the city slicker. Today, these beliefs are not sound advice or even charming fables: they are dangerous illusions. If readers and critics can locate and celebrate science fiction works that refute or question such attitudes, and thus help reshape the genre along those lines, then science fiction might truly become, as Gernsback once envisioned, "an important factor in making the world a better place to live in."[9]

Appendix: Methodology and Vectors for Further Research

To carry out this research I had to locate twenty works—ten of each type—that feature readily identifiable heroes and villains who speak frequently, preferably in long speeches. This was not easy, because as a narrative attains any level of complexity, the nomenclature of "hero" and "villain" can become questionable. Even in the works I selected, informed readers might well challenge my characterizations of Blackpool as hero and Gradgrind as villain, and Sir Isaac as hero and Phipps as villain. And to include Heinlein's "Solution Unsatisfactory," which features no major villain, I was obliged to examine the dialogue of three minor villains and average the results.

Fry's method calls for the random selection of three one-hundred-word passages from the beginning, middle, and end of a book to establish its readability. Clearly, I could not follow this procedure, since I had to locate speeches by particular characters that were at least a hundred words long. I sought uninterrupted speeches because I thought that in the give and take of ordinary conversation, statements tend to be unrepresentatively short, whereas a lengthy speech would better reveal linguistic preferences. In a few instances—more often in the case of heroes, who tended to make fewer long speeches—I was obliged to incorporate portions of previous or following statements in order to create a one-hundred-word sample; because of this, and because my selection was not truly random, there was unconscious bias in some of the results. I am confident, however, that the overall tendency I observed is valid.

To study the other factors I examined entire short works and portions of longer works. I first counted the total number of sentences uttered by the hero and the villain, seeking a sample of at least a hundred sentences by each character. If a phrase ended with a period, question mark, or exclamation point, it was counted as a sentence, regardless of grammar. In the case of ambiguous ending punctuation—ellipses or a dash—if the next word was capitalized, the previous phrase was regarded as a separate sentence. In tabulating uses of particular surface structures I regarded each sentence as a unit of thought and counted how many sentences contained *at least one use* of the given structure. I must point out, therefore, that it is not necessarily true, for example, that Barron issues twenty-five commands in chapter 9 of Norman Spinrad's *Bug Jack Barron*; rather, there are twenty-five sentences of dialogue that each contain at least one command; that is, the total number of commands may be higher.

To simplify the counting I employed standards that were straightforward and naïve. I counted every instance of the imperative mode as a command, even if the statement—for example, "Please come visit me"—did not really have the force of a command. I counted only first-person pronouns as self-references. For instance, when Raymond Chandler's hero says, "The name is Philip Marlowe," the statement was not counted. Negative constructions had to be marked by a word like *no, not, never,* or *nobody;* even though a statement like "I left without speaking" might be analyzed as having the deep structure "I left and I did not speak," I did not include such examples. I defined the passive voice as the use of a copulative verb followed by a past participle; in addition, there had to be a possible transformation—however unwieldy—of the statement into the active voice. Thus, "I'm engaged" counted, since one could conceivably say, "I have engaged myself in marriage"; but the colloquial "I'm gone" did not count, since that statement cannot be so transformed. Any sentence, regardless of its structure, was counted as a question if it ended with a question mark. I also tabulated how many of the questions were simple questions and how many were information questions, but I did not include that breakdown because no strong pattern emerged in their use.

In discussing how this type of research might be expanded or improved, I must first report the reaction of Norman Spinrad, who was present when a version of this paper was presented at the Tenth Eaton Conference. He vehemently argued that he had deliberately crafted Barron as a character who *spoke* in short, simple sentences but *thought* in more complex, convoluted sentences; thus, by examining only his speech and not his interior monologues, I was not properly representing his character. Certainly, one additional avenue of research would be to analyze differences between characters' speech and thought patterns. However, in this case I point out that Barron is, after all, a talk show host, and regardless of the way he thinks, readers will inevitably judge him according to the way he talks. In having Barron talk in a simplified manner, Spinrad was still in a way conforming to conventional expectations. In fairness to Spinrad, though, I was inspired by his reaction to include *Bug Jack Barron* in my detailed analysis and found some evidence for his assertion that he was attempting something different in the novel: Barron was the only hero who issued more commands than the villain, and while he met the other criteria for heroic speech, he typically did so by a narrow margin. My conclusion is that Spinrad was essentially creating a story with *two* villains, one of whom, Barron, ultimately wins the reader's sympathy because his faults finally seem insignificant compared with the heinous crimes of the other villain, Howards.

Other possibilities for continued research follow; some of them were raised in comments following my paper presentation.

It might be useful, as a control, to include with the analysis of dialogue an examination of the author's narrative voice, to distinguish general patterns in speech from idiosyncratic authorial preferences in writing.

A flaw in my profile is that it is essentially comparative; villainous language is defined only as it compares with heroic speech. By incorporating the control described above and building a large data base, one might be able to establish an absolute model of villainous speech, one that could distinguish a villain even without reference to a heroic counterpart.

The research could move beyond heroes and villains to include ambiguous, mixed, or neutral characters; their speech might reflect a mixture of heroic and villainous traits, or something different might emerge.

To avoid complicating factors, I deliberately did not include any female characters in my analysis and used only three pairings of human and alien; but one might fruitfully conduct research of this type to examine differences in the dialogue of women and men, and of humans and English-speaking aliens. (I have completely avoided the troublesome issue of alien languages.)

There are many other linguistic structures in speech that could be studied and counted, including the use of coordinate and subordinate structures, use of second-person pronouns, the subjunctive mode, use of interjections, and use of active and copulative verbs.

Finally, many of the differences I have noticed are rooted in the peculiar history of the English language, in which a native, largely monosyllabic language (Old English) gradually blended with two foreign, largely polysyllabic languages (French and Latin) imposed by a ruling class during the Middle Ages. Therefore, a tendency to associate complex speech with domineering villainy may simply reflect the situation in medieval England, where oppressed peasants mostly spoke English while nobles and clerics mostly spoke French or Latin. One would need to study the dialogue of heroes and villains in foreign-language works to see which differences are universal and which are unique to English.

Notes

1. Eric Frank Russell, "And Then There Were None," pp. 319, 355.
2. The method was first described by Edward Fry in "A Readability Formula That Saves Time."

    In addition to the Russell novella, science fiction works examined were: C. J. Cherryh, *Downbelow Station*; Charles Fontenay, *The Day the Oceans Overflowed*; Robert A. Heinlein, *Between Planets*; Ursula K. Le Guin, "The Word for World Is Forest"; C. S. Lewis, *Perelandra*; Ross Rocklynne, "The Men and the Mirror"; E. E. Smith, *Galactic Patrol*; Norman Spinrad, *Bug Jack Barron*; and Jules Verne, *Twenty Thousand Leagues under the Sea*.

    General works examined were: Chinua Achebe, *A Man of the People*; Horatio Alger, Jr., *Cast upon the Breakers*; Raymond Chandler, "Red Wind"; Charles Dickens, *Hard Times*; Ian Fleming, *Doctor No*; Zane Grey, *The Last Trail*; John Steinbeck, *In Dubious Battle*; Robert Louis Stevenson, *The Master of Ballantrae*; Lew Wallace, *Ben-Hur*; and Nathaniel West, *Miss Lonelyhearts*.
3. The theories of Gernsback and Campbell are examined at length in "An Idea of Significant Import" and "A Convenient Analog System."
4. Gernsback, *Ralph 124C 41+*, p. 153.
5. Campbell, Introduction to *Who Goes There?*, p. 3.
6. This definition was most recently offered by Brian Aldiss and David Wingrove in *Trillion Year Spree*, p. 26.
7. Ibid., p. 388.
8. Gernsback, "Science Fiction Week," p. 1061.
9. Ibid.

Works Cited

Achebe, Chinua. *A Man of the People*. 1966. Garden City: Doubleday, 1967.
Aldiss, Brian W., with David Wingrove. *Trillion Year Spree: The History of Science Fiction*. New York: Atheneum, 1986. An earlier version, by Aldiss

alone, is *Billion Year Spree: The True History of Science Fiction*. New York: Schocken Books, 1973.

Alger, Horatio, Jr. *Cast upon the Breakers*. 1893. New York: Popular Library, 1974.

Campbell, John W., Jr. Introduction to *Who Goes There?* Chicago: Shasta Publishing, 1948.

Chandler, Raymond. "Red Wind" (1938). In *Trouble Is My Business*. New York: Ballantine Books, 1972.

Cherryh, C. J. [Carolyn Cherry]. *Downbelow Station*. New York: DAW Books, 1981.

Dickens, Charles. *Hard Times*. Edited by George Ford and Sylvere Monod. Norton Critical Edition. 1854. New York: W. W. Norton, 1966.

Fleming, Ian. *Doctor No*. 1958. New York: Signet Books, 1962.

Fontenay, Charles. *The Day the Oceans Overflowed*. 1964. Israel: Bridbook Publishers, n.d.

Fry, Edward. "A Readability Formula That Saves Time." *Journal of Reading* 11 (April 1968): 513–16, 575–78.

Gernsback, Hugo. *Ralph 124C 41+: A Romance of the Year 2660*. 1925. New York: Frederick Fell, 1950. Novel originally published in *Modern Electrics* in 1911 and 1912.

———. "Science Fiction Week." *Science Wonder Stories* 1 (May 1930): 1061.

Grey, Zane. *The Last Trail: A Story of the Early Days of the Ohio Valley*. 1909. New York: Belmont Tower Books, n.d.

Heinlein, Robert A. *Between Planets*. 1951. New York: Ace Books, n.d.

———. "Solution Unsatisfactory" (1940). In *Expanded Universe*. New York: Ace Books, 1980. Story originally published in *Astounding Science-Fiction* in 1940.

Le Guin, Ursula K. "The Word for World Is Forest" (1972). In *Again, Dangerous Visions*, vol. 1, ed. Harlan Ellison. New York: Signet Books, 1973.

Lewis, C. S. *Perelandra*. 1944. New York: Macmillan, 1965.

Rocklynne, Ross. "The Men and the Mirror" (1938). In *Before the Golden Age*, ed. Isaac Asimov. Garden City: Doubleday, 1974.

Russell, Eric Frank. "And Then There Were None" (1951). In *Science Fiction Hall of Fame*, vol. IIA, ed. Ben Bova. New York: Avon Books, 1974.

Smith, E. E. *Galactic Patrol*. 1937. New York: Pyramid Books, 1964.

Spinrad, Norman. *Bug Jack Barron*. New York: Avon Books, 1969.

Steinbeck, John. *In Dubious Battle*. 1936. New York: Viking Press, 1963.

Stevenson, Robert Louis. *The Master of Ballantrae: A Winter's Tale*. London and New York: Cassell and Company, 1889.

Verne, Jules. *Twenty Thousand Leagues under the Sea*. Translated by Anthony Bonner. 1870. New York: Bantam Books, 1962.

Wallace, Lew. *Ben-Hur: A Tale of the Christ*. 1880. New York: Grosset and Dunlap, 1922.

West, Nathaniel. *Miss Lonelyhearts* (1933). In *Miss Lonelyhearts and The Day of the Locust*. New York: New Directions Publishing, 1962.

Westfahl, Gary. " 'A Convenient Analog System': John W. Campbell, Jr.'s, Theory of Science Fiction." *Foundation: The Review of Science Fiction* 54 (Spring 1992): 52–70.

———. " 'An Idea of Significant Import': Hugo Gernsback's Theory of Science Fiction." *Foundation: The Review of Science Fiction* 48 (Spring 1990): 26–50.

Chapter 4

Warfare Celestial and Terrestrial: Osip Senkovsky's 1833 Russian Science Fantasy

Louis Pedrotti

Osip Senkovsky arrived in St. Petersburg in the autumn of 1821, after traveling for nearly two years in the Near East and northern Africa, including Egypt. Senkovsky was born Józef-Julian Sękowski in 1800 in a village near Wilno, Poland (now Vilnius, the Lithuanian capital). After finishing his studies in classical and Near Eastern languages at the University of Wilno in 1819 he began a remarkable journey that took him to Turkey, Syria, Egypt, Nubia, and the upper reaches of the Nile. For much of this time he traveled as a native, disguised in Arabic garb and speaking the local dialects with those he met along the way. Acknowledgment of his great erudition in the Oriental world was not long in arriving. He was invited to return to his alma mater in Wilno to be professor of Oriental languages, but he declined the offer for a more attractive one made to him by the University of St. Petersburg, where he remained until his retirement in 1847.

Meanwhile he had become famous not only as professor of Oriental languages and literatures but also as witty author of one of the most popular books of his day, *The Fantastic Journeys of Baron Brambeus*, published in 1833. The three travel stories that make up this volume (*Poetic Journey over the Great, Wide World*; *Scientific Journey to Bear Island*; and *Sentimental Journey to Mount Etna*) made Baron Brambeus a household name in Russia during the 1830s and 1840s. In an age dominated by great poets such as Aleksandr Pushkin and Mikhail Lermontov, Senkovsky's works came to exemplify Russian popular prose literature. The success of his tales adapted from Arabic literature and of the satires he wrote under the pseudonym Baron Brambeus brought him to the attention of Aleksandr Smirdin, the proprietor of St. Petersburg's largest bookstore. In 1834 Smirdin invited Senkovsky to join him in a new enterprise, the publication of a literary and scientific journal, *The Library for Reading (Biblioteka dlya Chteniya)*. Within a few years even Senkovsky's literary enemies, among them Gogol, Belinsky, Druzhinin, and Chernyshevsky, had to acknowledge that *The Library for Reading* had become the most widely read and best-run periodical in the country.[1] Incidentally, Senkovsky used his powers as editor of this influential magazine to wage his own war on behalf of a genuinely Russian literary language in prose. No less tireless were his journalistic battles against what he considered the excesses of writers of the romantic school. Nor did Senkovsky confine himself to journalistic attacks on his literary foes. His prose too is filled with sarcastic antiromantic parody and satire.[2]

From his studies at the University of Wilno Senkovsky acquired a lifelong interest in science and mechanics. His scientific research became even more intense after he retired from his academic and editorial duties. He followed with great interest the accomplishments of Louis Daguerre in photography, and he himself experimented with galvanoplastics, a system of making impressions and copies of objects by coating them electrolytically with a thin layer of metal. In fact, he considered galvanoplastics a great improvement over the daguerreotype method. Senkovsky was also attracted to technological and commercial advancements. He discovered new methods of preparing flax and hemp and obtaining finer grades of tobacco, and he developed a new process of staining wood. He even designed all the furnishings in his home. His interest in astronomy and music led him to believe that the harmony of the spheres was not merely a poetic metaphor, but that the same mathematical laws that govern the production of sounds in music apply to the harmonics of the universe as well—in short, that "the system of spheres is the harmonic order of divine music."[3] Incidentally, Senkovsky's scientific experiments with physics and music led him to develop an instrument that he hoped would embody, as fully as possible, the elements of an entire orchestra. This idea was finally realized in his "orchestrion," an immense contrivance composed of wind and string instruments, with a complex keyboard, bows, bellows, and several pedals. The sounds it produced were unique in that they very nearly reproduced the effect of a chorus of human voices. Among his other musical inventions were a five-stringed violin and a piano with a glass keyboard that produced soft and melodious tones.

One of Senkovsky's aims in founding *The Library for Reading* was to popularize contemporary achievements in the scientific world. He wanted to do more than merely educate his readers in scientific phenomena; he also set about the task of making them use the scientific method to think. He goaded his readers into questioning all scientific discoveries and theories, no matter how hallowed the source. For him there were few sacred cows in the world of science. To this end he wrote numerous articles on scientific subjects for *The Library for Reading*, such as "Theory of the Natural Sciences" (1837); "The Animal Origin of Sea Sand" (1839); "General Deductions on the Essence of Galvanic Currents, of Electrical and Chemical Affinities, Crystallization, Light, Heat, etc." (1843); "The Latest Discoveries of Faraday" (1846); "Meteorites and the Earth's Internal Fire" (1847); and "Electrical Sounds" (1849). So extensive was Senkovsky's journalistic coverage of the scientific world that one of his biographers declared that the popularization of the natural sciences was his principal service to Russian culture.[4]

Senkovsky the novelist was no less industrious in his pursuit of scientific material; he combined fiction and science to create some of his most popular works, many of them satirical in nature. The plots of many of his stories center on topical scientific subjects such as Halley's comet (*The Scientific Journey to Bear Island*), the controversy over the deciphering of the Rosetta stone (*Mikeria, the Nile Lily*; *Scientific Journey to Bear Island*), and recent discoveries in the excavations at Pompeii and Herculaneum (*Arithmetic*; *Sentimental Journey to Mount Etna*).

Like most of the subjects treated in his fictional works, Senkovsky's handling of warfare and armed conflict was usually satirical, an attitude that infuriated his many literary opponents. When he published *The Fantastic Journeys of Baron Brambeus*, he made topical use of the widely predicted appearance of Halley's comet in the year 1835, the most publicized and most widely ballyhooed appearance of the comet to date. The event was eagerly awaited not only in Western Europe and America but also in Russia. The comet was talked about and written about years before it was due to appear.[5] Senkovsky, knowing a good vehicle when he saw one, jumped at the opportunity to use the comet's next return to carry his message.

In *The Scientific Journey to Bear Island*, Baron Brambeus, Senkovsky's fictional alter ego, sets out on an expedition of exploration in the frozen tundra of northeastern Siberia. Traveling with the baron is a learned naturalist (naturally of German background), Dr. Spurtzmann, who is somewhat skeptical about Baron Brambeus's system of reading Egyptian hieroglyphs, which he learned from studying with the noted French Egyptologist Jean-François Champollion the Younger. The explorers eagerly decide to undertake an expedition to Bear Island, which lies off the mouth of the Lena River in the Arctic Ocean, after they learn from the natives that something called the Room of Writings is located there. When the two adventurers arrive at the top of Bear Island, they do indeed find an immense cave whose walls are covered with what Baron Brambeus immediately recognizes as authentic Egyptian hieroglyphs.

He begins to read the inscriptions in accordance with Champollion's system, wall by wall, while Dr. Spurtzmann copies down his dictation. The writings, it seems, constitute a narrative inscribed centuries ago by the last man left after a great flood covered this region. The lone survivor tells of his love for a beautiful but unfaithful antediluvian girl named Sayana. One day, his story goes, a comet appeared in the heavens. All the astronomers of the country, a land called Barabia, made pronouncements about it, some saying that it would pass over harmlessly, others maintaining that it would strike the earth somewhere in the vicinity of Barabia. But the ominous presence of this invader from space did not deter the Barabian army from continuing its war with its neighbors to the west in a land comprising today's Arctic island groups of Spitzbergen and Novaya Zemlya, as well as with a nation to the southwest, in what is today the Kyrgyz Republic, at that time inhabited by blacks. But not all armed conflict was waged against the external enemies of the state. Driven nearly mad by the threat of the assault by heaven, various groups of Barabian citizens began plundering the homes of the wealthy and murdering on the streets anyone who might even slightly be associated with astronomers, believed by the rabble to be the cause of the dread comet's appearance. The hero related the bloody events of the urban strife that occurred while his guests were gathered in his home to celebrate his marriage to Sayana:

Soon even the splendid embankment of the Lena River, where my home was located, began to fill up with riff-raff. We watched with horror the violent mobs as they wandered about in the darkness and filled the porticoes of countless buildings with their howling, when suddenly a hail of rocks began to pelt my windows. My guests hid behind the walls and columns. Sayana threw herself tearfully on my neck. My mother-in-law fainted. My uncle yelled out that they had injured his leg. The pandemonium became incredible. When I heard that the raging mob was taking the festive illumination of my home as an affront to the public distress, I immediately ordered the lamps extinguished and the shutters bolted. We remained in almost total darkness, but nevertheless we took all possible measures to protect ourselves in case of an attack. The sight of the noisy crowd of servants, horses, elephants, and mammoths that were gathered together in my courtyard and that belonged to the illustrious people celebrating in my home kept the rebels from making any further attempts. Some time later the neighborhood around my home was cleared, but in other parts of the city the disturbances continued as before.[6]

Soon after the hero's marriage to Sayana the comet did indeed strike the earth, and all Barabia was shaken with great quakes and inundated with raging floods. After long wanderings and attacks by bands of roving street gangs, the hero was finally reunited with his bride (who in the meantime had run off with another man)[7] on Bear Island, which before the celestial invasion had been just another local mountain peak. Weak from suffering and privation, they finally came upon the cave. Senkovsky's caustic commentary on the human folly of war continuing even in the face of nature's incursion is given through the hero's scratchings on the walls of the cave:

After finding almost at the very top of the mountain a large, comfortable cave, the same cave on whose walls I am now drawing these hieroglyphs, we selected it as our abode. The rain, accompanied by a strong neosouthern wind, continued incessantly, and the water kept on rising, each day engulfing a few more mountaintops, so that by the sixth morning from the entire archipelago there remained no more than five islands, considerably diminished in size. On the seventh day the wind shifted and began to blow from the new north, our former west. Within a few hours the whole sea was covered with countless numbers of strange-looking objects that rolled about on the surface of the water—very long looking and round things, at a distance looking like black logs. Curiosity made us leave the cave to get a closer look at this floating mass. To our extreme amazement we recognized in these logs our splendid army that had marched against the blacks, as well as the naked black troops of our enemy. Members of both armies had been lifted onto the waves, probably during the battle. The sea cast onto our shore several long lances that had been used by the blacks. I grabbed one of them and drew toward me a beautiful flat chest that was floating right alongside the mountain. After breaking it open against a rock we found inside only a bombastic speech that someone had composed on the eve of the battle in order to arouse the valor of the warriors. We threw this pompous speech back into the sea. Meanwhile, the wind had begun to blow from another direction, and both armies, after changing their battle positions, were borne off to the east.

Needless to say, Baron Brambeus and Dr. Spurtzmann are overjoyed at their discovery. They dream of the great fame and fortune that will be theirs when they return to Europe with the astounding news that once upon a time a splendid Egyptian empire existed in the frozen wastes of Siberia, once a warm and beautiful subtropical land of green forests and camels, a land that was engulfed by the Arctic Ocean and turned into the frigid tundra regions of present-day Siberia. Unfortunately, they are informed by a mineralogist that the symbols on the walls are not hieroglyphs, Egyptian or otherwise, but merely crystallized stalagmites, the work of water and weather. The return trip to Europe is a gloomy one indeed. Baron Brambeus and Dr. Spurtzmann exchange barely a dozen words. The Baron is disillusioned and bitter. "It's not my fault," he complains, "if nature plays tricks in such a way that her stupid jokes make real sense, in accordance with Champollion's grammar." Baron Brambeus vows never again to undertake any more scientific journeys.

In another of the stories comprising *The Fantastic Journeys of Baron Brambeus* Senkovsky made use of topical scientific material and took the opportunity to lampoon man in his militaristic mode. The rage over recent excavations at Herculaneum and Pompeii prompted *The Sentimental Journey to Mount Etna*. In this story Baron Brambeus, in his pursuit of a beautiful Italian girl, falls into the crater of Mount Etna, eventually ending up in a land where everything is upside down. Here all customs and emotions are the reverse of those to which the Baron is accustomed. Even the local speech is topsy-turvy: Baron Brambeus recognizes it as German, the language used on the face of the earth in discussing the deep philosophical questions propounded by German speculative philosophers such as Kant, Fichte, Schelling, and Hegel. The local inhabitants, of course, believe that it is Baron Brambeus who is walking upside down. Even wars are waged here in a topsy-turvy manner. Here is how the Baron describes this dark side of man's nature:

One day I was walking peacefully, upside down, along the sidewalk, my hands behind my back, when suddenly several upside-down men grabbed me without warning and hauled me off to the army recruitment office. They gave me a rifle, gunpowder, and bullets and sent me abroad, along with some other soldiers. I asked one of my comrades, "Are we going off to war?" "No," he replied, "we're going off to shoot our friends." "What ever is this called, what we're doing to them?" I asked in astonishment. "Nonintervention," he replied. We came to a large fortress, we began to shoot and fight and kill and be killed, and we captured it. I could have sworn that we were waging a bloody war. But after we took the fortress, our opponents came up to us, shook our hands, and said that after this they were completely convinced of our good intentions and friendship. It was only then that I saw that we had been waging a bloody peace. In short, the upside-down world is completely contrary to our rightside-up world.

Incidentally, the Baron eventually returns to Naples via Mount Vesuvius, out of which he is blown by a series of underground explosions.

Senkovsky's work deserves to be better known, for he is an important figure in the development of modern science fiction. His works belong in that line running from Swift's *Gulliver's Travels* (1726) through works like Ludvig Holberg's *The Journey of Niels Klim to the World Underground* (1741), Voltaire's *Micromégas* (1752), and Rostand's *Cyrano de Bergerac* (1897), which blend fascination about scientific discovery with a propensity to satirize the pretensions of science. More important, he anticipated, in the sheer enthusiasm with which he embraced scientific advances, writers such as Jules Verne. Indeed, Baron Brambeus's *Sentimental Journey to Mount Etna* may have been a source for Verne's classic *Journey to the Center of the Earth* (1864).

Furthermore, Senkovsky can be seen as the originator of what remains today a thriving subgenre of science fiction—the comet story. Here the line runs from H. G. Wells's classic story *In the Days of the Comet* (1906), written in anticipation of the next scheduled appearance of Halley's comet in 1910, to present-day works like Larry Niven and Jerry Pournelle's *Lucifer's Hammer* (1977). The latter novel, anticipating yet another return of Halley's comet (in 1986), continues the tradition of celestial assaults on our planet and the ensuing spectacle of war and conflagration. Gregory Benford and David Brin, in their novel *Heart of the Comet* (1986), give a new twist to the old theme.

Although Senkovsky was not the first in Russia to work in the science fiction mode, he deserves credit for popularizing the genre in his country. Science fantasy (the term Russians normally use for science fiction) had been probed before him by Mikhail Shcherbatov, Vilgelm Kyukhelbeker, Faddey Bulgarin, Vladimir Odoevsky, and Vladimir Sollogub. But it was Senkovsky who made the fusion of science with fiction popular in Russia. The name of Baron Brambeus on any work published in the 1830s and 1840s immediately attracted the interest of a large reading public. Echoes of Senkovsky's fantastic tradition can be found in many of the works of later writers. Since everybody was reading his stories and writing about him, Senkovsky had a significant influence on the development of Russian literature. His literary rivals were quick to emulate the Baron's successes in the world of fantasy. Vladimir Odoevsky's *The Year 4338 A.D.* (published in 1835 and 1840) concerns the dire consequences predicted for Earth in a later return of Halley's comet in that far-off year. Even Tolstoy and Dostoevsky echoed the concern raised by Senkovsky's "cometophobia" in *War and Peace* (1863–69)[8] and *The Brothers Karamazov* (1879–80),[9] respectively. Senkovsky's particular combination of cataclysmic terrestrial warfare linked to the menace of celestial destruction—the intervention of a vastly more powerful force from without that halts our bellicose course either by destroying us or by scaring us into passive awe—echoes (in varying degrees) through the works of more recent Soviet fiction writers such as Aleksey Tolstoy in *Aelita* (1922–23), Evgeny Zamiatin in *We* (1924), Mikhail Bulgakov in *The Fatal Eggs* (1925), and even Ivan Efremov in his classic *Andromeda: A Space Age Tale* (1957). But the true inheritors of Senkovsky, in his unique combination of far-flung fantasy and sharply targeted, biting satire, are the Strugatsky brothers. The destructive folly of warfare, again magnified to a cosmic scale for satiric purposes, receives a Senkovskian treatment in their *Hard to Be a God* (1963) and in novels like *Second Invasion of the Martians* (1967). Another of Senkovsky's fortes—the satirical, fantastic treatment of scientific pretensions—is masterfully carried on in novels like *Monday Begins on Saturday* (1966), about the "Soviet Institute of Thaumaturgy," and *Snail on a Slope* (1966–68). Senkovsky's comico-serious treatment of this theme is brought to new heights in the Strugatskys' masterpiece, *Roadside Picnic* (1972), a work that greatly intrigued the Polish writer Stanislaw Lem. And indeed, Lem's own work, developing on a parallel track and itself, from its particular national viewpoint, also straddling the cultures of Western and Eastern Europe, also seems to echo Senkovskian themes and techniques: scientific pretension in *Solaris* (1961), the folly of cosmic warfare in *The Invincible* (1963), and the fabulous "journey" to a satiric country of the mind in *Futurological Congress* (1971). Indeed, it is in the Eastern European sphere that Senkovsky's influence has been most important and pervasive (e.g., Karel Capek's satirical novel *The War with the Newts*, 1937). His presence in Eastern European science fantasy is pervasive and deserves to be studied in detail.

Finally, we may see an ironic example of art anticipating reality, perhaps, in what happened at Tunguska in 1908, when a gigantic explosion occurred in almost the same region of northeastern Siberia where Senkovsky's fictive comet invaded Earth. This devastating cataclysm is still being investigated, and various explanations have been proposed. Controversy still surrounds what has been recognized as the brightest and most massive fireball on record. If, as some scientists maintain,[10] the huge explosion was caused by a comet entering Earth's atmosphere and disintegrating several miles above Siberia, then we may indeed regard Senkovsky's popular literary ventures into science in 1833 as not so fantastic after all.

Notes

I thank the Committee on Research of the Academic Senate, University of California, Riverside, for its assistance in the research of this project. I am grateful to George Slusser, curator of the Eaton Collection of Fantasy and Science Fiction, for his invaluable assistance in relating Senkovsky's work in science fiction to that of other writers of the genre.

1. N. V. Gogol, "O dvizhenii zhurnal'noy literatury v 1834 i 1835 godu," in *Sobranie sochineniy* (Moscow: Gos. Izd. Khudozh. Lit., 1950), 6:91; V. Belinskiy, "Nichto o nichem," in *Sobranie sochineniy v trekh tomakh* (Moscow: Gos. Izd. Khudozh. Lit., 1948), 1:191; A. Druzhinin, "O. I. Senkovskiy," in *Sobranie sochineniy* (St. Petersburg: Imp. Akademiya Nauk, 1858), 7:779; N. Chernyshevskiy, *Ocherki gogolevskogo perioda russkoy literatury* (Moscow: Gos. Izd. Khudozh. Lit., 1953), pp. 534–35.
2. For a discussion of Senkovsky's war on archaic language and the romantic style see Louis Pedrotti, *Józef-Julian Sękowski. The Genesis of a Literary Alien* (Berkeley and Los Angeles: University of California Press, 1965), pp. 102–3, 152–53, 160–62.
3. P. Savelyev, "O zhizni i trudakh O. I. Senkovskogo," foreword to O. I. Senkovskiy, *Sobranie sochineniy* (St. Petersburg: Imp. Akademiya Nauk, 1858), 1:cvii.
4. S. Stavrin, "O. I. Senkovskiy," *Delo* 6 (1874): 33.
5. Mikhail P. Pogodin, "Galleeva kometa," *Kometa Bely* 6 (1833): 1–23; Anonymous, "Kuplety iz vodeviliya: Na drugoy den' posle prestavleniya sveta, ili Kometa 1832 goda," *Molva*, January 26, 1833, pp. 29–30; G. Perevoshchikov, "O komete 1835 goda," *Molva*, February 5, 1832, pp. 41–44; Anonymous, *Moskovskiy Telegraf* 4 (1831): 297–98; "R.," "O komete 1832 goda," *Moskovskiy Vestnik* 9 (1828): 96–101; Anonymous, "O vliyanii komet na zemlyu i ee zhiteley," pt. 1, *Teleskop* 16 (1833): 354–81; Anonymous, "O vliyanii komet na zemlyu i ee zhiteley," pt. 2, *Teleskop* 17 (1833): 195–208.
6. The translations from Senkovsky's *Fantastic Journeys of Baron Brambeus*

are mine, taken from Osip Ivanovich Senkovsky, *Sobranie sochineniy* (St. Petersburg: Imp. Akademiya Nauk, 1858), 2:3–278.

7. A good part of the hieroglyphic narrative deals with "the woman question," as the Russians called the growing feminist movement in the early part of the nineteenth century. Senkovsky used the occasion to give voice to the demands of women for a more public role in Russian society.

8. L. N. Tolstoy, *Voyna i mir*, in *Sobranie sochineniy v 14-kh tomakh* (Moscow: Gos. Izd. Khudozh. Lit., 1951), 5:377 (translation mine):

It was frosty and clear. Above the dirty, ill-lit streets, above the black roofs, stretched the dark, starry sky. Only as he gazed up at the sky did Pierre cease to feel the humiliating pettiness of all earthly things compared with the heights to which his soul had just been raised. At the entrance to the Arbat Square an immense expanse of the dark, starry sky appeared before Pierre's eyes. Almost in the center of this sky, above Prechistensky Boulevard, surrounded and spangled on all sides by stars but distinguished from them all by its nearness to the earth, by its white light and its long upturned tail, shone the huge, brilliant comet of the year 1812—the comet that was said to portend all kinds of horrors and the end of the world. In Pierre, however, this bright star with its long, luminous tail aroused no feeling of horror. On the contrary, Pierre gazed joyously, his eyes moist with tears, at this radiant star which, having traveled in its orbit with inconceivable velocity through immeasurable space, seemed suddenly, like an arrow piercing the earth, to remain fixed in its chosen spot in the black sky, its tail vigorously poised, shining and disporting itself with its white light among the countless other scintillating stars. It seemed to Pierre that this star fully corresponded with what was in his own mollified and uplifted soul, now blossoming into a new life.

9. Fyodor Dostoevskiy, *Brat'ya Karamazovy*, in *Sobranie sochineniy* (Moscow: Gos. Izd. Khudozh. Lit., 1958), 10:172 (translation mine):

[The Devil, to Ivan:] But you know, our present earth has repeated itself perhaps as many as a billion times: why, it has died out, got itself covered with ice, cracked, broken to pieces, decomposed into its original component elements; and again there would be just "the water above the firmament," then again a comet, again the sun, again the earth from the sun—you know, this process can repeat itself infinitely and always in the same way, over and over again, to the minutest detail. How intolerably boring.

10. Mark Littmann and Donald K. Yeomans, *Comet Halley. Once in a Lifetime* (Washington, D.C.: American Chemical Society, 1985), p. 80.

Chapter 5

"The Evils of a Long Peace": Desiring the Great War

Laurence Davies

In that chilly part of our continent where I live, a local insurance company runs a series of ads showing happy golfers and blithe hunters under threat of imminent but unnoticed disaster. "My insurance company?" they say, "New England Life, of course"—just before they're crushed by a thousand pounds of boulder or an even greater quantity of moose or grizzly bear. Any modern student of future-war stories written in the period 1871–1914 must feel like the knowing reader of such advertisements. With very few exceptions (such as Wilhelm Lamszus, author of *The Human Slaughter-House*, which is so closely focused that it doesn't seem like speculation at all),[1] those who imagined the coming Great War got it wrong. The dreadful near immobility of the front in Western Europe, the struggles by attrition and atrocity on the Eastern Front, the victories by misadventure in East Africa, and the absolute futility of the Gallipoli landings bore little resemblance to the exciting military offensives and decisively catastrophic naval battles of fiction. After them, the real deluge.

But they were serious, weren't they—these authors of seventy or more years ago? Indeed. Many, perhaps most, offered an agenda: in general, the dangers of military unreadiness; in particular, whatever seemed most menacing—a shortage of men, battleships, or technical education, an abundance of spies, old-fashioned guns, cronyism and snobbery in high places. No doubt many writers believed that their calls to action would avert catastrophe. If armies were to exist at all, then in a local sense the authors were often right: modern warfare does call for more sappers and fewer hussars.

In a broader sense, of course, specific reforms are never enough and may even create a more disastrous complacency than the one they challenge; the view from a hobbyhorse is not extensive, steady thought is difficult in a bee-loud bonnet.

Yet the real issue is not a failure of the imagination; quite the reverse. Moving outside that portion of the literary cosmos where authors' aims are simple, rational, and explicit, one might argue that to write *about* future wars is to write *against* them. "Look at the horrible consequences of not listening to us," the books seem to say. "Don't prove us right." One might even look on such works as attempts to write warfare out of existence—to expunge the worst thing in the world by putting it down on paper. Imagining tragedies and disasters may be taken as a form of homeopathic magic, that kind of magic that makes bad events happen in magical space to stop them from happening in the world outside.

Nevertheless, I'm concerned with the risks involved in these homeopathic activities. I want to speculate about the ways in which future-war narratives before 1914—the I. F. Clarke period, it's tempting to call it—embody desires for war and its attendant destructiveness as much as a desire for peace. It's not my intention to blame the entire First World War on Lieutenant Colonel Chesney and his once-notorious *The Battle of Dorking*, nor even to curse the memory of such ruthless mongers of war and sensation as William Le Queux and Alfred Harmsworth, his appalling boss. It's not my intention, either, to put the reading public in the dock. However one wants to describe it—as reader response and writer response, as supply and demand, as base and superstructure—the relationship of cause and effect in cultural studies is ambiguous if not downright shadowy. Nor, finally, do I mean to suggest that the ideas and longings under discussion were universally welcome or universally held. Nevertheless, sometimes by subterranean routes, sometimes out in the open, enthusiasm for war and fascination with its possibilities snake through the landscape of late nineteenth- and early twentieth-century Europe and North America. Any resemblance to our own time and place is probably not an accident.

I. F. Clarke did a splendid job of presenting future-war stories in the context of political anxieties.[2] The development of new weapons and an unprecedented arms race involving Japan, the major European powers, and the United States opened up alarming prospects. Tensions over colonial expansion and competition for new markets produced crisis after crisis: Fashoda, the Venezuela-Guyana border, Manchuria, Agadir, and all the rest. Paranoia ruled the waves. Consider two quotations from a political commentator: "That there exists, in spirit if not in letter, a worldwide confederation against us has been plain to us, and to the rest of the world, any time since January, 1896." "Unless we increase our strength to a point that warns off aggression, we shall have either to give up all the sources of our greatness, or fight for them on conditions that will put a premium on defeat."[3] The author was British but might equally well have been French, American, or German. And whatever one's country, it was always the real victim, threatened and misunderstood by insolent foreign schemers—threatened and misunderstood, yet stoically taking on the task of international policeman with the cry "Who if not us?" Here is the voice of a high official of the Anglican church best known for his tearful children's stories: "While the world continues to be what it is, the suppression of all appeals to the decision of war would involve the certain and absolute triumph of robbery, oppression, greed and injustice."[4] Dean Farrar wrote those words during the Boer War, a conflict aptly described by one contemporary dissident as a brawl between two burglars.

What does not emerge so clearly from I. F. Clarke's study is that a noisy section of public opinion shamelessly welcomed the prospect of a bloody conflict; this section, furthermore, was by no means made up only of soldiers and sailors looking for work.

The cure for national effeteness, so the argument ran, was a purgative dose of cordite. Listen, for example to "Dux," a regular columnist in the *Manchester Sunday Chronicle*. The date is 1898: "The risk of war seems to me an excellent stimulant to a nation; it keeps the national fibre well strung and its men manly. . . . The war tax may be a heavy drain on commerce, but the war risk is a wholesome antidote to the enervating influence of the gold craze, and the art worship."[5] Note that his unsurprising dismissal of "the art worship" sits next to his more surprising disapproval of "the gold craze." The coming wars will be fought to protect commercial interests: "that we may be able to continue our trade better we must be ready to enter on the battle of shot and shell." Nevertheless—and here the double bind clamps shut—commerce is "enervating": "don't you think the huckster spirit will grow, as the martial spirit, which is after all a man's spirit, decreases?" Pity the manly man of the English 1890s, expected to lay down his life for commerce while hating it the while. Now listen to an *unexpectedly* intemperate voice, that of the otherwise gentle-mannered naturalist W. H. Hudson. He wrote, in 1913, to Edward Garnett, a left-leaning publisher's editor: "Still I hope to stay on to see the flame of war brighten in this peace-rotten land. It will look very beautiful to many watchers and have a wonderful purifying effect." Even by 1915 the slaughter hadn't changed his mind: "The blood that is being shed will purge us of many hateful qualities—of our caste feeling, of our detestable partisanship, our gross selfishness, and a hundred more."[6] The fires of Armageddon are necessary, cleansing, and—we should note for future reference—"very beautiful." *Götterdämmerung* will be worth the price of admission.

I, for one, would rather rot at leisure than be turned immediately into hamburger, but the notion that tranquillity corrupts was not simply an aberration of the nineteenth century. As far back as the second, Juvenal complained, "Nunc patimur longae pacis mala" ("Now we suffer the evils of a long peace").[7] Nonetheless, the claim that war improves society did not attract the late Victorians only as a classical commonplace suitable for beating into the minds of boyish boys who were soon to be manly men. To borrow Frank Kermode's phrase—with an admiring nod toward Warren Wagar's work on this topic—here was a society spellbound by the sense of an ending, listening for the century's death rattle. One of the 1890s' most widely cited works—an international best-seller—was Max Nordau's preposterous attack on the spirit of everything modern, *Degeneration*.

But an eagerness to turn degeneration on its head did not come only from residence in a dying century; the arrival of its successor meant more of the same. The social Darwinists, Teddy Roosevelt and the football coaches of America among them, taught that existence is a struggle from which only the fit march away triumphant. If the metaphor of life as battle could be made literal, the process of "natural" selection would accelerate. If, on the contrary, society made survival too easy, all kinds of undesirables would be kept alive. An article in *Blackwood's Magazine* (1898) objects to such tender-heartedness. It is titled "The New Humanitarianism":

> Civilisation is making it much too easy to live; humanitarianism is turning approval of easiness of living into the one standard of virtue. A wiser standard of civilisation would look, not to the indiscriminate preservation of life, but to the quality of the life preserved. A wiser humanitarianism would make it easy for the lower quality of life to die. It sounds brutal, but why not? We have let our brutality die too much.[8]

Also in the 1890s, M. P. Shiel wrote a detective story about a secret society dedicated to murdering the unhealthy. By a horribly prophetic irony, it is called "The S.S."[9]

To the martial mind, peace is dull as well as weakening. So great was the appetite for battlefield dispatches that it could not be satisfied by news of imperial campaigns in China, Burma, the Sudan, and West and South Africa. British newspapers devoted column after column to vigorous accounts of the Spanish-American, Graeco-Turkish, and Russo-Japanese conflicts. Encouraged by the availability of the electric telegraph, reporting became terser, more vivid, and more dramatic. Here is the Turkish army going into action: "Little dots of skirmishers, little clumps of main body, black lumps of supports began to dapple the brown. Slowly, slowly they moved—but they moved. The field began to be full of them. It began to be so full that the men seemed to be standing still and the field to be drawn slowly back through them, like the great brown roll of a musical box through the black teeth."[10] In descriptions like this, war becomes an aesthetic object. The decadents made fun of the doers for their utilitarianism and their admiration of what was ugly; in writing artistically about war, the ugliest and most utilitarian of all pursuits, the doers took their revenge.

War correspondents became journalistic celebrities who could travel on a generous budget. From Italy came Luigi Barzini, from England G. W. Steevens, from the United States Richard Harding Davis, Stephen Crane, and Cora Crane—the first woman in this noisily virile company.[11] In an age when the front was a long way off, these correspondents exercised a peculiar authority. They *knew*. They enabled the stay-at-home reader to experience "the real thing," to find out what life was "all about." Let me quote again from G. W. Steevens's *With the Conquering Turk*, which was assembled, like his other best-sellers, from dispatches to the London *Daily Mail*. This passage comes from a chapter called "What War Feels Like": "The preoccupations of peace had imperceptibly ceased to preoccupy; things that mattered everything had ceased to matter in the least. The sum of it was that everything artificial, conventional, social, had vanished and you were left the bare natural man."[12]

If, as the counterdecadents asserted, to do was better than to dream, war was desirable as the supreme form of doing—and, what was more, the supreme form of experience. Such ideas were popular among the philosophers of the yellow press, but they weren't entirely absent from the avant-garde. In its most extravagant form, the cult of war is exalted in the Futurist Manifest of 1909. Here are the first, part of the seventh, and the ninth points:

1. We intend to sing the love of danger, the habit of energy and fearlessness.
7. Except in struggle, there is no more beauty. No work without an aggressive character can be a masterpiece. . . .

9. We will glorify war—the world's only hygiene—militarism, patriotism, the destructive gesture of freedom—bringers, beautiful ideas worth dying for, and scorn for women.[13]

Top that if you can, Robert Heinlein.

But the real thing could so far only be found in such exotic locations as Cuba, Ethiopia, Thessaly, and the Transvaal; in order to be brought home—in both senses of the phrase—it had to become fiction.

Future-war stories, in other words, did not appear against a neutral backdrop. They appeared in a culture familiar with the notions that war was the great simplifier of issues and the great resolver, that war was exhilarating, spectacular, and purifying. No wonder that the pacifists found it hard to compete. No wonder that earnest military gentlemen with a point to make about the strategic value of heavy artillery got carried away. No wonder that even the most cynically motivated examples of the genre can insist on their own sublimity. As William Le Queux observed of a London devastated by *The Great War in England in 1897*, "The burning of Babylon was a sight of awful, appalling grandeur."[14]

Fictions of future war did not, however, corner the market in sublimity. Their visions of chaos come again showed a close affinity with two other kinds of narrative popular around the turn of the century: the fiction of natural disaster, in which great cities founder amid fog, flood, earthquake, or flame; and the fiction of political or personal terrorism, in which anarchists, revolutionaries, or mad scientists do the honors. These categories overlap: in George Griffith's *The Angel of the Revolution* (1893), for example, the alien armies besieging London and its "helpless millions . . . crowded within the impassable ring of fire and smoke"[15] are finally defeated by the airships of an anarchist air force, commanded by a Jewish genius who, despite his name (which is Satan spelled backward), wants to make the world safe for the Anglo-Saxon race.

The Angel was illustrated by Fred T. Jane, himself an impressive creator of mixed scenarios. It is hard to do justice to his *Violet Flame* (1899), enticingly subtitled *A Story of Armageddon and After*, a book that has everything: the activities of the Finis Mundi Society, a group of anarchists who, far from wanting a better tomorrow, are bent on finishing off humanity today; the mad Professor Mirzabeau, a.k.a. The Beast, who declares: "I am the man . . . I can destroy the whole earth. It is ill, diseased; the great tonic that I propose shall kill or cure it"; Mirzabeau's discovery, a wonderful ray capable of turning humans to stone and vaporizing London's largest train station; a comet that passes close to the earth, raising a tidal wave so vast that it engulfs London, drowning millions of Londoners and making the loss of a mere railroad terminal trivial; brutal riots among the survivors and orgies of looting that can only be put down by the fortunate arrival of the Royal Navy:

> There were ships in the Pool, some still floating, many lying in the mud. On some we saw bodies of looters, and we stopped every now and again to fire these. It was rather like rat-hunting.
> "Three of my crew are . . . crack shots," explained Bentham calmly, as he watched a sailor in the bow picking off the rioters one after the other. "Strange, is it not, the pleasure one soon gets in killing one's fellows?"[16]

Even if the categories of disaster fiction did not overlap, it would be revealing to discuss them side by side. The opportunities for luridly describing catastrophe are the same in each, as are the opportunities for moral posturing.

Besides, the disaster novels have one distinctive technique in common. However extravagant, however cataclysmic the events of the story, they must take place in a recognizable, preferably familiar, and often famous place. Chesney set the precedent in 1871 with his carefully worked out invasion routes through the tranquil Home Counties, rural yet dangerously close to London.[17] In 1915—still prewar in the United States—J. Bernard Walker's *America Fallen* put the climactic scene in New York's Woolworth Building, at that time the tallest structure in the world and the subject of many articles in the illustrated magazines:

> The stairs ended in space, and through a gaping hole, where the hollow-tile flooring had been blasted entirely away, he saw that the whole two stories, with their floors, outer walls, and inside partitions, had been blown clear into space, leaving the skeleton of the building—columns, floor beams, and braces—stripped as clean of its brick and terra walls as it was when the erecting gang had swung it into place, a few years ago.[18]

The more cynical operators in the genre could even provide military devastation to order. When Alfred Harmsworth stood as Conservative candidate for Portsmouth, he became the owner of a local newspaper just in time to carry William Le Queux's *Siege of Portsmouth*, a bloodthirsty invasion novel. I'm happy to report that neither the serial nor the special posters showing the Town Hall Square crammed with the dead and dying impressed the electorate enough to make them vote for the rising tycoon.[19]

Other kinds of catastrophe novel also localize the monstrous. In *The Doom of the Great City* (1880), William DeLisle Hay sends his narrator down from the safety of the Surrey Hills to his inner London lodgings. The entire population has been asphyxiated by a toxic fog. As the narrator advances through carefully specified suburban intersections, he finds buses loaded with dead passengers, the horses dead in the traces—one of those buses is vividly and gruesomely depicted on the binding. Farther in, he visits a tavern he had known: "There were the half-empty glasses upon the counter, those who had been drinking from them lying stark upon the floor; men in all the frippery of evening dress, the cigar or cigarette just fallen from their twisted lips."[20] These scenes and many more like them take their energy from the combination of known territory and unknown, or at least unexpected, terrors. The best and probably the most accessible examples are the scenes in and around London in *The War of the Worlds*. Wells and the others applied the same circumstantial realism to future horrors that Defoe, in his *Journal of the Plague Year*, applied to the horrors of the past.

The one critical advantage of keeping the future-war novel at arm's length from the other narratives of catastrophe is that one can then come up with a handsome pair of matching metaphors; thus war would signify ecological disaster and ecological disaster would signify war. But it is more enlightening to think in terms of metonymy and reinforcement. There's no denying the great variety of surface agendas—the need to keep an eye on anarchists differs from the need to keep an eye on artillery procurements and differs again from the need to keep an eye on killer fogs. Yet beneath the surface, all the catastrophe stories speak to similar anxieties and—to introduce a phrase that only *seems* incongruous—offer similar pleasures.

Anxieties first, pleasures later. The primary anxieties or discontents stemmed from the size, complexity, and moral condition of modern civilization. The moral issues concerned sexual identity and the privileges of gender, the use and abuse of riches, the distressing abundance of poverty, "idleness" and unemployment, the future of religious belief, and all the other symptoms and sicknesses of the national health—physical, cultural, and spiritual. On the issues of size and complexity, William DeLisle Hay makes a strong witness. Sixty years after the great fog of 1882, his narrator, writing from the pastoral safety of New Zealand, remembers "the monstrous proportions of the 'Great City.' For miles and miles around us on every side were streets and squares and endless ranks of houses, ever extending outwards, and absorbing suburb after suburb beneath stone and brick. The population—some four millions in number—was a nation in itself."[21]

Thus the issues of size, complexity, and moral worth converged: the places most evidently in need of purification were the great cities, growing ever larger, ever more intricate, ever more massive, yet ever more vulnerable. Here were the places that war, revolution, or natural calamity would purge and simplify.

And where was the pleasure in contemplating such relentless destruction of homes and such brutal savaging of human bodies? Some authors suggested that the aftermath would be worth the struggle. *The Angel of the Revolution* ends with the happy assurance that "there is not a regiment of men under arms in all the civilised world. The last battle has been fought and won, and so there is peace on earth at last." But the carnage in these books is always dreadful. Griffith again, this time in *The Outlaws of the Air* (1895). Showing some initiative, he has chosen Strasbourg for the hecatomb: "It was short, sharp, and terrible. The streets were swept with incessant storms of Maxim bullets, and shells began bursting in fifty parts of the city at once. The air-ships flew to and from far beyond the range of terrestrial weapons, and in an hour the city lay little better than one vast shambles under the hurricane of death and destruction that had swept over it."[22]

We'd be on surer ground if we invoked an aesthetic of the sublime, a late romantic craving for terrifying yet pleasurable grandeur. When they are not laying mountains low, sublime disasters in the early nineteenth century are usually located in sacred or secular history—as in John Martin's paintings of the Fall, the Flood, and the Day of Judgment, and Thomas Cole's of the course of empire. (Elaborations of the Last Man theme make a partial exception.) The later nineteenth century brought the sublime to the present-day streets of Paris, London, and New York. That is not to say that everywhere else escaped, mind you. When the sun loses its vigor in Gabriel de Tarde's *Underground Man*, "The entire population of Norway, Northern Russia, and Siberia perished; frozen to death in a single night";[23] frozen, one might add, by a few deft turns of the pen. But cities do become the principal arenas for such bloodier than gladiatorial displays.

I'm not convinced, though, that appealing to a notion of sublimity will uncover all that is hidden. There's so much moral gusto in these panoramas of retribution. Susan Sontag's valuable essay on science fiction movies provides the necessary supplement. The imagination of disaster, as she calls it, brews an intoxicating blend of wish fulfillment and punitive fantasy.[24] While summoning one authority, I'll call upon another—an uncle who watched his eighteen-month-old nephew playing with a wooden reel attached to a string, making it appear and disappear, *fort, da;* now you see it, now you don't. In this way, his Uncle Freud speculated, the child gained some power in an apparently unreliable world.[25] The whole catastrophe genre is a titanic game of *fort, da* played at the expense of great cities.

Fantasies of metropolitan collapse are not only motivated by the will to punish. They are also shaped by a longing for freedom. Disaster obliterates boundaries, suspends routines, and inverts patterns of behavior or tears them to shreds.[26] It allows all that is oppressively solid to melt or burn away. In more than one sense disaster unleashes; it sets loose all kinds of horrors, but it also sets free. Imagining disaster may work as homeopathic magic intended to avert everything undesirable, but it also permits the harmless enjoyment of what is secretly desired.

But no, not entirely harmless. To quote Friedrich Dürrenmatt's *The Physicists*—a play about imminent rather than actual catastrophe—"What was once thought can never be unthought."[27] The belief that society could be purged only by total cataclysm did not originate in the future-war genre, nor did it end there. But the genre did play its part in keeping that belief in motion. The coalition of authors and readers did not—could not—imagine the worst, but it helped—only *helped*—to make it come about. What is worse, the fictions in question bred a familiarity with violence that was dangerously inexperienced and thus too casual in its understanding of the consequences. And worst of all was the longing for drastic consequences, for a purgation that was "short, sharp and terrible," a longing all the more perilous for being unacknowledged.

Notes

1. *The Human Slaughter-House: Scenes from the War That Is Sure to Come*, trans. Oakley Williams (London: Hutchinson, n.d.).
2. In *Voices Prophesying War, 1783–1964* (London: Oxford University Press, 1966). See also his bibliographical study, *The Tale of the Future* (London: Library Association, 1972); Michael Moorcock's anthology *Before Armageddon* (London: Wyndham, 1976); and Bruce Franklin's *War Stars: The Superweapon and the American Imagination* (New York: Oxford University Press, 1988).
3. G. W. Steevens, *Naval Policy* (London: Methuen, 1896), pp. 189, 190.
4. F. W. Farrar, "Imperialism and Christianity," *North American Review* 171(1900): 291.

5. "Wars and Rumours of Wars," February 27, 1; "Dux" was the Fabian Socialist Hubert Bland.
6. Edward Garnett, ed., *153 Letters from W. H. Hudson* (London: Nonesuch, 1923), pp. 116, 129.
7. *Satires* 6:292.
8. *Blackwood's Magazine* 163:103.
9. Collected in *Prince Zaleski* (London: John Lane, 1895).
10. G. W. Steevens, *With the Conquering Turk* (Edinburgh: Blackwood, 1897), p. 171.
11. Phillip Knightley, *The First Casualty: From the Crimea to Viet Nam* (New York: Harcourt Brace, 1975); and Lillian Barnard Gilkes, *Cora Crane* (Bloomington: Indiana University Press, 1960).
12. Steevens, *Conquering Turk*, p. 311.
13. Filippo Tommaso Marinetti, trans. and ed. R. W. Flint and Arthur A. Coppotelli, *Marinetti: Selected Writings* (New York: Farrar, Straus and Giroux, 1972), pp. 41–42.
14. Moorcock, *Before Armageddon*, p. 115; the first of the many editions of Le Queux's story appeared in 1894 (London: Tower Publishing).
15. *The Angel of the Revolution* (London: Tower Publishing), p. 149.
16. *The Violet Flame* (London: Ward, Lock), pp. 59, 223.
17. In the same year, Bracebridge Hemyng imagined revolutionary mayhem in the fashionable streets of the capital itself; see *The Commune in London: Or Thirty Years Hence* (London: C. H. Clarke).
18. *America Fallen* (New York: Dodd, Mead), p. 104.
19. Hamilton Fyfe, *Northcliffe* (New York: Macmillan, 1930), pp. 90–91.
20. *The Doom of the Great City: Being the Narrative of a Survivor, Written A.D. 1942* (London: Newman, 1880), pp. 47–48.
21. Ibid., p. 9.
22. *The Outlaws of the Air* (London: Tower Publishing), pp. 369–70.
23. *Underground Man* (London: Duckworth, 1905; reprint, Westport, Conn.: Hyperion, 1974), p. 54.
24. *Against Interpretation and Other Essays* (New York: Farrar, Straus and Giroux, 1966), pp. 209–25.
25. Sigmund Freud, *Beyond the Pleasure Principle*, trans. James Strachey (New York: Norton, 1961), pp. 8–11.
26. For a phenomenology of such events, see Maurice Blanchot, *L'Écriture du désastre* (Paris: Gallimard, 1980).
27. *The Physicists*, trans. James Kirkup (New York: Grove, 1964), p. 92.

Chapter 6

Armed Conflict in the Science Fiction of H. G. Wells

Arthur Campbell Turner

After the death of H. G. Wells in 1946 his reputation sank into a trough. This is a common development when an author who has been very much in the public eye passes on. It happened to Anthony Trollope, to Wells's contemporaries Arnold Bennett and John Galsworthy, and more recently to G. B. Shaw and J. P. Marquand. Sometimes their stocks rise again in the marketplace of reputations, sometimes not. At any rate, it should not have surprised Wells, since it was something he expected and even, so he said, welcomed. "What I write goes now, and will presently die." He said this or something like it many times. He claimed not to be interested in being regarded as an artist, though in fact he had great literary gifts. Still, even he could hardly have welcomed the fact that his reputation, and his influence, had waned long before his death. His greatest popular success was *The Outline of History* in the early 1920s; his most ambitious and prophetic work was *The Shape of Things to Come* (1933). But from the middle 1920s through the two remaining decades of his life, it was not fashionable to take him seriously as a novelist, as a social critic, or as an advocate of causes.

More recently there has been a notable revival of interest, demonstrated, and no doubt propelled along, by a series of excellent works. Without any intention of embarking on a complete list, which would be fairly long, one must mention a few of the more significant. Since Wells's death, the outstanding disciple and leading champion of his *political* ideas has been the American academic W. Warren Wagar, who wrote *H. G. Wells and the World State* (1961), *The City of Man* (1963; only in part about Wells), and

H. G. Wells: Journalism and Prophecy (1964). As the dates show, Wagar was a pioneer. He began his discipleship when his hero's reputation was at its nadir: "When I first probed into the possibility of a doctoral dissertation on H. G. Wells in 1954, popular and scholarly interest in Wells was practically extinct."[1] The acquisition of Wells's papers by the University of Illinois, and the subsequent publication of the beautifully edited volumes of some of his correspondence, made a big difference. Then in 1975 came the splendid biography *The Time Traveller*, by Norman and Jeanne Mackenzie, followed in 1984 by *H. G. Wells: Aspects of a Life*, by Anthony West, Wells's son by Rebecca West (Cicily Isabel Fairfield, 1892–1983). Also published in 1984 was a posthumous book by Wells himself, *H. G. Wells in Love*, comprising autobiographical material too indelicate in substance to have been published during his lifetime. It was intended specifically by Wells to supplement his interesting but very patchy *Experiment in Autobiography* (1934). On the whole, this book made very little difference to Wells's reputation.

In these books on Wells and in various articles in periodicals there has been much debate about his fundamental worldview: was it optimistic or pessimistic? One view, which has become a rather widely accepted critical cliché about Wells, is the one put forward in varying terms by George Orwell, Virginia Woolf, and Rebecca West, inter alios, that he was for most of his life a rather superficial optimist who thought that mankind was heading for a utopia of mechanical devices and benevolently imposed universal order, only to be disillusioned by the Second World War, age, and illness into a bleak and total pessimism. The other view, argued at some length and with a touching sincerity by Anthony West, is that he was fundamentally a pessimist whose radiant prophecies were no more than whistling in the dark. There is a wealth of material in Wells's voluminous writings to back up each side in this not very profitable debate. Wells was well aware of the dark side of man's nature. *The Island of Dr. Moreau*, one of his earliest books (1896), is a piece of science fiction with profoundly disturbing undertones. The fact is that Wells had an energetic and volatile mind which bounced about rather easily from optimism to despair, and back again. This is relevant to his treatment of armed conflict. He was equally interested in war and peace: in the probability or the actuality of war (he displayed a fascination with the actual techniques, real or imagined, of conflict), and in the conflict-free new world, which, repetitively, he saw as becoming possible through, and only through, war. There is an aspect of his work here that perhaps has not been fully explored.

One example of the revived interest in Wells's work is the 1971 McGill symposium, which resulted in the admirable volume *H. G. Wells and Modern Science Fiction*, edited by Darko Suvin and Robert M. Philmus and published in 1977. It contains ten splendid papers (two of them bibliographical) dealing with aspects of the volume's title topic. Not one of them, however, deals with Wells's treatment of armed conflict. Much the same may be said of two other recent volumes that are well worth a mention: *H. G. Wells under Revision* (1990), a perceptive collection of the proceedings of the International H. G. Wells Symposium held in London in July 1986; and Brian Murray's *H. G. Wells* (1990).

And yet Wells had an enormous interest in—a virtual obsession with—questions of war and peace. A useful rough indicator of this is the number of times the words *war* or *peace,* or both together, occur in the titles of his writings. Among his books and pamphlets six titles incorporate the word *war: The War of the Worlds* (1898); *The War in the Air* (1908); *Little Wars* (1913), this along with *Floor Games* (1911), originally published as articles in the *Strand Magazine*, constitutes Wells's two classic contributions to the literature of children's games; *The War That Will End War* (1914), persistently misquoted as "the war that will end all wars," actually a weaker phrase; *What Is Coming? A Forecast of Things after the War* (1916); and *War and the Future* (1917). Three titles employ the word *peace: The Peace of the World* (1915), *Washington and the Hope of Peace* (1922), and *The Common Sense of World Peace* (1929). At least one title uses both key words: *The Common Sense of War and Peace* (1940).

Wells was not alone in his pre-1914 apprehensions about a coming war. As the long Victorian peace between the major powers frayed to its end, similar forebodings gave rise to a considerable body of literature in both fiction and nonfiction, some few items in which, notably Erskine Childers's *The Riddle of the Sands* (1903), are still worth reading as literature. Fear of a coming war certainly did not begin with the atomic bomb. Wells contributed much to this literature; he appropriately named volume 20 of the Atlantic Edition of his collected works (1926) *The War in the Air and Other War Forebodings.*

Among all these contemporary voices prophesying war, the one person who got it right, or nearly right, was the impressive Jean de Bloch (1836–1902), a Polish-Jewish industrialist and financier, and author of *La Guerre* (7 vols., St. Petersburg, 1897), which was published in England in an abridged form as *Is War Now Impossible?* (1899). Bloch made three important points: (1) he foresaw correctly the involvement of the whole population of the belligerent countries, both in the war effort and in suffering its consequences; (2) he foresaw widespread destruction; and (3) he prophesied correctly that in such a war, involving the mobilization of whole societies in industrialized countries, a decision would not be achieved easily or quickly. Wells was familiar with Bloch's work, and to those three basic points he added a number of guesses and *aperçus* of his own, some accurate, some not.

Wells's science fiction about war, and peace, generally follows a repetitive pattern. This is so deftly disguised by an exuberant inventiveness that the reader who knows only one or two of Wells's fictions in the genre might easily fail to note the underlying repetitiveness. Generally, Wells began with some description of the contemporary world: a microtreatment sometimes, such as the comedy of lower-middle-class life portrayed in *The War in the Air*, or a macrotreatment along the lines of *The World Set Free* or *The Shape of Things to Come*, but in any case leading, or about to lead, to war. Then comes the middle section, about which more in a moment. Finally, there is the description of the ideal future à la Wells—the ordered, scientific society, the world state.

Wells seems to have seized on this pattern, or to have had it forced on him, because he was not very good at transitions. A novel like Thomas Mann's *Buddenbrooks*, which traces the decline of a family over several generations, would have been quite beyond his capacity; so, for that matter, would any plot involving a slow, long-term improvement. This shows up just as clearly in his novels about private life, which are praised for their naturalism, as it does in the cosmic dramas about war and peace. The naturalistic novels are naturalistic only up to a point. As A. J. P. Taylor has noted, "Each book by Wells begins more or less realistically, usually in rather depressing surroundings, and then the principal character escapes by a miracle."[2] Mr. Polly finds the Arcadian perfection of the Potwell Inn and its motherly landlady. Kipps comes into a windfall fortune not once but twice. Uncle Ponderevo in *Tono-Bungay* escapes from want through the quasi-magical invention of a popular patent medicine. In a very typical short story, "The Purple Pileus," a henpecked and unsuccessful husband turns into the master of his home and a success because he happens to eat an edible fungus that puts him in a berserk mood for several hours.

In the large-scale stories about war and peace, the transition is equally violent, and equally improbable. Wells was totally possessed by the curious notion that Utopia could only be achieved on the basis of a tabula rasa; first there had to be nearly universal destruction to shake men free from bad thinking habits and the dead hand of existing institutions. Then Wells, like the Almighty in *Green Pastures*, "passes a miracle." The nature of the miracle, of course, differs from book to book.

In their excellent biography of Wells the Mackenzies have a footnote in which they remark, with perhaps a touch of sarcasm, that among seventeenth-century Puritans it was a point of argument "whether the world would end with a cosmic collision, a blinding explosion, or the arrival of the host of angels to establish the third Kingdom. Over the years Wells used all these forms of the Apocalypse—the first in *In the Days of the Comet*, the second in *The World Set Free* and the third in *The Shape of Things to Come*."[3] But one way or another, the miracle arrives, and humankind advances toward the world state. This, then, is the threefold pattern that is discernible in nearly all Wells's treatments of war and peace. Sometimes the pattern is incomplete or imperfect, but, really, there is no other pattern.

It would not be fair to suggest that Wells was more interested in one of these three stages in his typical scenario than in the other two, or that he typically scamped two-thirds of the structure. He was interested in all three. First, he was interested in painting, with great novelistic skill, an unfavorable picture of the present (that is, of the present when he was writing). Second, he was interested in technical aspects of war, the usual culmination of the first phase. It is here that his striking prophecies, some astonishingly accurate, appear. He was passionately interested in the processes whereby a better world can come about—even though the means may seem improbable. Last, he was concerned to present, in some detail, the resulting Utopia.

There is a point worth stressing about Wells's treatment of war. In contemporary science fiction—by which I mean anything published later than 1945—when the subject is war, the tone tends to be one of pessimism and desperation. No doubt the invention of atomic weapons accounts for this. With Wells, it is somewhat different. However grave the catastrophe being described, the tone is seldom one of total pessimism; there is also a certain zeal or gusto in the discussion of technical aspects. Clearly, the *Kriegspiel* enthusiast of *Little Wars* is present in the author of *The World Set Free*, *The Shape of Things to Come*, and all the other fictions of belligerence; just as he shows in the Wells who during both world wars strenuously claimed to be the inventor of the tank (on the basis of the story "The Land Ironclads" of 1903); and in the patriot who in both wars tried, usually vainly, to interest government departments in new devices for waging war more efficiently. (During the First World War these efforts were principally concerned with a scheme for transporting supplies up to the front by a system of telpherage; and in the Second, with antiaircraft devices.)

A survey of Wells's fiction about war shows him ingeniously ringing the changes on his basic formulas. One may begin with *The War of the Worlds* (1898), which is in fact somewhat *hors série*. It is really hardly a war. The Martians who invade England prove to be totally immune to attempts to deal with them by artillery or poison gas. They are defeated and killed by an immunity deficiency syndrome—not acquired but intrinsic: they simply have no defenses against Earth's bacteria. The short story mentioned above, "The Land Ironclads" (1903), is only a vignette. In it Wells takes an existing invention, the pedrail, invented by B. J. Diplock, and ingeniously applies it to an imagined armored military vehicle capable of traveling over rough ground—in other words, an accurate prevision of the tank. The story then shows the tank in action in a remarkable forecast of tank warfare.

When the Sleeper Wakes (1899) and the slightly modified version of 1910, *The Sleeper Awakes*, are not really concerned with international war but with a proletarian revolt along Marxist lines against the trusts that by 2100 have come to dominate the world. *Anticipations* (1910), a strange book that is partly Utopia, partly nonfiction discussion, stresses the necessity in the dawning century for efficient scientific research as the sine qua non of military success in the future. Also here Wells envisaged a new social class, the Efficients, the first sketchy version of a concept that he returned to again and again: the dedicated minority who see, à la Wells, what is wrong with the world and by their efforts impose the necessary changes on everybody else. Later versions of these include the Samurai, the Open Conspirators, the Star-Begotten, and the dictatorship of airmen in *The Shape of Things to Come*.

In the extraordinary and powerful short story "A Dream of Armageddon" (1903), the strangely moving narrative of a recurrent nightmare gives us, essentially, only the first part of Wells's basic "war" pattern. Mostly a personal story with some anticipations in its plot of the later *New Machiavelli*, it has the outbreak of world war without the "middle" step and the world state. However, *In the Days of the Comet* (1906) shows the full pattern exemplified for the first time. The world on the brink of war (Britain versus Germany) is saved by the passage of a comet, whose radiation has the miraculous effect of making everyone start behaving rationally; that is, they see politics and sexual matters (about which there is a good deal in the story) in the way that Wells saw them.

In *The War in the Air* (1908) German dirigibles attack New York, and as a (somewhat implausible) consequence, the political and economic structure first of the United States and then of the world breaks down into famine and pestilence.[4] There is no miraculous transformation here, no Samurai, and no quick-change evolution to Utopia. There is, however, the full formula in *The World Set Free* (1914), one of the most extraordinary and successful Wellsian previsions of war. Wells was familiar with the work in radioactivity that Frederick Soddy had been doing in the previous decade (1904–14) at the University of Glasgow, and in the novel we have for the first time the atomic bomb, including the very phrase itself. It is not quite the atomic bomb that was unleashed on the world thirty-one years later, however; it has a fairly long half-life and so goes on erupting with diminishing potency for months and years. At any rate, it has the cathartic effect of destroying existing institutions, and so, freed of the past and led by an enlightened foreign monarch, mankind advances to the world state.

The onset of war is seen once again in *The Autocracy of Mr. Parham: His Remarkable Adventures in the Changing World* (1930), a *jeu d'esprit* (though fundamentally serious) that I have always found rather amusing, though the Mackenzies thought it "neither funny nor convincing," but "boring and silly."[5] It is a roman à clef with the key kindly provided in the vigorous and amusing illustrations by David Low, the cartoonist. An Oxford don who looks like a taller version of L. S. Amery enters into an association with a tycoon named Sir Bussy Woodcock, who in Low's drawings bears a remarkable resemblance to Max Aitken, Lord Beaverbrook. Parham-Amery, whose mind is a sort of museum display of all the conventional ideas about power politics that Wells detested, comes to rule England as dictator, giving himself the title "Lord Paramount." He attempts to lead the rest of Europe in a crusade against Bolshevik Russia—his conversation with Paramuzzi (Mussolini) is hilarious—and finds himself involved in a series of deepening disasters. He discovers himself opposed by the Samurai in yet another guise, this time a group of enlightened businessmen who are, so to speak, sons of *Clissold* (1926). At this point the whole thing falls apart, Mr. Parham's rise to power being revealed as a mere séance-induced hallucination. The reader is left with a certain dissatisfied feeling of having been conned, as the viewer was in the matter of the illusory death of Bobby Ewing in *Dallas*.

In *The Shape of Things to Come* (1933) we have the fullest and most elaborate, and perhaps the most satisfactory, exemplar of the Wellsian fictional paradigm world war–miracle–world state. There is plenty of warfare here, and plenty of mistaken prophecies. Tanks are opposed by vast ditches ("slime pits") dug across Europe. Aerial bombing is opposed by vast concrete carapaces built atop the buildings of London, so that eventually buildings on the north bank slide into the Thames. It is not, however, really warfare that destroys existing society and governments so much as economic difficulties of the period 1929 and after. (In the 1935 film version, *Things to Come*, there is more emphasis on actual warfare.) This time, the transformation and the coming of the world state are brought about by a worldwide association of scientific and technical workers, in particular, of airmen, who create an Air Dictatorship as the first step in world reorganization. There are many prophetic misses here. Again, as in *The War in the Air*, perhaps the most fundamentally wrong prophecy is the expectation that existing states would rapidly disintegrate under the strain of war; one of the greatest and most unexpected lessons of the Second World War was how well existing state structures stood up even under extraordinary stresses. But there are some very palpable prophetic hits too, notably the forecast that the Second World War would break out in January 1940, over the Polish Corridor.

The novella *The Brothers* (1938) is in a sense about war—the setting is a civil war strongly resembling the one then going on in Spain—but it is hardly science fiction; it is an allegory about how the two opposing leaders in a civil war turn out to be twin brothers and discover there is a great deal of common ground in their objectives, too. Also in 1938 Wells produced the long novel *The Holy Terror*, marginally science fiction, about the rise to the position of world dictator of a paranoid and charismatic figure who appears to be Hitler with a dash of Stalin. As world dictator he inaugurates a régime of terror, but the world is rescued from him by the Samurai in yet another guise. There is a good deal about warfare and economic breakdown more or less along the same lines as in *The Shape of Things to Come*.

Such, then, is the very rich but highly individual contribution of H. G. Wells to the science fiction of armed conflict. In concluding, I suggest that it is time for a complete and well-edited edition of Wells's works. Neither the Essex nor the Atlantic editions were complete even in their day, and Wells lived and wrote for twenty years after they were published. The Wells archive at Urbana has yielded much fascinating correspondence. It is time for some great American university press to produce a complete or nearly complete annotated Wells to do appropriate honor to one of the most fertile, inventive, and influential minds of the century.

Notes

1. W. Warren Wagar, *H. G. Wells and the World State* (New Haven: Yale University Press, 1961), p. vii.
2. A. J. P. Taylor, "The Man Who Tried to Work Miracles," *The Listener* (London) (September 1966); reprinted in *Politicians, Socialism, and Historians* (London: Hamish Hamilton, 1980), p. 136.
3. Norman Mackenzie and Jeanne Mackenzie, *The Time Traveller: The Life of H. G. Wells* (London: Weidenfeld and Nicolson, 1973), p. 128n.
4. In light of the Second World War, this is a preposterously bad prophecy. Why should the political and economic structure of the United States, far less the world, break down because a few bombs were dropped on New York? In the Second World War, Britain, and especially London, was subjected to almost nightly bombing for months on end, and *nothing* broke down—not the government or the economy, or for that matter the railway system, the postal service, or the BBC. Even in Germany things did not break down seriously before the spring of 1945. See the fascinating diaries of Princess Marie Vassiltchikov, *Berlin Diaries, 1940–1945* (New York: Alfred A. Knopf, 1987).
5. Mackenzie and Mackenzie, *Time Traveller*, p. 358.

Chapter 7

Fights of Fancy: When the "Better Half" Wins

Rosemarie Arbur

Conflict in science fiction serves two ends: technically, it generates development of character and plot; thematically, it dramatizes or makes concrete the opposition of ideas, values, and ideological perspectives. Oversimplification at the intellectual level—at the technical level the process is not "over"-anything; it is simply what happens when authors necessarily create concrete situations and characters—permits readers to experience the elements from which themes are generated very nearly as actual. That is, the reader usually sympathizes with the viewpoint character to the degree that threats to that character's well-being are felt as threats to the reader's own person. When characters or groups of characters are portrayed, at the literal level, in armed conflict with one another, the perceived threats become severe.

Inverting this sympathetic response in the context of gender conflict permits us to identify and examine those elements in "the battle of the sexes" which, presented as strategies and tactics, authors use to frighten readers into a recognition of the severity of the threats posed by men-versus-women and women-versus-men habits of thought, speaking, and actual behavior. If, in a narrative, "they" attack "us" in a literally warlike way, "we" perceive a severe threat to our continued existence. Despite our intellectual habits of avowing pacifism, of seeking facilitative instead of confrontational behaviors when we are threatened, our midbrains and endocrine systems still function atavistically; if we feel threatened, our instincts command us to flee or to fight. And if we can do neither—as we generally cannot while we sit quietly and read a novel—we are at the very least *engaged*.

During the past semester, a man in my science fiction course asked me the reason for the emphasis the selection of texts places on feminism.[1] My selection had little or nothing to do with a feminist agenda, but my student was obviously affected or engaged by what he had been reading. For his sake and mine, I hope this young man someday realizes that his question arose from his not-yet-identified cognitive dissonance, the result of his being a *woman's* student in a place and time when most professors are men, and of his nascent recognition of the second-class-character status of the few women he has encountered. My student's question superficially was "Why does this course have a feminist orientation?" But the question was really a statement: "I have noticed that women are not, in literature and in society, considered normally human."

Few men make statements like that, however obliquely. That they do not, even now when every sensitive, intelligent, and minimally educated adult has the means to discern the factuality of such statements, may cause writers of speculative fiction to fashion outrageous metaphors for gender conflict, either to shock readers into acknowledging the intensity and gravity of the subject or to embody and thereby express the artists' own Medean rage. Often, these metaphors are misread as literal renderings of wish-fulfillment fantasizings, and the misreadings have led some feminist writers—not all of them women—to construct narratives so obviously mythic that the truths they embody and their linguistic embodiment of these truths effect a fight-or-flight response in readers of both sexes. The following example "is not a man's story. It is for women." The woman character who tells it does so to a group of men and women, but only after another *woman* specifically asks.

> In the beginning was the act. . . . and the act was within the womb of god. But there was neither flesh nor fiber, neither soil nor stone, neither clear air nor cloudy mists, neither rivers nor rain, to make the act manifest. So god reached into her womb with her own hand and delivered herself. . . .
>
> When god had made her a world of sweet winds and fierce storms, gentle showers and lashing rains, fierce animals and songful birds, she said . . . "let me make a woman of my own shape, to praise me, to adore me, to hear my words, and to ascertain by inspection and reflection the wonder of the act. . . ."
>
> And so god took of her own flesh and made . . . the first woman. And god loved . . . and suckled her at both breasts. [And god gave woman] all the world

for her pleasure, and commanded all the animals to obey her and the weather to warm her, and [woman] prospered; and the daughters of [woman] prospered; and the tribes of [woman] filled the world and praised the wonder of god and the act. And there was soil and rock, fiber and flesh, rain and river, clear winds and cloudy mists to manifest the act; and all this [woman] praised and god was happy.

[But, as in our own creation myths, god's created sought a companion, and god created another woman and soon the two women sinned, chiefly because of the second woman's pride of intellect. And god was angry, and beat the second woman with] two trees from the ground, one of lithe, live wood and one of hard, near-dry wood, . . . god beat her bloody about the face and breasts and loins. And where god beat her on the face, coarse hairs sprouted; and where god beat her on the throat, her voice roughened and went deep; and where god beat her about the breasts, the very flesh and organs were torn away so that she could no longer suckle her daughters; and where god beat her about the groin, her womb was broken and collapsed on itself, and rags of flesh fell, dangling, from her loins, so that when they healed, her womb was sealed and useless, and the rags of flesh hanging between her legs were forever sore and sensitive, so that [the punished woman] was forever touching and ministering to them, where upon they would leak their infectious pus.

Then god said: ". . . I have beaten you until you are no longer a woman. . . . You have praised neither me nor the act well." And so [the second woman] bowed her hairy face and covered her poor, ropey genitals, and was called no longer woman, but 'man, which means broken woman. And she was called no longer she, but 'he, as a mark of her pretention, ignorance, and shame.

[And then god began to punish the first woman for her part in the sin and] raised her two trees and struck her across the groin: and she drew blood, as the daughters of [woman] had bled, every month, ever since. . . . [And god said:] "Go woman and 'man, and roam the earth, the hills, the forests, and the seas. Go in shame."[2]

This myth comes not from a woman's novel but from a man's. It is reasonable, and explanatory, and unsettling to read. It makes men angry, and it makes women uncomfortable. It does violence to our masculinist Judeo-Christian perceptions. *And yet it is for men almost exactly what our orthodox creation myth is for women.* It is blasphemous only if "he" is the appropriate pronoun for the deity. It is degrading only if women—never men—are inherently weak, prone to evil, and the source of *Man*kind's imperfections. If a "normal" man reads this myth and becomes angry (wants to fight) or throws down the book in disgust (wants to flee), the "normal" man's reaction demonstrates how effective this creation story is. His response—as if to physical threat—is a tacit acknowledgment of the intensity and gravity of the metaphorical war between the sexes, for this myth belongs to the literary-religious tradition of a nonexistent culture whose women have decisively won that war.

The student who asked about the feminism of my reading list was unaware of the myth recounted in the preceding quotation, but he was concerned about or threatened by hints of gender warfare that he found on the back cover of *A Door into Ocean:* "world of women . . . highest ethical evolution" versus "place where soldiers are honored above all things."[3] A man in a man's world, he should feel threatened by the postulation of a female human race with the moral power to pass judgment on the very humanity of the male and female people who live on their sister planet, because *A Door into Ocean* is one of the most recent and best accounts of how Man's "better half" wins the war.

Despite the obviously fictional nature of narratives that relate one or another version of the battle of the sexes, and despite the additional aesthetic distance from actual gender conflict that science fictional narratives provide, persons reading them cannot help feeling threatened. Men do not want to be reminded that they benefit (at least superficially) from the inequalities of the status quo. Women do not want to be reminded that they benefit (at least superficially) by not being personally responsible for the impending horror of thermonuclear catastrophe or ecological devastation. No one of us is neutral, yet nearly all of us prefer to remain detached. The portrayals of gender conflict in the women's works I examine here are calculated to shatter our detachment.

With the raising of American consciousness about twenty years ago, and then with the subsequent vehement denial of almost everything of which a "raised consciousness" became aware, feminist speculative fictions have been growing more bellicose. At one time the "men versus women" mythos was regarded as a semiserious comment on conflict between the sexes, but "*vive la différence*" prevailed. Their sisters' works having been unheeded, feminists writing science fiction more recently have embodied the conflict more obviously; "hysteria" is a euphemism for the descriptions and epithets that were elicited by these more earnest calls to arms.

The largely negative reaction to the proposition that the more radical feminists may be right is partly illustrated by an accident of plot in Pamela Sargent's *The Shore of Women*.[4] Birana is a young woman exiled from the Enclave; prior to her disgrace (by association with her mother), this woman had enjoyed, among other sports, horseback riding: "she had galloped through our parks on horseback while the rest of us kept to the paths at a trot," her onetime friend remembers.[5] Yet—I do hope this is a textual accident, but I fear otherwise—when Birana and Arvil are wandering the outside world with stolen horses, Arvil, the young man who has had *days* of experience with horses compared with Birana's *years,* Arvil it is who takes the reins of their mounts, talks soothingly to them, and leads them calmly over treacherous footing or quietly through woods where enemies may be listening for the iconoclastic heterosexual couple. There is no justification at all for Arvil's exercising his masculine-by-our-standards prerogative with respect to this take-charge, keep-a-cool-head behavior. Nor is it probable that Birana, trained athlete that she is, could so quickly become so gender-codedly dependent. After Arvil saves her from attack by a large wildcat, Birana narrates: "A few paces from the cat, I found the carcass of a small deer. I could not lift it; at last I began to drag it forward by the legs. The effort soon made me pant." And this in response to Arvil's unspoken command: "He gestured with his head. 'The game I have found lies there. You must get it back to the shrine.'"[6] *Come on!* I want to say; this "aspect of the Lady" takes orders from a mere male? This woman who could swing up onto a horse's back cannot *drag* the body of a *small* deer without panting? The incident has at least the virtue of demonstrating how unthinking adherence to gender-coded behavior is literally exhausting even for a woman character who is an athlete.

Almost exactly contemporaneous with *The Shore of Women* is the remarkable novel by Joan Slonczewski, *A Door into Ocean.*[7] Like Urras and Anarres in Ursula K. Le Guin's *The Dispossessed*, Valedon and Shora constitute a double-planet system. On the former, a terrestrial world, people live as we do: women and men, husbands and wives, secretaries and soldiers. On the latter, an entirely pelagic world, an ancient race of women-only human beings live—in harmony with their fragile environment, at peace but not at some evolutionary dead end, with a strange language in which all verbs are "share" words, active and passive simultaneously, so that "share deceit" means both "to deceive" and "to be deceived": "*Deceiver/Deceived*—the same word, in Sharer tongue" (83). When those of Valedon "discover" Shora and, profit in mind, begin to exploit the world and its people, Merwen and her lovesharer, Usha, travel to the more populous planet, where people live on land, away from "a strange sea, . . . with its floor jutting out hard as a whorlshell," on the "endless edge of dry [ocean] floor." They go to terrestrial Valedon to find out whether or not the two-sexed Valans—particularly the "malefreaks" among them—are truly human. Merwen believes they are. On the sea-plus-land planet, "in Chrysoport, a small, quiet place, she might find out. And that answer would save her own people" (3). This novel affirms the humanity of men just as strongly as Sargent's does, but the affirmation comes from a nonmasculinist perspective. Because it does, because the experience of *women* is the novel's thematic norm, and because from a masculinist point of view the Shoran women "win" the war that is inevitable and brutal and not at all romanticized, its deep-structure theme (first, *women* are the human ones, and, second, men are, too) is all too easy to devalue. *Wimmintrash*, Marion Zimmer Bradley told me, is a word that describes and dismisses the novel and its theme.[8]

Wimmintrash or wisdom, fiction by feminists that dramatizes gender conflict as actual warfare, or at least overt hostility, demands not only our attention but a kind of revaluation. The affirmation of men's humanity by Slonczewski's novel is an important thematic act. Prior to it, moreover, there have been equally important treatments of "the war between the sexes." Hindsight discloses that just as *A Door into Ocean* depends on *woman*like *non*violence—like that of Thoreau, Ghandi, and Martin Luther King, Jr.—in order for the right side to achieve victory, other feminists' "battle fictions" also use particularly "feminine" strategies to achieve their thematic ends.

Once upon a time, when it seemed that the work of Elizabeth Cady Stanton, Susan B. Anthony, and others was being taken up again two generations after it had been deflected by the constitutional amendment that affirmed American women's right to vote, Joanna Russ employed the indirect (and thereby "feminine") strategy of "make 'em laugh" in her *Female Man*. Surely no one would read about the future "war" between Manland and Womanland without realizing how silly, how comical, almost—one might say—how quaint Russ's depiction of Alice Reasoner's (or Jael's) environment truly is. Over there, the men, literally at war with the women for the control of the planet. Over here, the women, who use guerrilla tactics to gain what they cannot, "naturally," obtain by brute force. Guerrilla tactics are "feminine," not fair in Manland's war game. By using them to win, Jael is no less than her conarrator Joanna a "female man."

Despite her cyborg adaptations (as an assassin, she needs them), Jael Reasoner is quintessentially feminine. Of the Manlanders she observes:

Astonishing how each of them has to be reassured. . . . They're not very bright, are they? . . . Besides, they've been separated from real women so long that they don't know what to make of us; I doubt if even the sex surgeons [in Manland, one of seven boys undergoes transsexual surgery to satisfy the atavistic need of some "real-men" for "real-women"] know what a real woman looks like. The specifications we send them every year grow wilder and wilder and there isn't a murmur of protest. I think they like it. . . . I think these men are not human. No, no, that's wrong—I decided long ago that they weren't human. Work is power, but they farm out everything to us without the slightest protest—Hell, they get lazier and lazier. They let us do their thinking for them. They even let us do their feeling for them. They are riddled with duality and the fear of duality. And the fear of themselves.[9]

Her vocabulary is somewhat better, and her grasp of the philosophical issues involved is more sophisticated, but Jael's observations are otherwise quite similar to what one might hear listening to housewives hanging their wash out on lines affixed to the fire escapes of the tenements in which they live, discussing the frailties of their muscular husbands who work in the steel mill or brewery or slaughterhouse.

Jael has two significant sexual encounters. One is with a citizen of Manland, of whom she tells us: "These men play games, play with vanity, hiss, threaten. . . . It sometimes takes ten minutes to get a fight going. I, who am . . . only an assassin, only a murderess, never give warning. They worry about *playing fair,* about *keeping the rules,* about *giving a good account of themselves.* I don't play" (180). Jael's potential sex partner

was muttering something angry about his erection so, angry enough for two [she says], I produced my own—by this I mean that the grafted muscles on my fingers and hand pulled back the loose skin, . . . and of course you . . . have guessed that I do not have Cancer on my fingers but Claws, . . . a little more dull than wood brads but good for tearing. And my teeth are a sham over metal. Why are men so afraid of the awful intimacies. . . ? I raked him gaily on the neck and chin and when he embraced me in rage, sank my claws into his back. You have to build up the fingers surgically so they'll take the strain. [Then I] scored him under the ear, letting him spray urgently into the rug; . . . at her feet he bowed, he fell, he lay down dead. (181–82)

Jael admits to her monomania, her adrenalin high, her failure: "No business done today, God damn, but once they get that way, . . . you have to kill them anyway, might as well have fun. There's no standing those non-humans at all, at all" (182).

Then Jael goes home for her second encounter: "Davy was there. The most beautiful man in the world." In Jael's Vermont home, "It's warm enough for Davy to go around naked most of the time, my ice lad in a cloud of gold hair and nudity, never so much a part of my home as when he sits on the rug with his back against a russet or vermillion chair, . . . his drowned blue eyes fixed on the winter sunset outside, his hair turned to ash, the muscles of his back and thighs stirring a little" (185). And eventually, Jael, who reminds us that she's really an old-fashioned girl, makes love to Davy—languid, unhurried, sensual, satisfying sexual love. And then she turns him off. Literally. He is an android ("The original germ-plasm was chimpanzee" [199]). And Jael is just an old-fashioned girl.

Russ's book was no doubt meant in parts to be outrageous, but it was optimistic, a then-designed metaphor for the old days written by a woman almost certain of better things to come. It is a book that can produce pure laughter only if the reader transports herself to a world where men are proved to have been human after all. In the years since *The Female Man*'s publication, men have not notably so proved themselves, nor have they recognized women's right to do the proving. The delicious humor of *The Female Man* has hardened with the years into farce.

Meanwhile, a retired schoolteacher-psychologist-adventurer named "James Tiptree, Jr." (and sometimes, I imagine for the fun of it, named "Racoona") was telling stories of the same "war" in a quieter, somehow more deadly, tone of narrative voice. Alice Sheldon's women characters make their own conscious decisions (unlike Russ's Janet, woman from Whileaway, who doesn't really know—or can't with her relatively optimistic and naïve turn of mind admit—how it came to be that there are no male people on her planet). Sheldon's "Women Men Don't See"[10] are women who exercise the primordial right of any mammalian female: to choose among available males, to accept a partner in copulation, to have the last word about which set of genes will be joined with hers in her offspring. Thus Sheldon's women characters employ "feminine" tactics to win battles their adversaries are unaware of, and the winning is the most basic kind of victory: perpetuation of the species, or, for mothers and daughters anyway, survival.

"The Women Men Don't See" is a strangely understated novella, powerful precisely because the chief women characters are the sort of human beings who are invisible to more conventional women as well as to most men. They are not decorative, so they cannot be even office furniture in the Washington, D.C., bureaucracy. They are more like keys on a typewriter or folders in a file. Unlike these mundane associative metaphors for them, however, Sheldon's women have a vitality that office equipment cannot have after the offices are empty. Not only do they choose mates, they choose their destinations. The narrator, stunned at the conclusion, cannot even "see" their motivations: "*I'm used to aliens....* [He repeats her words bemusedly, then realizes] She'd meant every word. Insane. How could a woman choose to live among unknown monsters, to say goodbye to her home, her world?" (164). Had the narrator truly seen Ruth, he would have seen also that she could not live for long among unknowing "monsters," and that the world she left had never been her home.

"Houston, Houston, Do You Read"[11] is a later chapter in Sheldon's history of the war between the sexes. The novella is strategically feminine—the women characters show almost sisterly, almost motherly, compassion for the last survivors of the war—yet tactically female; the women characters do not let sentimentality interfere with their duty to humanity, all eleven thousand female genotypes of it. So the rescued men must die. Their genes might have been salvageable, but the risk is too great to take. Besides, the enemy is no longer necessary—not for pleasure, not even for reproduction. The war between the sexes is not only won by women in Sheldon's fictive future, it is obviated. There can be no contest, nor even a true contestant, when only one side is left.

This fictional end to gender conflict is not funny, although one must smile, at least, at the women's interest in Bud's (the would-be rapist's) physiology. " 'Is he going to emit sperm now?' Connie whispers" just before Bud's premature ejaculation; and when a "small oyster jets limply" into the free-fall environment, "Judy's [Bud's victim's] arm goes after it," her hand having held the specimen bag ready throughout the scene. It is repellent, the rape, but dutifully "Judy swims through [Bud's legs] bagging the last drops" of the last sperm sample ever (90–91).

Sheldon's thematic cry of outrage is devastating, almost impossible to ignore—but not quite; Phyllis Schafley's voice and message were easier to hear. The Equal Rights Amendment was not ratified. The women in our work force were led to believe that gender discrimination was a phantom memory, a thing entirely of the past. How were they led to believe? Maybe by use of the Big Lie, a heavy-handed (and thereby "masculine") tactic, but maybe by the use of well-intentioned ("boyish" if one needs a polite word for it) obfuscation of the issues: how can one, after all, determine that one has been the object of sexual harassment in the workplace when that term insidiously suggests a discrete pattern of identifiable actions, when one's experience is of on-the-job situations, most of which are indefinably unsettling and almost all of a piece? How can a woman point to this and that behavior by her masculine colleagues as "harassments" when these and those behaviors are the norm, the way things get done, the way they've always been, the—well, who does have a word for it?

Suzette Haden Elgin does, and did, in *Native Tongue*.[12] In a headnote to chapter 2 we learn that a "*lexical encoding* refers to the way that human beings choose a particular chunk of their world, external or internal, and assign that chunk a surface shape that will be its name; it refers to the process of word-making." We also learn that when the women Linguists of the novel "say 'Encoding,' with a capital 'E,' [they] mean something a little bit different. [They] mean the making of a name for [what] has never been chosen for naming in any human language, and that has not just suddenly been made or found or dumped upon your culture" (22). We also notice how unpretentious is the language of this headnote; yes, it is the transcription of a part of a woman character's textbook. And, if we reflect upon "language," "their world," and "women Linguists," all in combination, we are halfway to the solution: major Encodings in the world of *Native Tongue* are words made to name *women's* gender-specific (though not gender-exclusive) perceptions, perceptions of things that go unnamed in all the languages of Man.

As a child, Nazareth Chornyak began her own notebook of Encodings. One of them defined the following: "To refrain from asking, with evil intentions; especially when it's clear that someone badly wants you to ask—for example, when someone wants to be asked about her state of mind or health and clearly wants to talk about it" (29). When older Linguist women learn of this and other woman-specific perceptions-given-a-name, they realize that Nazareth is going to contribute enormously to their secret project: the creation of a separate language for women, which, by its nature, will reorder and redefine everything perceived by those for whom the women's language will be a native tongue. Years have to pass before Nazareth can become privy to the barren women's secret. *Native Tongue* is structured around the double mastectomy and hysterectomy that make Nazareth, mother of nine, incontrovertibly barren—and free. The older women's hopes prove well founded, for on the very day that Nazareth learns of the "woman-language" in the Chornyak Barren House, she summarily declares it ready for use and shocks her women relatives into implementing what becomes the last word in women's liberation.

At the end of the novel, the Linguist men can stand no longer the—they have no word for it, for what the women (now using their own language secretly, altering their previously all-but-intolerable lives) have become. At the meeting called because of the strangely docile, agreeable women who grew out of their formerly dissatisfied wives as if by magic, the men articulate what they can about their displeasure: "Can a man point a finger at a woman and say to her, 'I accuse you of never frowning, or never complaining, of never weeping, of never nagging, of never so much as pouting?' Can a man demand of a woman that she nag? Can he demand that she sulk and bitch and argue—in short, that she behave as women used to behave?" (289).

What has happened is that the Linguist women—and soon, any other women who want to learn how—have reordered their perceptions so that their demanding, petulant, overbearing husbands and fathers and brothers and other male relatives and associates are little more than minor irritants, which, once named, cease to irritate. If humans are at least in part defined as those animals which speak, then Elgin's women's "native tongue" *did* effectively change the reality they lived in. Men were no longer "oppressors" and other nasty irritating English words; they were something else—some*thing* for which the women's language had a satisfying Encoding. By focusing their attention on the trivial matters that only women notice, by using their schoolgirl gregariousness in the Barren Houses to play at making up new words, by exercising their gender-coded facility with language, Elgin's women have quite effectively seceded from mankind. Elgin's play with language is as funny as Russ's farce, but less offensive. It is as alienating as Sheldon's re-creation of the human race, but less overtly hostile. It is, though science fictional, grounded in what we know of language, what we know about ourselves. It is probably possible.

And suddenly, apocalyptically, we come to understand just how important the phrase *male chauvinist* really was and is. Twenty years before the publication of *Native Tongue*, Betty Friedan's *Feminine Mystique* drew our attention to "the problem that has no name." Then, with the news media's promulgation of "male chauvinist," what Friedan could not put a word to finally had a name, an encoding: if not for the problem, at least for the everyman (and everywoman) who self-righteously stands in the way of a solution.

One criticism of Elgin's *Judas Rose* (sequel to *Native Tongue* and set approximately sixty years later) is that it does not display the "woman-language" that most of the Linguist women have been using since childhood, and that we are not aware of the power of that language except by inference. The criticism is unfair insofar as it demands that Elgin do actually what her most gifted Linguist character could not accomplish by herself, even in a fiction: create an entire language, write a novel in it, and then back-translate the novel into English we can read, English the shortcomings of which gave rise to the women Linguists' need for a new language in the first place. Yet at some level the criticism addresses a thematic concern shared by feminist war fictions I have discussed and those I have not: the women who read these accounts of gender conflict are demanding a solution.

They are not satisfied by their vicarious murders of the leading citizens of Manland, nor do they take much pleasure in the verbal "victory" that *The Female Man* creates by its ironic humor. Neither do they want, except metaphorically, the wholesale replacement of Mankind that Sheldon's "future history" offers. Women can—and do—use language that achieves some of the aims of Elgin's fictional one, but women are not really satisfied by the frighteningly alienating outcomes of science fictional wars between the sexes, nor are the men who read them threatened only by the speculated loss of power, of being needed, of being paid the attention due another human person.

Feminist or not, woman or man, the reader of what happens when the "better half" wins the war is personally dissatisfied, frustrated, and plain scared, for our culture seems increasingly unconscious of what these narratives are all but shouting at us. These narratives, quite simply, are telling us that we had better start speaking the same language, lest Mother Eve, the Blessed Virgin, and the legion of uncanonized housewife saints permit our species to do what none has ever done before: sever one half from the other, lose the common language, and tacitly declare itself extinct.

Notes

1. That day, we had begun our study of *A Canticle for Leibowitz*; the week before, we examined stories by Lucius Shepard, Connie Willis, and Ian Watson. Before that, the class had read *Brightness Falls from the Air*, stories by Gregory Benford and Michael Bishop, *Startide Rising*, *Starship Troopers*, *The Integral Trees*, *Memoirs of Alcheringia*, *The Tombs of Atuan*, *The Forgotten Beasts of Eld*, and *A Wizard of Earthsea*. Later—the inspiration of his question—we read *The Judas Rose* and *A Door into Ocean*. But the course ended with the study of stories by Robert Silverberg, John Crowley, and David Zindell. All the novels mentioned are in mass market paperback editions; the

stories are in *Terry Carr's Best Science Fiction of the Year #15* (New York: TOR Books, 1986).
2. Samuel R. Delany, *Tales of Neverÿon* (New York: Bantam Books, 1979), pp. 168–74. The author dedicates this work, aptly, to his daughter and to Joanna Russ.
3. Avon mass market paperback; see subsequent citations.
4. Pamela Sargent, *The Shore of Women* (New York: Crown Publishers, 1986).
5. The more available Bantam paperback edition (New York, 1987), p. 5.
6. Bantam edition, p. 226.
7. Joan Slonczewski, *A Door into Ocean* (New York: Arbor House, 1986). Citations are from the Avon paperback edition (1987).
8. Private correspondence, not dated, late January 1988.
9. *The Female Man* (New York: Bantam Books, 1975), pp. 169–70.
10. Originally published in *The Magazine of Fantasy and Science Fiction*, December 1973. Citation here follows the text in *Warm Worlds and Otherwise* (New York: Del Rey, 1975).
11. In *Aurora: Beyond Equality*, ed. Vonda N. McIntyre and Susan Janice Anderson (Greenwich, Conn.: Fawcett, 1976).
12. Suzette Haden Elgin, *Native Tongue* (New York: DAW Books, 1984).

Chapter 8

Vietnam and Other Alien Worlds

Joe Haldeman

In discussing the subject of armed conflict in science fiction, I prefer to speak not as a scholar but as a piece of raw material on display. I speak as a Vietnam veteran and as a writer marked by this real-life battlefield experience. I do have my opinions about other authors' science fictional excursions onto the battlefield, but they're about as biased and skewed as you might expect any combat veteran's to be: if it didn't happen that way to me, it couldn't happen. That doesn't help my usefulness as a critic. What I *can* discuss with some authority is how fighting in Vietnam molded my own fiction, and risk some generalizations from there. Let me apologize once for indulging in autobiography; but I think it's appropriate.

Every fall semester, I teach workshops in science fiction and genre writing at MIT. It's an interesting environment, as you might imagine: most of the students are hyperintelligent, hyperactive, unpredictable, and not overburdened with social graces. Last semester one of them asked me, out of the blue but not completely irrelevant to the classroom context, "How many people did you kill in Vietnam?"

Oddly enough, I don't recall anybody ever asking me that before. My pacifist sympathies are pretty obvious, at least to my friends and most of my students—even to most of my readers, I hope.

Technically, the answer to the question is "None." (In fact, I once refused a direct order to kill a man, which is another story.) But the actual answer, as far as the victims themselves were concerned, is twenty or thirty people,

North Vietnamese Regular Army troops. Maybe more. The next question is "How did you feel about it?" And the terrible true answer is "Neutral."

That requires some amplification. In real life, a person who kills twenty or thirty people and feels neutral about it will cop an insanity plea, go to jail, and get a best-seller out of the experience. I've only done one of these things.

Actually, I never killed anybody in the sense of pointing a weapon at him and pulling the trigger. In fact, I tried to forestall the necessity of finding out whether I could or would do that, at several levels.

First, I tried to register as a conscientious objector. The draft board required a letter from a minister. Atheists don't have ministers, though, and I was politically naïve enough to let it go at that. (A year later, the law was challenged in the courts and, of course, was declared unconstitutional.) I tried for alternate service in the Peace Corps but got drafted while the papers were being pushed.

In response to a bulletin board notice at basic training camp, I waved my physics degree at the army and offered to sign up for four years of nuclear power plant operation. True, I'd have to spend one year, maybe two, in a radioactive underground bunker in Antarctica, but it sounded safer than Vietnam. They said I was overqualified for the position.

Finally, sent to Vietnam, I found that you could volunteer to be an unarmed combat medic or assistant medic, and I tried to be reassigned. But they said they didn't need medics; they needed combat engineers. When I finally got to the field, I told the sergeant that I couldn't kill anyone. He said, in effect, "Sure."

What does all this have to do with science fiction? There is a connection. Because I got through the war with a clean conscience. I didn't realize—or admit—that I had killed those twenty or thirty people until long after they were dead.

You can't compel any two scholars, or any two readers, to agree on a definition of science fiction, even though the energy expended on arguing over it since Hugo Gernsback's day would power a spaceship to the moon. Most people would be willing to concede that it has something to do with science, and something to do with human nature—and here's a list of two hundred exceptions to whatever you were going to say.

Well, the science part is just wrong, as is occasionally pointed out, even if you first disqualify stories set in the future that have only to do with history, religion, politics, or other nonscientific stuff. With few and interesting exceptions, even "hard" science fiction deals not with science but with technology, which relates to humanity in a totally different way. In the physical sciences, if you are limited to a natural human language, you can only approximate truth; the actual verities have to be expressed in the various dialects of mathematics. As the life sciences move into smaller and more subtle realms, this becomes true for them as well. Even the behavioral sciences move away from natural language as they evolve toward precision, or at least the appearance of it.

Technology is another matter. Plenty of cold numbers and equations are used up in design and manufacture, but a finished product radiates a kind of secondary humanity, because it was designed for human needs. We sense this radiation even when we're not sure of the thing's function, as is often the case with obscure medical or scientific equipment, or the arcane utensils of the chef, the mechanic, the artisan—what Gerard Manley Hopkins delightfully praised as "all trades, their gear and tackle and trim"—and we become nervous around artifacts that are patently antifunctional. Dadaist sculptors and their descendants have capitalized on this tension, and there's a comical avatar of it in the Boston Museum of Science: a machine the size of a small room that is constantly busy, with hundreds of moving parts and no observable function whatsoever. It's interesting to watch people watching it. They giggle and point things out to each other: "Watch what happens when the ball gets to the bottom of this spiral ramp. See? Now the bell's gonna go off."

This childlike, more or less *boy*like, fascination with machines is a dominant motif in science fiction, especially the subgenre of military SF. Can you think of a single military SF story of any length that doesn't describe, usually in loving detail, the tools of the future soldier's trade? I can't offhand, though it's such an obvious direction for a story that I'd be surprised if it hasn't been done more than once. But I'm no expert; I don't often read military SF novels any more, or mainstream military novels, for that matter. They don't seem to speak to my experience, about which more later.

The machines, though. Like most American boys of my generation and previous ones, my childhood was dominated by weapons-oriented play: cowboys and Indians, cops and robbers, soldiers. Some enlightened parents nowadays try to prevent their children from acting out these unhealthy fantasies; I would be inclined to do the same if I were a parent. But I suspect that prohibition, predictably, just makes it that much sweeter when the child sneaks out to do it in secret.

When he grows up somewhat and steps off the bus to get his head shaved, his eardrums bruised by a surly sergeant, and his identity excised in a hundred large and small ways, the confused man-child is offered one positive thing: guns that actually shoot. That's no small boon for the majority, who never handled the country boy's .22 or the inner-city boy's zip gun. I was not exactly a boy, having been sheltered from the draft by academe up to the ancient age of twenty-four, but I liked this new thing of shooting almost as much as the impressionable kids did. Rifle marksmanship was a physical and mental challenge, and the occasional experience with more exotic weapons—bazooka, machine gun, grenade launcher—was a flamboyant exercise in pyrotechnic power. I don't recall ever contemplating what these things would do to human flesh, which I suppose is what psychologists call "avoidance," but until I actually received orders for Vietnam, I was sure the army would find a computer, or at least a typewriter, to put me behind.

Instead, wading through the snow of a hard Missouri winter, I learned how to construct hasty bridges, build roads, tie knots, use a jackhammer and a Skil saw, and do various other things that the book says an army engineer should be able to do. We never even saw the only things we would, in a few months, actually be using in the jungle heat: pick, shovel, axe, machete, chain saw, plastic explosive, M-16, napalm. You think of napalm as something dropped from airplanes. It's not always. But let me not get ahead of myself.

It's an eighteen-hour flight from the West Coast to Vietnam, and we were about an hour from landing when I first had the sense of entering an alien world. It was about one in the morning; I woke up from a light, nervous sleep and looked out the porthole. I couldn't recognize any of the stars. That was profound: I had been interested in astronomy, sometimes to the point of fanaticism, since the age of eight or nine, and the constellations were as familiar to me as the faces of family members. But I'd never been to the tropics. For the first time in my life I was looking at the Southern Cross, Alpha Centauri, the Magellanic Clouds. I stared for a long time, transfixed, and the plane began its descent. Soon there were lights on the ground as well, the red spray of tracers and smoky orange billowing napalm. The base where we were landing was under attack.

We landed without incident—the fighting was going on at the other end of the large base, several miles away—and entered yet another alien world, a surreal one. They herded us into a mess hall and someone handed me a large spoon, and for an hour I served instant mashed potatoes to hundreds of people who didn't seem to notice that there was a war going on outside. I felt like I was caught in the middle of a Harold Pinter play. After my shift

I spent a couple of hours sitting behind the mess hall, sipping warm beer and watching the helicopters bob and weave, spitting flame, firing rockets. Men dying under alien stars, literally.

There followed a couple of weeks of growing tension while people tried to cram into us the training we should have had in the States. In jungle warfare in the sixties, the main function of a combat engineer in the field was to carry on his person enough high explosive to level a city block. It was a dead dangerous weight until you ran into the enemy. Then, ideally, while the fighting raged, you would take a couple of riflemen and drop back a ways in order to clear a landing zone for helicopters, which would evacuate the wounded and bring in supplies. To do this, you affixed explosive to the largest trees and blew them down, then cleared out the smaller stuff with axe and machete, hoping that it hadn't occurred to the enemy to circle around and see what was going on. It wasn't the safest job in the world, but, at least for me, it was psychologically easier to endure than most combat positions, since you could tell yourself you were engaged in saving life rather than taking it.

But we also learned how to use other people's weapons—even Russian and Chinese weapons that we might scavenge on the battlefield—and how to call in artillery and air support. Because if enough of the infantry were killed, the engineers would have to take their place.

The next alien world was alien primarily in an existential way, though the surroundings were strange enough. That was when I was first sent out into combat.

I was sitting in a fire base, a semipermanent camp in a secure valley, learning how to take apart and clean chain saws, when the sergeant came running up and said, "You, you, and you, saddle up and get down to the pad." I was given five hundred extra rounds of ammunition and a case of beer and told we were going to a "hot LZ"—a landing zone that was under fire, so the helicopter wouldn't actually land. It would come within a few feet of the ground, and we were to jump out and land running.

It was terrifying. As we descended, you could hear the gunfire even over the throbbing of the helicopter's straining engine and blades. I didn't know that the gunfire was all from our side, trying to keep the enemy's collective head down while the chopper came in. It was no more than twenty yards from where we jumped out to where a GI was waving from behind a stack of sandbags; I don't believe my feet touched the ground three times in those twenty yards.

None of us was hurt coming in. I hunkered down behind the sandbags and passed out the beer and ammunition, both appreciated, and tried to will myself to relax. I couldn't. The firing stopped but the smell persisted. The unit had been in the same position for two days, and the jungle all around was full of enemy dead, rotting in the damp tropical heat. We had a few dead ourselves, decently tucked away in body bags, including the man I'd been sent to replace. With less than a month left in Vietnam, he'd been shot through the heart by a sniper.

The guy who told me that, as if to even things up, took me off to see the latest treasure, a freshly killed enemy scout whose body and gear they had dragged inside our perimeter. I'd never before seen a dead person who hadn't had the benefit of an undertaker's ministrations. I steeled myself for the experience—but someone had moved the body, which made me feel relieved and annoyed and obscurely weirded out. The Walking Dead and all. But I got to hold his rusty, bloody rifle and sort through the sad mementos he'd left behind. A letter, presumably from home, unfolded and refolded many times, a wallet with a little useless currency, a military ID that said he was only sixteen years old.

Then the enemy machine guns started up again, from a new angle, and we ran for cover, bullets whirring around. I spent the rest of the afternoon in or near shallow makeshift bunkers while sporadic gunfire probed the invisible perimeter. Just before dark the artillery started, a salvo coming in every few minutes to protect us, crashing just beyond the perimeter. But it was a double-edged sword; the shrapnel sometimes whined overhead, and a piece the size of a dessert plate opened up the back of a lieutenant's hand as he slept. I had a feeling I wasn't going to get much sleep that night, and I was right.

That's when I visited another alien world, and as I've said, it was existential as much as physical. The other soldiers helped; they all said some version of, "Hell, this is nothing; you should've been here last week"—and I didn't know enough about human nature to realize I was being hazed. In fact, it was the heaviest action they'd ever seen. To me, though, lying there wide awake while the jungle shook and flashed with explosions, while the air sang with bullets and fragments and stank of the dead, while wounded men cried and muttered, desperate men whispered into radios and belly-crawled from position to position—I was seized with an absolute conviction that I was going to die. Nobody could live through a year of this. It was just as certain as the doctor snapping on the X-ray viewer and saying, "Maybe a year, maybe a month, maybe tomorrow; there's nothing we can do."

I'm tempted to say that once you visit that world, you never come back from it. The truth is less dramatic. It's more like the memory of a hometown: easily recalled, not far below the surface, but not profoundly present in everyday life. At least not for me, at least not now.

After that eventful day we did have the gruesome chore of searching and disposing of bodies, the description of which I will spare you, and we did draw fire occasionally, but it was obvious that things were cooling down. After a few weeks, I came to realize that it might be possible to survive the whole year. We had significant contact with the enemy only a couple of times a month. The death rate was high, a lot higher than news reports indicated, but it looked like you had about a fifty-fifty chance of leaving the country alive. As it turned out, of the thirteen people who joined the company the day I did, only three were left after a year. I was the sole survivor of a squad. But both disproportions were unusual.

And what about the machines? It became obvious that there were two ways to die in Vietnam. Either you ran out of luck and got killed by the enemy, or you did something stupid and got killed by your own equipment. Stories abounded. The guy who scratched behind his ear with a .45. The guy who jumped aboard a personnel carrier with hand grenades safety-pinned to his tunic. The guy who leaned too far out of a helicopter or tried to fire a weapon full of mud or dropped an armed mortar round or slept under a tank. My demolition outfit circulated a warning picture of what was left of a man's face after he'd tried to crimp a blasting cap with his teeth. We lost one man in a bizarre chain-saw accident and another (just before I got there, actually) who had gotten blasé about explosives, neglected to take cover, and was killed by a piece of debris from his own blast, a wood chip that struck between his eyes at the speed of sound.

(This doesn't even count the problems caused by the septic and hostile natural environment. One man was bitten by a Russell's viper. He died before antivenin could be dropped. Another was mauled by a tiger, and people were constantly being poleaxed by malaria and gruesome intestinal parasites. During the rainy season we tended to look like refugees from a George Romero movie, covered with suppurating leech wounds and green patches of jungle rot.)

The machines were not simply, or primarily, dangerous, of course. They were the only thing between you and the enemy, and you got pretty close to them. The relationship with the M-16 was a love-hate one, well documented, because it was too delicate a weapon for the conditions (and how it wound up that way is a fascinating study in bureaucratic incompetence and greed)—but there were other weapons that always did the job, and soldiers' attitudes toward them covered the spectrum from approval to veneration. In my experience, those were the new army hand grenade, the size and shape of a baseball; the workhorse .45 automatic; the M-79 grenade launcher; and the LAWS one-shot rocket launcher. Some unofficial weapons, like the Soviet AK-47 assault rifle, the Thompson submachine gun, and the Colt Python .44 Magnum, commanded respect for relative rarity as well as dependability.

Napalm was very popular with our outfit. We walked around the jungle in small groups, trying to make contact with the enemy. Once we succeeded in getting pinned down, we would call in artillery and air support, attempting to kill more of them than they killed of us. (This is an admittedly myopic version of what was doubtless a more sensible, or at least more grand, overall strategy.) It was common for us to be outgunned and surrounded, so we were always glad to hear that help was on the way. Air support was more welcome than artillery, though, because we knew that jets or helicopters would make the enemy flee. Artillery sounds impressive, but if you have a trench only a foot deep, you're safe from even a surprisingly close hit. You can hear it coming, duck down, and then pop back up and shoot GIs.

You can't duck from napalm, though. The forest turns into an inferno and you don't even have time to scream. The first intake of breath kills you. Therefore it was also supposed to be a pretty humane weapon, or at least a quick one, even though the baked remains were hideous to look upon. For whatever reason, the enemy sensibly tended to fade into the woods when it started to rain jellied gasoline.

Napalm proper is not flammable; it's the name of a soap powder (a mixture of naphthenic and palmitic acids, in case you want to go out and whip some up yourself), which, when added to gasoline, forms a sticky syrup. I hadn't known that before, but one morning we walked back into the fire base from a search-and-destroy sweep and found dozens of drums of gasoline stacked around. A sergeant rounded up all us engineers and showed us how to make "foo-gas" bombs (I later learned it was a French word, *fougasse*). First you put a measured amount of this purple powder, napalm, into the fifty-five-gallon drum of gasoline; then you stir it around for a few minutes, until it has the consistency of thin Jell-O. Try not to let anybody near who's smoking. Then you take a white phosphorous grenade and tape it to a brick of plastic explosive—this was starting to sound real dangerous—and you carefully unscrew the detonator from the grenade, and carefully screw in an electrical blasting cap, and most carefully lower the whole thing down to the bottom of the fifty-five-gallon drum of jellied gasoline. Then put the top back on the drum and with the help of a few other guys carry it carefully to the perimeter, trying not to stumble over the trailing wires; then dig a deep hole at a forty-five-degree angle and bury the damned thing. For this we got an extra $50 a month, demolition pay. Then you splice the trailing wires to a claymore plunger and deliver it to the machine gun bunker overlooking the site. Tell the guy in charge not to squeeze the plunger until he sees the whites of their eyes. It's sort of like the Strategic Defense Initiative: you don't get to test it and you can only use it once.

This hilltop base had been graced with foo-gas because Intelligence had divined that it was going to be the target of a so-called human wave attack, like the Japanese banzai raids in World War II. Intelligence was usually wrong, fortunately, and no one had actually experienced a human wave attack, so people weren't too worried. There was no doubt that the enemy concentration was increasing, though; there were lots of small-unit contacts in the area, and almost nightly mortar and sniper harassment on the hill.

I was called over to an adjacent hill to do some emergency demolition and wasn't able to get a helicopter back by nightfall, for which I was most grateful, because that night Intelligence proved to be right for a change: the artillery on my new hill started pounding away, and I asked what was up, and someone said, "Human wave attack on Brillo Pad." I watched it through binoculars from about ten miles away. You couldn't see any individuals, but you could see the flashes from weapons, and especially the pyrotechnic display of the foo-gas, which seemed to work perfectly. I took a kind of craftsman's pride in it, assuming that one of them was the one I had put together.

Which circles back around to MIT. It was some weeks before it occurred to me that, in a sense, I was now an accessory to murder. I had refused to kill people directly, but I wasn't reluctant to apply technology and expertise to the same end. The twenty or thirty people who were engulfed in flames when the plunger was squeezed died as much from my actions as from those of the infantryman who triggered the bomb. Of course, if I hadn't done it, some other demolition man would have; the outcome would have been the same. But following that line of reasoning carries you back to the moment you open your draft notice and have to decide between the army or prison or exile. Even if the army uses you for typing or rolling bandages, you have freed another pair of hands for killing.

Of course, you can go even further, as radical rhetoric did in the sixties, and point out that merely paying income tax made you an accessory to the murder of Vietnamese; civil disobedience was the only moral alternative. If I'd known then what I know now, that may have been the route I'd have taken. Speculation is idle, though. There are no time machines, and history doesn't quite repeat itself.

A month or so later, I was severely wounded and spent five months in a couple of hospitals, the second of which introduced me to another alien world, the mundane one of drug dependence. I had more than a hundred bullet and fragment wounds, more than twenty of them serious, and the army wouldn't give me enough painkiller to dent a migraine. Army hospitals have more pushers than doctors, though, and I floated through three months on a cloud of hashish, Demerol, marijuana, opium, amyl nitrite, and alcohol. I could have had all the heroin I wanted, cheap as beer, but I tried it and, fortunately, didn't care for it.

Through all this succession of alien worlds I was aware of being a stranger in a strange land, moving through physical, emotional, moral, and existential terra incognita. What I wasn't ready for was returning home and finding yet another alien world.

Part of it was political. Having been away for the year 1968, I missed most of the events that polarized the country over Vietnam. A larger part, though, must be something that anybody goes through who has learned to survive combat, and by learning I don't mean the business of remembering to clean your rifle and not light a match at night. You become attuned to danger, living every second as if you were in somebody's sights. And you can't turn it off simply by traveling ten thousand miles. For a couple of years I treated the real world as if it were a suburb of the war; land mines between the sidewalk cracks, ambush lurking behind McDonald's. It was absurd, but that's not an argument you can use with your subconscious. What it takes is years of the sidewalk not blowing up and Ronald McDonald not opening fire.

So I was okay after a few years, and then not okay again, with a classic case of Post-Traumatic Stress Disorder, which yielded either to two years of psychotherapy or two years, period; I'll never know.

I guess that's my solar system, the alien worlds that I've explored and reported back about in the form of novels. Most novels that are any good are "about" a lot of things, not all of them accessible to the author, but for the record and for the hell of it, let me record which is where. *War Year* is a realistic, naturalistic novel simply about Vietnam. *The Forever War* is an extended metaphor on Vietnam, mainly about the alienation of soldiers, veterans, from the culture they risked their lives to protect—and also about the tendency of powerful weapons to bite their owners. *All My Sins Remembered* is about guilt associated with socially condoned murder. *Worlds* and *Worlds Apart* are about stress and survival. A novel in progress, *1968*, is about all these things, and more.

I've been out of uniform for nearly twenty years, but in a way you never stop being a soldier, any more than you stop being a mother after your children leave home, or you stop being a child yourself when you begin to shave or menstruate, or even when your hair turns white or falls out. All of us are everyone we've ever been. Being a lot of people is probably a good thing for a novelist; it certainly seems to be an easier and more natural occupation for an Ernest Hemingway than an Emily Dickinson.

Let me close with a coda: an observation that a friend made. I was at the University of Iowa, studying at the Iowa Writers Workshop, walking down a hall with Vance Bourjaily. Vance's first novel was *Confessions of a Spent Youth*, a memoir of his World War II experiences. We'd been talking about Melville or someone, when all of a sudden he asked, "Do you know if any of the other men in the workshop are Vietnam veterans?"

I said I was pretty sure they weren't; nobody had said anything.

He looked thoughtful. "What the hell are they going to write their first novels about? Graduate school?"

Chapter 9

Evolution and Salvation: The Iconic Origins of Druillet's Monstrous Combatants of the Night

Paula Rea Radisich

The illustrated, or "comic book," narrative is, quite rightly, both touted and decried for its ability to depict violence. This is not simply because such narratives are graphic in the strong sense of the word. It is also due to the power of this medium not only to exploit the images of an increasingly violent contemporary world but to stylize these images into something like icons in the deep sense of the word, or to invest them with an aura of tradition and history. Philippe Druillet's *La Nuit* may have taken this icon-making process to its limit. Druillet calls his work a hymn to death, and in it he depicts the final combat of armed bands of degenerate humanoids in the equally disintegrating urban landscape of some SF future. Readers are struck, on one hand, by the sheer rage and violence of Druillet's vision; the battle is waged not only among images but against the power of the graphic image as medium of control. For they are treated to a crescendo of forms—human and nonhuman alike—exploding and dissolving into near-shapeless configurations of color and line. On the other hand, however, one is struck by Druillet's obvious desire to evolve from this chaos a larger framework. This is a frame less of traditional icons than of iconic suggestiveness. What it suggests is that Western art's search for order would operate here if it could only step back from the chaos of forms that continually assail it. The tension in this text, between disorder and the nostalgic dream of an organized tradition of order, tests the nature and function of the icon as few works of art have done before.

Druillet's "night" is an example of iconic nostalgia. It suggests (or wants to suggest) Armageddon, a structure of images that will show us a final clash of the armies of the night followed at daybreak by the endless silence of the tomb. The "armies" in this case are motorcycle gangs, soldiers whose iconic identity is blurred by a mishmash of forms: the uprooted and meaningless fetishes of the urban outcast—tattoos, swastikas, crosses, chains, leather garments. They have, like heroes of old, a quest. But that quest is for drugs—a substance whose shape and identity are confounded by a plethora of slang terms from different languages, English terms further deformed in French transliterations. The heroic words of these warriors are obscenities and monosyllabic grunts, their chants and litanies are misunderstood lyrics from a Rolling Stones song, "Brown Sugar." Over this landscape of violence, drugs, and despair drifts the specter of atomic radiation, but in no identifiable iconic form; there is no bomb or mushroom cloud. Its presence is working rather in the very fabric of things, disintegrating structures, causing human and animal forms to hybridize, to devolve into visual chaos. Yet against this drift of narrative and of image we see Druillet fascinated, even obsessed with, the plastic power of the frame. More than any other artist in this *bande dessinée* medium, perhaps, he stretches and expands his frames to contain the riot of imagery within. On Druillet's page I see, vehicled by the themes of war and night, confrontation on the higher level of the creative act itself—a "battle" between symbolic and nonsymbolic forms, between the traditional signs of Christian apocalypse and a bikers' "rumble."

Despite the newness of his comic-book medium, in his framings and distribution of images Druillet suggests a continuity of "iconicity" that reaches back to Christian art. By means of this suggestion, he is in effect carrying the Christian worldview into the SF future of his tale. Underlying a process we recognize as organic devolution, we see at work several traditional modes of Western iconic representation. We recognize two specifically: hierarchization and hybridization. The former, as it continues to impose traditional structures on human existence, points back from the spectacle of a pointless destruction of forms to their possible salvation. The latter, however, suggesting a continuity of icons on a level more in tune with the evolution of SF itself, may offer Druillet's viewer-reader the means of resolving the tension between Christian and modern that fills his text. For the connection here is one that takes place specifically within the tradition of SF illustration, and one that holds out the possibility of transforming the hybrid monster—in this case the beast combatants of the Book of Revelation—into figures that incarnate a new form of "grace": evolution as it is aided and "shaped" by human science and reason. To trace this connection I will compare the animal-men depicted in an illustrated edition of Restif de la Bretonne's *La Découverte australe*, written in the late eighteenth century, with those in Druillet's text. Similarities may indicate a continuity of purpose between such apparent opposites as Restif's utopia and Druillet's dystopia—a continuity that derives from a shared, but hardly apparent, iconic tradition.

"What are these things, Mom?" my twelve-year-old son asked. "They're weird." He had picked up a photocopy of Louis Binet's 1781 "Elephant Man," an illustration for Restif de la Bretonne's utopian novel *La Découverte australe*, and was scrutinizing it with the serious attention he normally reserves for an *Amazing Spider Man* comic book. The first volume of Restif's four-volume *La Découverte australe par un Homme-volant ou le Dédale français: nouvelle très-philosophique*,[1] I explained, narrates the story of Victorin, a young eighteenth-century Frenchman who invents an amazing contraption made of silk and whalebone that enables him to fly. With the aid of this device he carries off the daughter of a nobleman to an isolated mountaintop, where he begets many children and forms a utopian community. The illustrations that had snared my son's interest are in volume 2, at the point in the story where Victorin and his offspring explore the austral, or southern, territory by air and discover pockets of fantastic creatures like the elephant-men, bear-men, monkey-men, lion-men, and snake-men. My son's curiosity about an illustration to a novel that most readers today would find intolerably opaque and boring prompted me to reconsider the nature of these images.

Louis Binet's plates are among the earliest examples of science fiction illustration. At the time *La Découverte australe* was published (1781), book illustration in general was by no means common. In fact, Restif had written sixteen books before one was accompanied by illustrations in 1777.[2] What are the constraints of SF illustration that these early limners, in the absence of a long-established tradition on which to draw, faced? Certainly, hybrid monsters are not new to Western art. Chimeras, satyrs, and sirens, for example, are familiar representations in the art history of the West.

Binet's elephant-man differs from these traditional hybrids by a pretense of plausibility that defies simple categorization. It is that pretense, nonetheless, that seems to set off the creations of the science fiction illustrator. In this genre, the reader-viewer accepts the likelihood of the depicted confrontation between the protagonist and an alien culture as a real event.[3] I say "reader-viewer," as opposed to "reader," because today, science fiction illustration finds one of its most distinctive outlets in the comic-book adventure, a uniquely twentieth-century form of expression that communicates less by words than by pictures, a fact that explains, to some extent, the ease with which an American youngster in the 1980s could "read" the illustrations of Louis Binet with such obvious delight.

Ironically, though, Binet's pictures were conceived according to radically different expectations regarding the relation of image to text. Like most eighteenth-century book illustrations, they rely on the text for their coherence and intelligibility. For example, the representation of the serpent creatures is accompanied by a lengthy caption located at the base of the opposing page that explains: "A male and female-serpent, in anger, dart their tongues out at the flyers. Hermantin throws a net over the male. One sees the tails of other serpents who flee."[4] Binet's plate is designed to clarify this episode by a straightforward visual illustration of the text. My son's response to these images, however, raises a more complex question about how they communicate as pictures, independent of a text. What representational codes and conventions of visual culture did Restif and Binet call into play to picture these encounters between man and beast?

To construe a plausible creature that was part man and part reptile, the Frenchmen drew on their own cultural vocabulary, which was heavily imprinted with the heritage of the Graeco-Roman past. One of the most well known and celebrated sculptures of antiquity, *The Laocoön*,[5] served as the visual substratum for the representation of the snake creatures. Binet seems to have borrowed the V-shaped composition, the placement of the undulating coils, the articulation of the torso, and the upraised hand from engravings of the famous statue representing the Trojan priest and his sons being destroyed by two huge serpents. The statue's chilling visual tangle of human bodies, grimacing visages, and convoluted appendages provided a model for the integration of serpentlike and human features in Binet's illustration. Connotative of the deadly and the sinister, the *Laocoön* source image expressed the nature of the loathsome snake beings in Restif's story, who remained incorrigible and fearsome in spite of human efforts at domestication. Any instruction they acquired from the flying men was lost, according to Restif, during hibernation each year.

The pretense of plausibility in *La Découverte australe* is due in some measure to the imagery and to the terminology of scientific exploration that marks this section of the novel. In the book's preface, Restif mentions with approval the recent expeditions of Captain Cook, that "voyageur philosophe."[6] Like the real explorers who traveled with Cook, one aim of Restif's flying men is to collect specimens from the austral regions. This collection serves a far more exalted purpose, however, than one might initially suppose, for one theme that emerges from the novel is the mixture of species. Snared and brought to the utopian community for instruction, these animal-men, once educated, are deemed fit to be mated with humans. In this fashion the progress of civilization is furthered (or should I say fathered), and new men of the future are created. This quixotic turn is wholly consistent with Restif's philosophical view of man as a passionate and unstable being who relates to the external world by feelings, not by reason.[7]

It comes as no surprise, then, that some of the representations produced by Louis Binet for volume 2 borrow from the lexicon of eighteenth-century ethnographic illustration. In the picture of the elephant-men, male and female stand frontally posed in nearly identical attitudes, rather like the "Two California Women" engraved for George Shelvocke's 1726 *Voyage around the World*.[8] The setting is carefully delineated, for in this tradition environmental factors were believed to affect the growth and character of a species.

Besides presenting a detailed visual account of the elephant's physical appearance, Binet's illustration shows the animals to be naturally disposed to courage, for they neither flee nor hide from the intruders, unlike the snake-men.[9] In addition, they are able to manipulate their environment intelligently, applying water defensively. The warm and pleasant tropical ambience in which they live corresponds to their own good nature. Once trapped and transported, these elephant beings become avid students of human civilization; they become conversant in French and prove to be almost as intelligent as Europeans. Configuring the elephant-beings with an ethnographic visual idiom accentuates Restif's confidence, reflected thematically in the novel, in the beneficent role played by European man in the civilizing process.

In one of the narrative's most overt instances of this missionary zeal, a character named Hermantin expiates on the theme before a pack of cat-people, utilizing their "crude" language of signs, snarls, and simple words: "Me, my Others," he exclaims, "me wishes good you, wish peace, friendship. Me man-man, you brave lion-man. Me in knowledge, you far from knowledge." The reader is conveniently furnished with a translation of this speech by the author: "I am entirely a man," he writes, "you, on the contrary, are half man and half lion. I possess an infinity of knowledge of which you have no idea and I will share this knowledge with you so you may procure all the pleasures of life."[10]

A most amusing image illustrates this episode, for Restif and Binet have cleverly posed the powerful, predatory male lion-creature standing next to Hermantin in the courtly stance of a European gentleman.[11] This comical posturing of the mighty lion alongside the pretentious European aristocrat also expresses an idea dear to the intelligentsia of the eighteenth century—the noble savage. When ethnographic illustrators wished to emphasize the natural grandeur of the aborigine warriors they were sketching, they often depicted the armed natives in this same stance as a means of communicating the idea of innate nobility.[12]

The king of beasts in this picture, moreover, displays an uncanny resemblance to a most specific French aristocrat. Restif and Binet have given the lion-man the visage of the most powerful male in the pack of the Bourbons, Louis XIV, a man admired at the end of the eighteenth century for his feline qualities of strength, courage, and sexual vigor.[13] Such a visual reference was certainly intended as a compliment to the memory of Louis XIV. The flattery has a sharp edge to it, though, for the perceptive reader would recognize that the grand pornographer (as Restif was known to his contemporaries) was inviting a comparison between the lionlike ruler in the illustration and the Bourbon king who ruled over the French in 1781. Louis XVI, according to the libelous pamphlets of the underground press proliferating at the time, was a bumbling, loutish man, cuckolded by his own brother, the duke of Artois. He was more a pussycat than a lion; the contrast is a pointed one.

As the use of this visual reference suggests, Restif's lion-men have a kind of nobility in spite of their brutish nature. Regrettably, they are not easily civilized, a factor intimated by their crude, halting, and inarticulate speech patterns. The word reigns supreme in Restif's cosmos as an attribute of civilization, just as the word provided the foundation in the eighteenth century for science, philosophy, and art.

What of present-day illustrated science fiction? If we are to compare the Restif-Binet enterprise with one of its more interesting contemporary manifestations, we must take the comic-book format seriously, as the French do. There, *la bande dessinée*, or the B.D., as it is known, is considered a significant literary and artistic form.[14]

Let us now turn to Philippe Druillet's *La Nuit*.[15] Druillet is one of the founders of *Métal hurlant*, a French graphic magazine specializing in science fiction and fantasy, and one of the forces behind the sophistication and refinement characteristic of the French *bande dessinée*.

Oddly enough, Restif's predatory lion-men, antagonists in his novel, have become the new protagonists in Druillet's story. Heintz, Leon, and Frankie, all members of a motorcycle gang called the Lions, dwell in what the author describes as the "dead city of the future." Their role has been upgraded to center stage in the Druillet narrative, but their nature remains untransformed. When a gang member speaks, which is rarely, it is with short, crude, stock obscenities. As with Restif's lion-men, the inarticulateness of the Lion gang signifies their savage state. They are barely able to string two or three words together in a sentence and are unable to express either complex ideas or feelings. Druillet reinforces this point by the uneven, spindly lettering in the balloons and the frequent misspelling of words. Graphically, the Lion gang members are configured to resemble men, but they are oddly textured, and their flesh is green.

The story of *La Nuit* is a simple one. At daybreak the planet the Lions inhabit will be destroyed. During the night, though, the gang's destination is the Blue Depot, where they hope to procure some "shoot." To reach the Blue Depot they must overcome monstrous Polars, military forces of the City, as well as other motorcycle gangs. At the end of the sixty-page saga, the gang reaches the Blue Depot, only to be annihilated by light crystals called "the pale ones."

The comic book is a form of expression that plays with time, space, and narrative progression in a totally unprecedented way. The result is a whole that is more than the sum of its parts—the narrative and the images are so closely interlocked that the eye sweeps across the page in spite of itself, guided by rhythms of shapes and colors. The reader-viewer is cued during this process by a highly specific set of conventions, all directed toward creating that impression of plausibility so central to science fiction illustration. *Plausibility* is a weak term to describe the visceral level at which the viewer is engaged by the typical comic book adventure. Noises, movements, ruptures of time and space can all be graphically conveyed as serial or simultaneous sensations in the blink of an eye. In one panel the reader is made to understand that the gang is in motion because of the cluster of parallel lines extending around the heads of the figures. Time in the comic book can be accelerated or suspended, moved forward in a linear sequence or backward in a flashback. For example, a later panel seems to represent the same moment as the first, but experienced from a different perspective, that of a hidden enemy.

Toward the middle of the narrative, Druillet begins to play with some of these conventions in striking ways. The frame no longer breaks the action into standardized, rectangular units, but compresses it into triangular formats, for example, which provide a series of steep, angled views on the same action, a design visually suggestive of the gears of a motorcycle or the impact of two masses crashing together. A trademark of Druillet's style is his use of the double page as a compositional field. He may pile the figures on one side of the composition into a narrow, vertical, stovepipe shape and frame the horizontal spread of the panorama next to it with a massive, undulating, spiky silhouette suggestive of a tank. Working with the two open pages as a field, Druillet channels the eye in a spiral movement rather than plotting it through the traditional linear sequence that shapes and structures the reading experience.

One noteworthy aspect of *La Nuit* is the frequency with which the author periodically disrupts the narrative action, meager as it is, to present the reader with a page that serves only as visual display. The first of these occurs about a third of the way through the graphic novel, when a double-page spread entitled "Brown Sugar" abruptly severs the reader's narrative engagement, for the book must be turned clockwise on a vertical axis in order to look at the picture from the correct point of view. The intrusion of the picture as an end in itself, rather than as a means of telling a story, is a particular feature of Druillet's style. In his most compelling images, a tense and taut balance is maintained between decoration and narration. On one page Druillet depicts the faces of Heintz and his allies as they stare at the massed forces of the enemy, unfurling them horizontally in a narrow upper register. Superimposed on the chest of a huge frontal figure in enemy armor posed beneath them is another view into the distance showing the opposing army molded into a sinister, skull-like formation. The frontality and centering of the rendered objects, the pentagon-shaped composition that repeats the outline of the framing edge, and the broken spatial continuity combine to create a highly decorative page. But juxtaposed with the upper row of faces, the image ultimately continues to work in tandem with the story line. It oscillates very effectively between surface and content.

Throughout most of the saga, *La Nuit* coheres as a narrative, although it is possible to read it on different levels. The travails of the gang can be read as a fantasy adventure, or the hallucinatory wanderings of a disordered mind, or a drug trip.[16] In the last dozen pages of the story, however, Druillet breaks with the familiar conventions of graphic narrative and withholds verbal cues from the page.

In one image, Heintz and the gang reach the Blue Depot, visualized as a fantastic iconic formation with the face, breasts, and arms of a woman but the insides of a smoking furnace. One character asks, "Where are the givers of shoot?" "Killed by the pales," is the reply. The gang yells obscenities as it surges forward. In the bottom panel, a figure trembles on seeing the pales approach, and on the next page the deadly crystals appear. Although the pales seem to symbolize bad dope, the reader-viewer is never absolutely certain what they represent. This ambivalence is the point. The pictures must be deciphered, an extraordinary demand entirely antithetical to the norms of comic-book form, in which easy legibility and a finely tuned integration of image with narrative are highly valued principles.

How do these images communicate as pictures, we may ask, in the absence of any explicit textual referent? In one double-page composition Heintz is centered above a series of horizontally layered inset panels containing depictions of the deaths of gang members. The delineation of his centralized silhouette set against the light draws on traditional imagery of the Crucifixion. In the *Calvary and Last Judgment Diptych*, by Hubert and Jan Van Eyck, to cite one example, the eye is led up a similar step-by-step progression of light and shadow to focus on the isolated figure of the crucified Christ looming above.[17] Furthermore, Druillet's design is inscribed within the splayed form of a spidery monster, another convention associated with Western religious imagery, notably scenes of the Last Judgment. In Van Eyck's *Last Judgment* panel a devil in an identically splayed-out posture sucks the contorted bodies of frail and pathetic human beings into the depths of Hell. "Death is everywhere," states a barely legible caption at the base of the Druillet composition, but salvation, if we read the iconography of the image correctly, may be at hand for a chosen few.

The diagonal rays of light shooting out from behind Heintz's head likewise signify in Western visual traditions a state of spiritual grace. Rembrandt's etching of *The Three Crosses* is a fine example of how light and dark can be manipulated to express this symbolic value.[18] Seen in terms of this visual convention, the pales, with their diagonal beams of light, acquire a spiritual connotation. This is the light that destroys in order to redeem.

On the last page of *La Nuit*, Druillet represents Heintz, his arm raised in a victorious salute and his body suffused with light, in an image of apotheosis like the resurrected Christ on the Isenheim altar piece.[19] At the bottom of the page Druillet has written: "The end . . . slowly a strain of music mounts." But it is not quite the finale, as viewers familiar with the source of Druillet's image will understand. The themes of salvation, rebirth, and hope for humankind are subtly suggested by this particular visual configuration of a disintegrating Heintz. And so the author directs us on to the sequel, for "Dawn, caress, death" is written in one balloon to the right of the figure, and beneath it we see "life?"

Druillet, we conclude, is not so very far removed from Restif in his essential optimism about the transformation of the animal-man into some as yet unimaginable other form.

Notes

1. Nicolas-Edmé Restif de la Bretonne, *La Découverte australe par un Homme-volant ou le Dédale français: nouvelle très-philosophique*, 4 vols. (Leipzig, 1781; reprint, Geneva: Slatkine, 1979).
2. Binet was recruited as Restif's illustrator in 1780, and a lifelong collaboration ensued between the two men. It is generally agreed that Restif was the actual inventor of the images that illustrated his books; he conveyed his desires in very concrete terms to his friend Binet, who then produced the pictures. On Binet, see J. C. Courbin-Demolins, "Les femmes féïques de Binet," *L'Oeil* 81 (September 1961): 22–31.
3. Jean Giraud (known as Moebius) explained in a recent interview that the genre of science fiction offers infinite possibilities to create this confrontation with another culture in the absence of "legalized" space—conditions that also prevail in westerns. Jacques Rendu, "Moebius: 'J'utilise mon art comme réflexion sur ma vie,'" *Journal Français d'Amérique* (February–March 1988): 24.
4. Restif, *Découverte*, 2:370.
5. *The Laocoön* is reproduced in Francis Haskell and Nicholas Penny, *Taste and the Antique* (New Haven and London: Yale University Press, 1981), p. 245.
6. Restif, *Découverte*, 1:12.
7. On Restif and science fiction, see Mark Poster, *The Utopian Thought of Restif de la Bretonne* (New York: New York University Press, 1971); and Charles A. Porter, *Restif's Novels or an Autobiography in Search of an Author* (New Haven and London: Yale University Press, 1967), chap. 6.
8. Rüdiger Joppien and Bernard Smith, *The Art of Captain Cook's Voyages*,

vol. 1, *The Voyage of the "Endeavour" 1768–1771* (Melbourne: Oxford University Press, 1985), p. 14.
9. The imagery of the snake-men and the elephant-men may also have a phallic connotation, as Eric Rabkin pointed out. The repellent snake creatures are characterized by limp phallic imagery, a quality consistent with the disapprobation in which they are held, while the happily ejaculating elephant-men are literally bursting with vigor. Such a sexual pun is entirely in keeping with Restif's obsessive interest in the subject.
10. Restif, *Découverte*, 2:398–99.
11. See, for example, Rigaud's 1707 portrait of Louis XIV and the print of Jacob Riis, in which both men are identically posed; both are reproduced in Ragnhild Hatton, *Europe in the Age of Louis XIV* (New York: W. W. Norton, 1969), p. 130, fig. 139; and p. 50, fig. 47.
12. For an illustration, see Joppien and Smith, *The Art of Captain Cook's Voyages*, 1:22. The authors compare the pose with that of the *Apollo Belvedere*.
13. See Nanteuil's engraving after Mignard's portrait of Louis XIV, reproduced in W. H. Lewis, *The Splendid Century, Life in France of Louis XIV* (Garden City, N.Y.: Doubleday Anchor Books, 1957), p. 149.
14. See, for example, Yves Frémion, *L'ABC de la BD* (Tournai: Casterman, 1983); and Pierre Fresnault-Deruelle, *Récits et Discours par la Bande. Essais sur les Comics* (Paris: Hachette, 1977).
15. The full title is Philippe Druillet, *La Nuit* (Paris: Les Humanoïdes Associés, 1981). Several of the illustrations used in the novel had been published earlier in *Métal hurlant*. On Druillet, see Phillippe Bronson, *Guide de la Bande Dessinée* (Paris: Editions temps futurs, 1984), p. 58; and Yves Frémion, "Phillippe Druillet," *L'Oeil* 233 (December 1974): 44–47.
16. Druillet called *La Nuit* a passionate ode to death and dedicated it to his wife, who died of cancer halfway through the novel's creation.
17. Today in the Metropolitan Museum of Art in New York City; reproduced in Erwin Panofsky, *Early Netherlandish Painting*, 2 vols. (New York: Icon Editions, 1971), vol. 2, fig. 301.
18. Rembrandt's print reproduced in Horst de la Croix and Richard Tansey, *Gardner's Art through the Ages*, 8th ed., 2 vols. (New York: Harcourt Brace Jovanovich, 1986), 2:749, fig. 19-53.
19. By Matthais Grünewald, reproduced in de la Croix and Tansey, *Gardner's Art through the Ages*, 2:686, fig. 18-35.

Chapter 10

You're History, Buddy: Postapocalyptic Visions in Recent Science Fiction Film

Peter Fitting

A number of people who don't ordinarily go to science fiction movies have nonetheless seen Paul Verhoeven's *RoboCop*. Here a Dutch director, with no background in SF, consciously attempted to both use and critique some of the forms of popular American film so that it would attract two rather different audiences. On the one hand, through its mix of humor and violence it appealed to mass market tastes; at the same time, because of its political framing—particularly through the TV spots—it was able to satirically depict a Reaganite near future, a stance that drew more politically conscious viewers and introduced them to this subgenre of violence-oriented SF. In the following I will offer four overlapping and rather politicized readings of the violence portrayed in several recent films from within this tradition which are without the ostensible political stance of *RoboCop*: James Cameron's *The Terminator* (1984) and George Miller's three Mad Max films (*Mad Max* [1979], *Road Warrior* [1981], and *Beyond Thunderdome* [1985]).[1]

The pleasure we take from films that are seemingly without aesthetic value or any progressive political content poses a dilemma for me, one whose workings and components provide the focus of this paper. If the following can be considered a form of analysis of the "social unconscious," an attempt to "deconceal" the repressed fears and hopes of the popular imagination, it must also be understood as an attempt at understanding the ways society shapes my own desires and perceptions. There is no "out there," no impersonal and objective stance from which to observe and comment.

In one way, these films might best be compared to so-called sexploitation movies, except that here it is not prurience that overlays the original SF premise (e.g., *Flesh Gordon* [1974]) but an apparent pandering to the audience's taste for violence. Narrative and generic conventions are used as the vehicle for *special moments,* like the nudity or couplings in sex films, which are held together rather than generated by the plot. The organizing principle of such films lies in the frequency and spacing of these moments rather than in the unfolding and outcome of the narrative. Moreover, in the case of the SF film itself, there are also special moments specific to the genre. The SF film reached a first peak in the 1950s with the various creature and invasion movies, which were related to the larger social and political climate of the period (the cold war, the bomb).[2] In addition to these popular hybrids of the SF and horror film, there is a second, "ideas," current in SF, perhaps best illustrated by the long success of the television series "Star Trek" (79 programs from 1966 to 1969, and in reruns a regular feature of non–prime time television). With the Arthur C. Clarke–Stanley Kubrick collaboration on *2001: A Space Odyssey* (1968), which was also the culmination of the "ideas" SF film, special effects became SF's main attraction.[3] Although our ability to be dazzled by special effects has begun to wane (primarily because of their now repetitive character), SF films have been firmly established as money-makers since 1977 and the phenomenal success of *Star Wars* and *Close Encounters of the Third Kind*; the studios' earlier reservations have been replaced by wholehearted enthusiasm.

This intensification of particular moments could be written just as easily, for instance, using the history of the car chase scene, which is not without some relevance to the Mad Max films: from *Bullitt* to the spectacular chase in William Friedkin's *The French Connection* (which subsequent films have continually tried to outdo, as in his own *To Live and Die in LA*), such a study would go on to consider the development of the "car movies" (*Smokey and the Bandit* or the TV spin-off, "Dukes of Hazard"), "trucker" films (*Convoy*), and again, the overlap into SF (*Death Race, Damnation Alley, Battle Truck*).

What makes the films under study interesting to me is not the moments of violence themselves but their location in a future in ruins following World War III. This setting is made most explicit in the opening sequences of *Road Warrior,* which tell of the final clash of "two great warrior tribes" and the resulting chaos and destruction. *Mad Max*, on the other hand, is set in the context of a worsening energy crisis and the fight for gasoline to power people's cars, but the larger nuclear war–postapocalypse background that interests me is hardly mentioned.[4] In *Road Warrior* the city is gone and we are in the "Wasteland," where Max plays out a western scenario: helping a group of decent people besieged by a gang of sadistic bikers. *Beyond Thunderdome* follows Max into two further models of emerging postholocaust communities (although neither future seems to be the outcome of the escaped settlers in *Road Warrior*): the first, "Bartertown," is a social Darwinistic view of life after the apocalypse in which only the toughest survive; and the second provides a glimpse of a utopian new beginning.

The first future is that of the myth of the origin of the state: the frontier town before the arrival of families, churches, or morality; one based, moreover, on a premoney economy, where we see not only the "superstructure" (Auntie Entity [Tina Turner] and her cronies, or the various items and services for sale) but also at least an aspect of the "base": the production of methane gas from pig shit. Nor does the pertinence of this economic model stop there, for the film also embodies the geopolitical reality of the late twentieth century, in which the base is increasingly centered in the cheap labor and natural resources of the Third World. This geopolitical reference is made explicit through the "embargo" when Master turns off the power, reminding everyone where political power ultimately lies. In the context of the film, the embargo forcefully demonstrates what an exploitative superstructure needs Max for—to control through violence the rebelliousness of the masses, in this case to kill Master's protector (Blaster). At the same time the embargo also reminds the film's First World audience of their dependence on the continuing ability of the developed countries to exploit Third World energy. Like the oil crisis of the mid-1970s, the image of Bartertown grinding to a halt resonates far beyond its immediate diegetic function through its indirect evocation of the lines at the gasoline pumps during the crisis. As in *Road Warrior*, then, there is an overemphasis on energy and the energy crisis, which, paradoxically, leads to a vision of the future in which there is an excess of available energy at the same time that many of the other features of advanced technological civilization have disappeared. There are few books, no television or household appliances, and little technology apart from that involved in keeping the cars running.

If Bartertown is the future of the attempt to reconstruct technology, the second future of *Beyond Thunderdome* is that of the no-longer-understood traces of technology. Max is expelled from Bartertown and abandoned in the desert when he refuses to kill Blaster. There he is rescued by a group of children who live in a pastoral Eden, awaiting the return of the savior—Max—who will lead them out of the wilderness, back to the wonders of civilization. But as Max tries to tell them, all this has been destroyed. Yet, as the film ends, we see some of the children now living in the abandoned buildings of a great city where they camp like nomads among the ruins of a technology whose meaning and functions will be lost within another generation.

The vision of the collapse of civilization, where people move among the ruins of a technology they no longer understand, is an important subset of the postholocaust future in written and film SF, and it begins with evocations of the ruins of *other* (nonterrestrial) collapsed civilizations—most familiar to us in the remains of the civilization of the Krull in the film *Forbidden Planet* or in the many films and novels that depict Mars as an older dying planet, one on which, by extension, civilization has blossomed and died, as in the Martian novels of Edgar Rice Burroughs. This thematic current may be juxtaposed to visions of a future Earth where our descendants wander in the rubble, no longer understanding the remnants of technological civilization, from H. G. Wells's *Time Machine* (1895, film version 1960) through Jack Vance's *Dying Earth* (1950) and Russell Hoban's *Riddley Walker* (1980). (This category might also include the "lost civilizations" of A. A. Merritt and H. Rider Haggard, and by extension "sword and sorcery" of the Conan type, although such works are increasingly distant from the vision of a lost *technological* civilization, which is my starting point.) Images of collapsed terrestrial civilizations are not so popular in film—except as the result of nuclear war—although the ruined Statue of Liberty in *Planet of the Apes* is a striking visual representation of that theme.[5]

Finally, the theme of world destruction and world rebuilding *after* nuclear destruction is a staple of SF writing. (This theme is exhaustively cataloged in Paul Brians's recent *Nuclear Holocausts: Atomic War in Fiction, 1895–1984*.) Films that deal with these themes range from more "serious" treatments, such as *Dr. Strangelove*, *The War Game*, *The Day After*, *On the Beach*, and *Fail-Safe*, through films closer to the mood of *Road Warrior*, such as *A Boy and His Dog*, *Panic in the Year Zero*, *Damnation Alley*, and *The Ultimate Warrior*, and include some particularly awful Italian Mad Max imitations: *Exterminators of the Year 3000*, *The New Barbarians*, and *Stryker*.[6]

The Terminator is set primarily in the present. A few years into the future, nuclear war has broken out and the "defense network computers" have taken over and decided to exterminate humans. Against overwhelming odds, human resistance to the rebellious machines is nonetheless on the verge of success. In a last-ditch attempt to change their imminent defeat into victory, the machines send an android killer into the past to kill the mother of the leader of the resistance as a way of altering their present! In turn, the resistance sends a man back to protect her and to kill the "terminator." This is the background to the film's focus on the terminator and its mission, although we are given glimpses of the future in which the battle still rages, as gigantic war machines fly overhead blasting everything that moves, while a ragged guerrilla band of humans fights on.

"Vehicles of Liberation"

Is it still necessary to state that not technology, not technique, not the machine are the engineers of repression, but the presence, in them, of the masters who determine their number, their life span, their power, their place in life, and the need for them? Is it still necessary to repeat that science and technology are the great vehicles of liberation, and that it is only their use and restriction in the repressive society which makes them into vehicles of domination? (Herbert Marcuse, *An Essay on Liberation* [1969], 21)

The aspect of these films that raises the ire of many of the critics of popular culture is the large place given to violence. On one level, the question of violence is a sociological or anthropological one: these representations may be designed to produce an effect, although probably not the "incitement to violence" sometimes described by sociologists.[7] Our society is permeated with images, games, and rituals of violence, from comic books and TV cartoons through the sham brutality of wrestling and the ambiguous ferocity of our supposedly nonviolent sports, as well as the increasing bloodiness and gore of contemporary cinema and television. Arguments that attempt to blame the omnipresent spectacles and representations of violence for an increasing level of violence in "reality" do little to explain either the causes of social violence or our fascination with its repeated representation. To the contrary, it seems more reasonable to see these representations as symptoms of something else, and I am particularly interested in explanations of this "imaginary" violence which see it as an attempt to "manage" socially produced angers and frustrations, although sometimes such displaced imaginary resolutions are—in terms of the status quo—unsuccessful, and the rage and frustration erupt into the real.[8]

Much popular art serves to maintain the status quo by stimulating our repressed hopes and fears; then, rather than permitting those awakened feelings to become knowledge or praxis, it sets out to defuse this nascent recognition of social contradiction by redirecting and draining off those threatening emotions. These representations of violence provide only an incomplete satisfaction for the anger and frustration we feel when confronted with a world of plenty in which science and technology and the fruits of human labor are squandered in the intensifying race for new forms of destruction.

In the Mad Max films, that rage is fixed on the automobile itself, for the automobile embodies many of the basic contradictions of contemporary capitalism. Automobile production is the essential industry of the most developed capitalist countries. It was here that the techniques of the advanced capitalist mode of production—the assembly line—were developed and perfected. When it became a consumer good—the *private* automobile—this development intensified and hastened the growth of the U.S. economy for half a century. Today, as a result of competition from abroad, the North American economy's dependence on the automobile industry has been a primary cause of the recession of the last fifteen years. It is the "commodification" of the automobile, the conversion of the U.S. public away from a reliance on public transportation to a "need" for private automobiles, which, since the Second World War, has had a greater impact on our daily lives than that of any other technological development. The car is the quintessential totem of American (and one supposes of Australian) culture. Moreover, this conversion from public transit was based on the selling of a "preference" for private transportation which encapsulates our resistance to *collective* answers to social problems, an ideological blindness to certain kinds of solutions directly attributable to and orchestrated by corporate interests. (The classic case of this "impact" is the motorization of public transport in the United States, of which the most famous example is General Motors's purchase of various municipal trolley and railway systems—most notoriously in Los Angeles—which were then converted to motor buses manufactured by GM.)[9]

Our relationship to our cars is at the core of the Mad Max movies, for what is more important in the first two films than keeping the cars running? And what is more important or pleasurable to the spectator than watching those cars be destroyed? Behind the appeal of violence is a secret fascination with representations of the destruction of that which best sums up our "life-style" for the rest of the world. For viewers in the developed countries, these films speak to the underlying recognition of the contradiction between a society of abundance in which so much is wasted and squandered, and the daily experience for many of increasing immiseration. The spectator's anger and resentment are here *displaced* from an identification of the systemic causes of inequality and exploitation, and from a recognition that alienation and suffering are the result of corporate decisions based on profit calculations, to the objects that incarnate that wasteful life-style.[10]

This redirection of the spectator's rage, away from the people who profit from this "preference" for private cars and toward the machines that have been used to exploit and enslave us, is made explicit in *Terminator*, in which the machines have become the enemies of humanity, bent on eradicating the human species from the planet. If the raison d'être of the Mad Max films might be said to be the cars or their destruction, here the figure of the "terminator" itself is the film's center. The objectified physique of body-builder Arnold Schwarzenegger itself becomes a gleaming machine, which is gradually disassembled and reduced to a metal skeleton before it is finally destroyed.[11] His weak acting and his notorious woodenness here become assets insofar as they work to suggest a machine trying to pass as human (best summed up in the scene in which his computer-brain searches for and then finds the appropriate reply to the landlord of the sleazy hotel where he is hiding: "Fuck you, asshole").

From the explanation of representations of violence as a way of managing resentment and anger which might otherwise threaten the status quo, I now argue that these films also raise questions about violence and the state. For the postholocaust setting gives us a world without a state, and thus without the dilemma posed by state violence outside the boundaries of the law, as epitomized in the justifications presented by some of the witnesses during the Iran-contra hearings. This extralegal violence stems not from a psychological "need" for violence but from the structural contradiction between the capitalist state's "need" to protect free enterprise (at home or abroad) and its ostensible commitment to democracy. On another level, the frustration of the partisans of free enterprise when confronted with legislative attempts to protect consumers is figured in film in the frustrations of the policeman trying to preserve a society in which criminals have too many rights (Clint Eastwood in the Dirty Harry movies).

Road Warrior is a classic western in which "real" values only emerge when the veneer of society and its rules falls away. But like Shane and similar western heroes, Max disappears at the end; society must try to maintain itself without recourse to violence.[12] In this vein, *Terminator* offers two visions of violence beyond the law which are then sanctioned by the principle of self-defense: in the future setting, when the state has collapsed, through the depiction of armed resistance to the machines; and in the present setting, when the police are unable to protect Sarah, through the celebration of individual courage and force akin to the visions of Clint Eastwood or Oliver North. *Beyond Thunderdome* also demonstrates attitudes toward the state and violence, for with Bartertown it tries to imagine the reemergence of the state in social Darwinist terms, one based not on any innate or learned system of morals or laws but functioning solely on economic conventions. The economic system of Bartertown, however, as I have already tried to show, is itself riven by the contradiction between an emergent state apparatus and the actual "producers" of power—many of whom, by the way, are indentured slaves or prisoners, a rather brutal description of what a free-enterprise society might look like without even the veneer of bourgeois legal rights and freedoms.

After World War III

The fall of outdated social systems, and of great empires based on them, makes some people imagine that the world is coming to a catastrophic end, and their terrified visions often take the form of art. (Bruce Franklin, "Chic Bleak in Fantasy Fiction," *Saturday Review*, July 15, 1972, 42)

Since at least World War II there has been a decline in positive, utopian visions of the future and an increase—particularly in science fiction—of visions of imminent decline and disaster. Fictional and filmic images of mass destruction have been a staple of the popular imagination, and critical strategies for "reading" such visions have often lain with demonstrating and understanding their relationship to the historical moment that produced them. In dealing with works that take the bomb or its aftermath as a theme, there are certain conventions that determine the critics' reactions. Visions of a postholocaust landscape are deemed acceptable insofar as they are used as warnings about the dangers of nuclear war, for instance, while works that simply use such settings as a pretext for something else are not.

Indeed, one of the principal objections made against "trash"—whether in the name of high art or in terms of the "politically correct"—follows from the absence of an implicit moral standard which, in the case of the thematics of nuclear disaster, either depends on a work's mobilizing force as a warning or, by extension, on the realism of the portrayal of the disaster ("this is how it could happen," as in Peter Watkins's *The War Game*); or even at a further remove, by the use of this theme as a contextualization for other legitimate themes and stories that illustrate the eternal qualities of the human condition. What critics criticize in such films as *Terminator* or *Road Warrior* is their trivialization of this magisterial theme—their all-too-obvious utilization of this setting as a pretext for the scenes of excessive and stereotyped violence at their core. Although *Road Warrior* and *Terminator* do attempt to explain how this predicament came about and do portray a stereotyped struggle between good and evil, they are not perceived as really dealing with such moral issues, and certainly not as serious statements about the near future or the aftermath of World War III.[13]

An illustrative example of this critical expectation about the correct treatment of apocalyptic themes can be seen in the reversal of the conventional treatment of a closely related theme in J. G. Ballard's "worlds" trilogy (*The Drowned World* [1962], *The Drought* [U.S.: *Burning World*] [1964], *The Crystal World* [1966]). There in each case the familiar scenario of a worldwide disaster is distorted in a troubling and "unacceptable" fashion. The workings of this theme—a cousin to that of the aftermath of a nuclear war—are familiar to us through many of the SF films of the 1950s, beginning with the awakened monsters in the films of Inoshiro Honda in Japan (*Godzilla*; and in the United States, *The Beast from 20,000 Fathoms*), through various U.S. "creature" and invasion films. In many of those films, the world—or some important part of it—is threatened and the film recounts the collective struggle against the marauding invader. Without going into a detailed description of the historical significance of these threats, what interests me here is the almost universal narrative trajectory of these films: from threat to collective struggle to the defeat of that threat. (There are, of course, exceptions which prove the rule: films in which the threat is not defeated, and this failure is used to intensify the film's warning quality, as in the original *Invasion of the Body Snatchers* [1956].)

In his novels Ballard portrays the human community in the context of worldwide cataclysms (e.g., an increase in temperature followed by the melting of the polar ice caps and a subsequent flooding in *Drowned World*) where, in opposition to the official struggle against the disaster, the main character turns against that effort and embraces the destructive force. Although there have been attempts to read Ballard's novels in some "positive" way (e.g., as elaborate Jungian metaphors of transformation), many of his readers within the science fiction community are extremely hostile to these works, even as they trigger new enthusiasms in other readers (and have led in part to the "new wave" in science fiction). Readers react to the inherently "wrong" ethical treatment of the theme, although Ballard continues to go about his heretical rewriting of terminal landscapes in a very different vein than in the films under discussion.[14]

Returning, then, to Mad Max and *The Terminator*, they share both the postcataclysmic setting and an "unacceptable" treatment of this context. Rather than using the disaster as a warning, or even presenting it "realistically," these works use this setting as a pretext for the spectacle of violence.

Yet I would like now to reverse my position. For between the ethically acceptable treatment of a future postholocaust setting, based on a work's attempts to warn us, and the unacceptable trivialization of the theme of the all-too-possible destruction of our world, there is another, third, way of reading those terminal landscapes. This reading situates the blasted, ruined settings not in a possible or probable future—the usual terrain for most discussions of these films—but *in the present*: as the scandalous images of a disaster that has already happened and in whose ruins we can already walk, although only if we are prepared to actually visit the collapsing inner cities of the great metropolises of the United States (Watts or the south Bronx). Like the light from Shelton's nova, an explosion that happened thousands of years ago and whose light is only reaching us now, these films give us temporally dislocated images of a present of which we are only dimly aware. In both cases there is a crucial misperception, so that we misinterpret temporally what we are seeing: as we gaze at the stars, we think that faraway explosion has just happened, and as we watch these films, we think they are referring to a collapse yet to come. Yet such positivistic thinking, which limits itself to the evidence of the senses and which resists more complex modes of thought, is a form of willed ignorance, a deliberate flight from the reality of the present, a temporal blindness that can be compared with that of the central figure in Philip K. Dick's novel *Time Out of Joint* (1959), in which, in a neurotic escape from the present, the main character carefully constructs a world from his past, a happier time from which the tensions and disorders of the present are banished. Like the manifest content of our dreams, which emerge only in heavily censored and coded representations, these filmic images of the future are displaced signals from the social unconscious. Distorted so as to be unrecognizable, these indications of major troubles in our present, signs of its fractures and contradictions, work their way to the surface more easily in these less-censored popular films, while the catastrophes of which they speak are not to be talked or thought of in polite society—nor in the great art of the canon, I might add, from which the "ideological" and the "political" are banned in the name of an art that stands outside time, and, when it does depict moments of social upset and strife, can only show the "eternal" values of the human race.

> The avant-garde is always a way of celebrating the death of the bourgeoisie, for its own death still belongs to the bourgeoisie; but further than this the avant-garde cannot go; it cannot conceive the funerary term it expressed as a moment of germination, as the transition from a closed society to an open one; it is impotent by nature to infuse its protest with the hope of a new assent to the world: it wants to die, to say so, and it wants everything to die with it. (Roland Barthes, *Critical Essays* [1972], 69)

Let us return now to *RoboCop* and to the ways the films I discussed above image the future. Through its deliberate choice of political satire, *RoboCop* places itself outside the "unconscious" framework I have been using. Moreover, its attempt to consciously critique the SF genre leaves the film without an implicit alternative vision of the future. We are left instead with the image of a decaying inner city where the only apparent solution is an increased and more heavily armed police force—albeit one that will apply the law more equitably. The society of *RoboCop* is indistinguishable from the present, or from the media portrayal of the inner cities; the film depicts a society on the verge of collapse. The actual moment of collapse is, as we have seen, the setting of *Mad Max* and *The Terminator*. From this first moment, one can posit a historical narrative underlying these films which moves from the moment of collapse to the efforts to set out and rebuild in *Road Warrior*—an effort that is partially realized in the social Darwinist frontier of Bartertown. Collapse and rebuilding are then followed by a third moment—the radically different future glimpsed at the end of *Beyond Thunderdome*.[15]

Another version of this "narrative" can be seen by working back through the issues I discussed above. I began by arguing that we need to ask what the violence in these films is directed against. I answered that it is the automobile, and in a larger sense the machines of *The Terminator*, which have become the displaced targets for the anger and frustration of the spectator. Rather than take that reading further, however, I turned to the social context of this violence and discussed the films as reflections on the question of violence and the state at a time when the Right is increasingly dissatisfied with the too-liberal legal rights and restraints of capitalist bourgeois democracy. These concerns find expression in a narrative that again attempts to "manage" the spectator's repressed anger by identifying social problems with the myth of an overly lenient justice system and the concomitant feeling that if we could take the law into our own hands, we could somehow deal with those problems (for example, Clint Eastwood in the Dirty Harry films, or better, Charles Bronson in *Death Wish*). The violence in the SF movies under discussion is, I argued, a manipulation of the spectator's anger by turning the viewer's attention away from the *final* causes of frustration and exploitation and focusing it instead on their *instrumental* or material causes.

The world of the children in *Beyond Thunderdome* is, on the other hand, a glimpse of a society beyond the violence and exploitation offered us in the Reaganomics of Bartertown. It is now time to link utopia and violence, time to turn my argument around again and say that these films are not so much fantasies in which violence is used as a solution beyond the boundaries of what is sanctioned by the state, but fantasies of the destruction of the state itself—the recognition of the necessity of overthrowing our present social forms in order to build an egalitarian future. And the final, shocking step in such a reading is to suggest that here the representation of global disaster, in its most terrible, appalling form—nuclear destruction itself—may be seen as figuring our mixed feelings, our real hopes and fears for a radically different future. Let me hasten to add that such a reading is not meant to downplay the real threat of nuclear destruction or the urgency of combating exterminism. I am attempting, rather, to articulate the repressed, irrational side of those visions. As these films suggest, a different society will not grow "naturally" out of the present, just as a better public transportation system could not grow out of decisions based on corporate profit. That new future, as glimpsed at the end of *Beyond Thunderdome*, can only follow from the destruction of capitalism. And the narratives I have outlined, from collapse through rebuilding efforts to the brief glimpse of a utopian society, make clear how painful that struggle will be; without, moreover, any definite idea of what that other future would be like. As the Beatles put it in their reworked version of "Revolution" (the "white album"), "When you talk about destruction, you know you can count me out/in." There is a fundamental ambivalence toward violence in these films. I share it. In a happier society of the future (*Beyond Thunderdome?*), I would hope that violence will have disappeared. But for the present violence seems, in some situations, unavoidable, if only in the face of the brutal suppression of peaceful strategies for social change: from within (in South Africa) or from without (in Nicaragua).

My analysis cannot stop here. The destruction of this society guarantees nothing. My point is not to argue that these films are somehow "progressive," that seeing them will shake capitalism to its roots. To the contrary, I have tried to show that even as—in a vision somewhere between dream and nightmare—these popular works nourish utopian hopes for what R.E.M. calls an "end to our world as we know it," even as they raise the possibility of a qualitatively different future, they also disarm and contradict such hopes by draining off the spectator's anxieties and energy into imaginary solutions and violent satisfactions. In describing these works I have tried to bring out their contradictory functioning as both ideology and utopia. I would like to be able to conclude by referring again to the utopian moments in these works, by pointing to their endings as signs of a better society which will rise from the rubble. But they stop on the threshold, as it were, with the destruction of this world. This is so even in *Beyond Thunderdome*, where, in the final scene, we see the children who went to live in the city, years later, huddled in a cavernous building lit only by candles, as Savannah repeats the now-ritual telling of "history back" and how they came to be there. But the film's final shot is of Max—like Toshiro Mifune at the end of so many samurai movies—standing alone, his back to us, with a sword over his shoulder.

Moreover, Savannah's importance at the end serves to remind us that until *Beyond Thunderdome*, the Mad Max films reflected an older cinema in which women were relegated to fairly minor and stereotyped roles; and certainly Tina Turner's character (like that of Grace Jones in the second Conan film) can hardly be seen as a breakthrough. It is in *The Terminator* that we see the "new" woman of the eighties (although not perhaps as "new" and tough as Ripley, Sigourney Weaver's character in the two Alien films). After a fairly conventional beginning in which Sarah is portrayed as fearful and indecisive (huddled behind a desk in the police station, for instance), her character is transformed, and at the end she becomes an independent, self-sufficient woman who heads south into the desert to hone her survival skills in preparation for the "coming storm."

Like *Beyond Thunderdome*, *The Terminator* also ends with the voice of a woman, as Sarah speaks into a tape recorder, giving advice and information to her not-yet-born son (who, remember, will grow up to lead the resistance against the machines). This moment of transition, this vision of a present pregnant with the future, is a potentially powerful image of a new beginning whose full implications are avoided in these films. As my conclusion, then, I would have liked to have been able to compare Sarah with those women who are prepared to fight for an alternative future, as in Lizzie Borden's feminist utopian film *Born in Flames*; or to the warrior women of recent feminist utopian novels (like Joanna Russ's *The Female Man* or Marge Piercy's *Woman on the Edge of Time*), works that not only speak of the need to destroy this society but go on to imagine an egalitarian future beyond the distortions and exploitation of capitalist patriarchy.[16] But I cannot offer such a conclusion. Sarah's role is only an instrumental one, and a modest one at that, because she will not so much give birth to the future as to the preservation of the past: for she serves as an intermediary between two men, the father and the son, both of whom, in a paradoxical rejection of the utopian politics of feminism, leave her to the present, while they are, if only in the regressive terms of this film, the men of the future.

It is this temporal paradox that perhaps best sums up the ideological limits of these films; for, in attempting to imagine the future, they must keep returning to the past. Sarah's son will be born, fight, and die; and on the verge of military defeat, the machines will send the terminator into the past to kill her. But she will be saved by a man from the future who will also father that son who will lead the resistance against the machines and then die again. Unlike this despairing, cyclical narrative of a perpetual return to barbarism, I have tried to sketch another narrative, of the unfolding of a different future, one that will not happen automatically but must be fought for and won. These films will certainly not change the outcome of that struggle, but a critical attention to the repressed hopes for an escape from that temporal loop, with its social Darwinist explanations of the immutability of human nature or the limits of our human future, may serve as the first step in the call for an art which, like the feminist utopias to which I just referred, speaks more explicitly of the contradictions of the present and of the possibility of a future of our own choosing.

Notes

This is a revised and expanded version of an article originally published in *Cineaction* 11 (Winter 1987–88): 42–51. I thank David Galbraith for his many comments and suggestions.

1. Of course, the director of the Mad Max films—George Miller—is an Australian, but while Verhoeven's status as an "outsider" is apparent, I think, in the peculiar mix of violence and political satire, there is no such perception of

an outsider's hand at work in the North American reception of the Mad Max films (although the first of the series could perhaps be called an Australian film). Updating this in 1992, I should add that in the interim, Paul Verhoeven has become the preeminent Hollywood director specializing in cinematic violence: *Total Recall* (1990) and *Basic Instinct* (1992).

2. Among the many books on SF and film, the most recent is Vivian Sobchack's *Screening Space: The American Science Fiction Film* (New York: Ungar, 1987). For more encyclopedic reference works, see Phil Hardy, ed., *Science Fiction* (New York: Morrow, 1986); and David Wingrove, *Science Fiction Film Source Book* (London: Longman, 1985). For a brief history, see also my "The Other Alien," *Science Fiction Studies* 7 (1980): 285–93, 302–3. For an attempt to situate the films of the 1950s in their social context, see Peter Biskind, *Seeing Is Believing: How Hollywood Taught Us to Stop Worrying and Love the Fifties* (New York: Pantheon, 1983).

3. For the question of special effects, see Michael Stern, "Making Culture into Nature; or, Who Put the 'Special' into 'Special Effects'?" *Science Fiction Studies* 7 (1980): 263–69; and Manfred Nagl, "The Science Fiction Film in Historical Perspective," *Science Fiction Studies* 11 (1983): 262–77; as well as the final chapter of Sobchack's *Screening Space.*

   The shift to special effects also explains the relative failure of the Star Trek films, for the original appeal lay in their situations and ideas. The films work only in reference to the TV series, for what is primarily a public of loyal fans. Although SF films are now acknowledged as money-makers, popular wisdom is that SF will not work on television, a mistaken idea that will only be confirmed by the new TV "Star Trek."

4. Because *Mad Max* addresses the energy crisis without really addressing the issue of nuclear war or a larger conflict, I confine my remarks to *Road Warrior* and *Beyond Thunderdome*. *Mad Max* feels like a film that is still finding its way. In this discussion I also exclude films like *Aliens* (1986), which certainly shares the violence of the others but does not share the postapocalyptic setting.

5. *No Blade of Grass* (1970) is perhaps the best known postdisaster film in which the disaster was not caused by war. Based on the John Christopher novel, *The Death of Grass*, the film portrays the moment of collapse after a virus destroys most of the world's crops. In tone and mood, the disaster is, as I argue for *Road Warrior*, more of a pretext than a serious look at a postholocaust world.

6. See the special issue of *Science Fiction Studies* (13 [July 1986]) edited by Bruce

Franklin on "Nuclear War and Science Fiction." For a discussion of many of these themes in written SF, see Eric Rabkin, Martin Green, and Joseph Olander, eds., *The End of the World* (Carbondale: Southern Illinois University Press, 1983), particularly Gary Wolfe's "The Remaking of Zero" (pp. 1–19), in which he proposes a five-stage "narrative formula" in fictional end-of-the-world stories: "(1) the experience or discovery of the cataclysm; (2) the journey through the wasteland created by the cataclysm; (3) settlement and establishment of a new community; (4) the reemergence of the wilderness as antagonist; and (5) a final decisive battle or struggle to determine which values shall prevail in the new world" (p. 8). Particular stories may pass through all of these phases or be limited to one or more moments. I cannot deal here with the differences between his model and my own, particularly since I am dealing with only a few films while he is attempting to generalize about a large body of works.

7. For a critique of this research see Thelma McCormak's "Making Sense of the Research on Pornography," in *Women Against Censorship*, ed. Varda Burstyn (Toronto: Douglas and McIntyre, 1985), pp. 181–205.

8. My approach is based on the work of Fredric Jameson, most specifically on his "Reification and Utopia in Mass Culture," *Social Text* 1 (1979), and on the discussion of 1950s SF-monster movies at the end of his *Marxism and Form* (1971), pp. 404–6. There—in a gloss on Susan Sontag's "Imagination of Disaster"—he argues that the viewer of these films is caught up in contradictory feelings of anger and anticipation. The anger is directed at the society in which he or she was imprisoned and exploited, an anger that vented itself in the monsters' rampages; while, at the same time, glimpses of a repressed utopian alternative may be seen in the collective struggle against the monsters, and in the figure of the scientist, as an image of a nonalienated kind of work.

9. For an interesting discussion of the decline in public transportation in the United States as the result of a "preference" for the private automobile, see David St. Clair, *The Motorization of American Cities* (New York: Praeger, 1986), particularly his discussion of the "conspiracy theory" of Bradford Snell, according to which General Motors "purposefully sought to destroy electric public transportation in the United States by forcing an inferior technology on them—that is, the motor bus" (p. 16).

10. There are numerous instances in art of the celebration of the car, and of its destruction. This has been one of the major preoccupations of video artists like "Ant Farm," as in their *Cadillac Ranch*, a film that "documents the creation of the Cadillac Ranch in Amarillo, Texas, where ten Cadillacs were buried in

a wheat field on Route 66 as a monument to the rise and fall of the Cadillac tail fin" (*Art Metropole Videotape Catalogue* [Toronto: Art Metropole, 1982], p. 2).

One could also speak of the popularity of various entertainments that feature exaggerated features of the automobile and their destruction, as in the various "monster" cars and trucks.

11. There is, of course, a filmic subset that combines these themes, namely films about cars coming alive, from Walt Disney's *Herbie* to the more sinister cars of *Killdozer*, Spielberg's *Duel*, or Stephen King's *Christine*.

The specific prototype of the android that hunts a human who tries to run and must eventually turn and fight is, of course, the cowboy robot (played by Yul Brynner) in *Westworld* (1973). In the earlier film, the chase is the result of a malfunction; in the sequel *Futureworld*, the robot has been programmed to hunt and kill.

12. These themes are raised in a similar way through the setting of many of the Japanese samurai movies of Akira Kurosawa during the "time of troubles" of a collapsing feudal system. These more problematic moral dilemmas are vastly simplified in Western borrowings from Kurosawa, from the moral simplicity of *Star Wars* (*Hidden Fortress*) to the more cynical and nihilistic rip-offs of *The Seven Samurai* or Sergio Leone's reworking of *Yojimbo*.

13. There is little sense of how people actually live in the future in the films under discussion. Some more modest postholocaust movies have paid more attention to images of how people in the postholocaust future live, as in *The Ultimate Warrior* (1975) or *Escape from New York* (1981)—both set in New York—or *A Boy and His Dog*. These three films give us more worked out visions of how people's lives are organized around daily survival, although all of them fall into the "exploitation" category as well.

For a reading of the Mad Max films that argues their "serious" nature—in contradistinction to movies like *Damnation Alley* "where the nuclear aftermath is only a pretext for the adventure" (p. 322)—see Peter C. Hall and Richard D. Erlich, "Beyond Topeka and Thunderdome: Variations on the Comic-Romance Pattern in Recent SF Film," *Science Fiction Studies* 14 (1987): 316–25. By attempting to apply Northrup Frye's "mythic patterns," the authors empty these works of their historical specificity while falling into the trap of accepting the categories and values of the established canon and then trying to show how some films rise above the dross to meet these standards.

14. The work of J. G. Ballard is in the process of being rediscovered, thanks to the success of his "mainstream" novel *Empire of the Sun* (1984) and Stephen

Spielberg's recent film version. When that novel was short-listed for the Booker Prize in Britain, his portrayal of the British in the Japanese internment camps in Shanghai provoked the same sort of negative comments I have been talking about: instead of showing the heroism or noble suffering of the internees, he instead used this harsh setting as a pretext for his own aesthetics. For an overview of his work close to my own perspective, see the special issue of *Re/Search* on J. G. Ballard (8–9, 1984).

15. An important precursor for the theme of collapse and rebuilding after a (nonnuclear) war is the 1936 Menzies-Wells collaboration, *Things to Come*. Part 2, set in 1967–70, depicts the emergence of a small, authoritarian society based on harsh social Darwinist principles analogous to those of Bartertown, although here the "chief" has consolidated his position through his strict enforcement of a decision to kill all victims of the highly contagious "wandering sickness" rather than through the physical might–energy production dialectic of Bartertown. There is, however, a major contradiction at the core of this portrayal of the shining technological future of 2036, which is built on the ruins of the "old world," although it is rarely mentioned by critics. While the film explains the familiar transition from war to the ruined Everytown of 1970, no explanation is given of how the highly advanced, enlightened "freemasonry of science"—made up of "the old engineers and mechanics"—which has "pledged [itself] to salvage the world," has managed to emerge from the war years without the destruction and barbarism shown in the depiction of Everytown.

16. Contemporary utopian fiction represents a range of attitudes toward violence, particularly in the transition to the new society, from the peaceful strategies of Sally Gearhart's *Wanderground* (1978), to attempts to displace inherent violent tendencies through ritualized violence (Ernest Callenbach's *Ecotopia* [1976]), to more brutal assessments of the continuing presence of some violence in our lives: Joanna Russ's *Female Man* (1975), or Marge Piercy's *Woman on the Edge of Time* (1976). For a further discussion of these novels, see my " 'So We All Became Mothers': New Roles for Men in Recent Utopian Fiction," *Science Fiction Studies* 12 (1985): 156–83.

Chapter 11

The Apocalyptic Mirage: Violence and Eschatology in *Dhalgren*

David Clayton

The action in Samuel Delany's *Dhalgren* (1975) takes place in a city that has somehow been placed outside ordinary historical time. The city is Bellona, a name that seems, a priori, terribly relevant. For if it is true that Delany has taken the modern American city with all its seething rivalries and simply removed the forces of order that now contain them, then this is indeed the war goddess's world. Nothing now, apparently, can stop the urban armies of the night from mutually annihilating themselves. And just as Bellona's brother is Mars, so Delany's city has a larger context of strife for its internal warrings: the omens of millennial destruction that fill its urban sky—a huge red sun and fires of conflagration. Delany seems to be staging the apocalypse.

And yet, if Bellona and its red sun are props, where is the "play" in this novel? For if the signs and symbols promise much, little really happens, either in terms of war in the streets or in terms of final destruction and Second Coming. Traditionally, apocalypse comprises a punishment and a judgment. As Delany seems to promise with Bellona, evil will be allowed to wage a final war, which will accomplish the final winnowing of the wheat from the chaff. In *Dhalgren*, however, both punishment and judgment, if constantly promised, are always deferred.

What is Delany doing then? This question takes on additional significance if we consider the novel in another context that it constantly evokes and yet defers—that of science fiction. Many readers contest calling the novel SF. Yet Delany's situations—indeed, the apocalyptic "imagery" he uses throughout the novel—insist on the SF association. Delany is purposely raising the question of SF's relation to the apocalypse: Is this the literary form that most insistently evokes the apocalypse, and why does it do so? This in turn raises the question of the social implications of apocalyptic fictions in general in relation to the material reality of a culture (here, Delany's 1960s–1970s America) capable of imagining these wars to end all war. SF purports to be a literature of open-ended promise and future development. And yet, is it so fascinated with the symbols and story structures of eschatology, of the predetermined and violent end? Delany's story of Bellona, SF that constantly promises total destruction only to defer that promise constantly, exposes a crucial association in our culture between fight and flights of fancy. Let us look at Delany's apocalyptic mirage.

Dhalgren has proven a hard nut for the critics to crack. Like its locale, the fictional city of Bellona, it occupies the position of a blind spot on the literary horizon. Yet in spite of its length (almost nine hundred pages), the demands it makes on the reader, and the unfavorable reviews that greeted its publication, the novel has had an astonishing success. Published in 1975, the novel had gone through thirteen printings four years later, making it Delany's best-selling work to date and giving it unusual prominence in the field of science fiction paperbacks. While one might ascribe some of its popularity to the freewheeling sexual antics of the main characters, one can also surmise, given its intrinsic difficulties (for which the erotic passages furnish a meager compensation), that *Dhalgren*, in common with certain other innovative works emanating from the mass culture industry—for example, Robert A. Heinlein's *Stranger in a Strange Land* (1961) and Stanley Kubrik's *2001: A Space Odyssey*—owes its resonance to having articulated a dimension of experience its audience felt had been ignored, if not directly refused, by the quotidian offering of goods in the entertainment marketplace.

Appearing seven years after *Nova* (1968), Delany's previous book-length work, *Dhalgren* marked an important turning point in his career. In his earlier works he often adopted a playful attitude toward the sclerotic conventions of traditional science fiction, juxtaposing space opera situations with characters and occurrences totally foreign to them. *Babel-17* (1966), the most interesting of the pre-*Dhalgren* creations, features a female spaceship captain who is also a renowned poet and skilled linguist, and who unravels the secret of an intergalactic pirate's identity by decoding a hitherto unknown language. Clearly such a work takes the reader far off the path well trodden by Campbell, Heinlein, and Asimov, yet Delany by no means treats the materials bequeathed to him by his predecessors with contempt; Delany forces us rather to ask ourselves why science fiction—which ordinarily depicts life in the future—continues to rely on clichés from the nineteenth-century adventure story. Such an approach clears the ground for more imaginative and more sophisticated explorations of the genre's potential at the same time that it tacitly points up the ideologically dubious functions of the majority of these clichés. Why should the commander of a spacecraft be a white—probably Anglo-Saxon—male with a stiff upper lip and a degree in engineering who barely betrays a twinge of emotion, much less of sexual desire, and not a Rydra Wong?

As if sensing the risk of facile aestheticism, Delany chose to abandon this vein of comically laudatory spectacle, substituting the vast, stagnant panorama of *Dhalgren* for the glittering tableaux of the earlier novels. A dense, ambitious work even measured by the standards of serious non–science fiction writing, the novel announces Delany's maturity as a literary artist and reveals—by its attempt to at once cover the grounds of communication, poetics, social behavior, sexuality, and psychology—striking parallels with Herman Melville's *Mardi* or Gertrude Stein's *The Making of Americans*. Although Seth McEvoy claims that "when you get past the first 20 or 30 pages of *Dhalgren*, the story reads like any other novel,"[1] the conventional fictional ingredients—plot, character, setting—Delany employs serve primarily as lures to entice the reader farther into the labyrinth of the text, not to orient his or her understanding of it. To Bellona, nearly deserted, afflicted by a catastrophe of unknown origin, partially destroyed by a conflagration that smolders on throughout the narrative, visited by celestial wonders such as two moons and a solar disk that fills the entire sky, comes a young wanderer who no longer knows his own name. But this time no Rydra Wong helpfully appears to decipher the hero's identity and to clear up the mysteries her creator has evoked.

In breaking so emphatically with his past, Delany reevaluates it in two important ways. First, *Dhalgren* offers a highly critical view of the sixties counterculture scene that had evidently provided much of the inspiration for his earlier works and that Delany describes in his memoir, *Heavenly Breakfast* (1979). Where he had tended before to idealize familiar types from the American underground, such as the vagabond poet Mouse in *Nova*, Delany now focuses on sharply accurate portrayals of the fragile dynamics of social groups and the misery of individuals who have drifted away from the mainstream of middle-class life. More important, Delany carries on the interrogation of the science fiction genre begun in his previous fiction and in his critical essays, shifting his attention from out-of-date generic conventions to a far more crucial issue: How do we recognize and identify a given work as science fiction?

Prima facie, *Dhalgren* lacks any of the signs that would enable one to assign it to the science fiction genre—so much so that the publisher, having slapped the rubric "science fiction" on the book's spine, apparently felt compelled to supply a highly misleading blurb on the jacket which refers to the "dying days of earth." How does one then recognize science fiction? Is a book science fiction because the author labels it as such? If Delany had previously called into question specific conventions, in *Dhalgren* he goes a good deal further by removing the props indigenous to the genre. When a writer fails to provide fancy technological gadgets combined with feats of derring-do performed in outer space centuries hence, does he or she cease to produce science fiction? Or does not the furor aroused by their absence, which no doubt contributed to *Dhalgren*'s hostile reception by fanzine reviewers, point instead to a possible confusion about the aims of the genre?

Looking for a definition that would justify labeling *Dhalgren* science fiction, one might appeal to Darko Suvin's suggestive description of science fiction as "*a literary genre whose necessary and sufficient conditions are the presence and interaction of estrangement and cognition.*"[2] Unfortunately, in practice the key terms in the definition most often stand in an antagonistic relation to one another; cognition undermines the critical role of estrangement, or the latter usurps the former's position, immersing us in a stream of inexplicable happenings. Delany anticipates this problem when he writes of Bellona: "Very few suspect the existence of this city. It is as if not only the media but the laws of perception themselves have redesigned knowledge and perception to pass it. Rumor says there is practically no power here. Neither television cameras nor on-the-spot broadcast function. That such a catastrophe as this should be opaque, and therefore dull, to the electric nation!"[3] From the beginning Delany accents the negative: the discrepancy between the estranging reality of the city and the socially mediated process of cognition. To the extent that Bellona resembles any typical large American metropolis, what we see taking place in it represents less an extreme case of urban decay than facts constantly before our eyes that we usually protect ourselves from seeing. In this way, the book has parallels with Stanislaw Lem's remarkable parable about ideology, *The*

Futurological Congress (1974), whose hero finds himself projected into what seems to be a paradise but turns out to be an enormous drug-induced hallucination. *Dhalgren* effectually inverts this premise, since in it the absence of media camouflage, or in a larger sense of ideological distortion, allows the characters to see things as they really are—a revelation that not a few of them experience as if it were a psychic episode. Returning to Suvin's definition, we could say that true cognition—stripped of parasitic ideological components—must necessarily manifest itself in the maximum of estrangement.

In a passage deleted from the final version of his novel *Triton* (1976) but printed in an appendix, Delany inserts into the mouth of one of the characters the arresting proposition that "the episteme was *always* the secondary hero of the s-f novel—in exactly the same way that the landscape was always the primary one."[4] This paradigm suggests another way of looking at *Dhalgren*: as paradox.[5] In Bellona, landscape and episteme violently clash with one another; the always uncured ailments of the body politic—poverty, racism, exploitation—that emerge in full force once the apparatus of power no longer keeps them out of public view cry down the technological achievements of a society capable of conquering the moon and yet incapable of guaranteeing a better-than-subsistence level to its citizens. But science fiction has always thrived upon this paradox, whether it depicts a future in which this opposition has reached unbearable proportions, as in Lem's novel or in H. G. Wells's *The Time Machine* (1895), or even where it degrades it to the cheap promise of a happy ending safely placed centuries away from the present. By bringing this conflict closer to home than science fiction usually does, *Dhalgren* reminds us how much the genre follows the motto *De te fabula narratur*.

The protagonist's quest for identity and the eponym *kid* bestowed on him evoke memories of the picaresque novel, and one might describe *Dhalgren* as an example of the epistemological picaresque. The comparison, however, serves mainly to point up differences essential to an understanding of Delany's work. The picaresque hero's quest culminated in an act of synthesis, the subject's integration into society; as a bourgeois epic, the picaresque novel offered the collectivity as the true goal the hero or heroine reaches after having vainly chased after its illusory—usually criminal—substitutes. Delany, starting from the thesis of a fundamental discrepancy between the social landscape and the epistemological—in this case, scientific—frame of reference, must necessarily take a far more difficult reverse journey, that of undoing the process of socialization. To his credit, Delany

Violence and Eschatology in *Dhalgren*   137

rejects the ludicrous idea that one can attain this end by simply turning on and dropping out; long before the capitalist era, Western culture had indisassociably tied together reason and personal identity, the latter equated with knowledge of one's proper name. Undoing this knot requires an act of negation equal in power to that which produced it, conjuring up the specter of madness whose approach the hero so fears—with "reason," one could ironically add.

Dhalgren is divided into seven chapters, but the seventh consists of fragmentary entries from Kid's notebook which partially continue the narrative and partially obscure it. Among these is an enigmatic scrap which presents for the first and only time in the novel a sense of "normal" life. One might speculate, since Delany furnishes a number of plausible explanations for the events that occur in *Dhalgren*, that the book actually corresponds to an intentional denial of what the character "really" sees around him, reconstructed as a narrative. In this case, Delany would have carried off a dialectical tour de force and would have completely changed the assumptions of naïve realism: the Kid grasps the truth by sacrificing the real, even at the price of his sanity. Whether the hypothesis holds does not basically affect our reading of the novel, but it should warn us away from precipitously imposing answers on such a problematic text.

The aspect of *Dhalgren* most likely to strike the average reader of science fiction is the apocalyptic. Delany, certainly not without humor, has cooked up an American nightmare designed to send chills down the spine of followers of Howard Ruff and *The National Enquirer*: after the city's abandonment by the forces of law and order, a hippie commune sets up in the park, people engage more or less publicly in promiscuous sexual acts, a juvenile gang called the Scorpions roams the streets and pillages at will, and, last but not least, a black man named George who has raped a WASP maiden becomes the object of an incipient cult. In contrast to end-of-the-world stories that depict the struggles of a handful of survivors, *Dhalgren*—the advertising notwithstanding—consistently emphasizes the uniqueness of Bellona's lot; outside the enchanted city, life goes on as usual. Here again, Delany upsets the conventions to make his point. If this apocalypse, which combines natural and social disasters, represents the last judgment for many white middle-class Americans, one can no more hope to find it parading around in broad daylight than one can hope to glimpse the true, complex visage of urban life except in a moment when its defenses have totally fallen.

But the funniest thing about Delany's apocalypse is that either it never takes place or it occurs over and over, like a needle stuck in a record groove. The book offers more than one candidate for this event. There is, first of all, the catastrophic day on which Bellona's troubles commence, the day on which George rapes June Richards during an electrical storm that possibly sets the city afire. This action, however, takes place before Kid's arrival in Bellona, and he hears about it from the newspaper peddler Joaquim Faust. Second, there is the day on which the sun entirely fills the sky, perceived by Kid as a harbinger of the end if not its fulfillment: "Perhaps, he thought, we are all going to die in moments, obscured by flame and pain."[6] Finally, there is the conflagration that ensues just before the end of the novel and sends Kid and a handful of Scorpions in flight from the city.

At this point the difficulties set in. A careful comparison of the last apocalypse with the first shows them to be identical, including a repetition of the attack on June. Does Kid leave the city at the end of the book only to suffer amnesia, hear of the apocalypse he has already endured, and then undergo it again at the novel's conclusion and return amnesiac to Bellona? Or is the end really the beginning? Does the apocalypse "really" happen at the end, and do the characters live through it again and again in a kind of afterlife? Then what is one to do with the second apocalypse? Or are all of these simply rehearsals for a main event yet to come? The book offers us at least three alternatives, none compatible with the others, and each with equal claim to probability. Evidently the law of the excluded middle has, like most other laws, ceased to operate in Bellona.[7]

One can come up with various explanations for the pluralization of apocalypses, ranging from the limp one that Delany is supplying another piece of evidence to show how screwy Bellona is to the more sophisticated one that the writer wants to emphatically demarcate a work of art from real life. The latter explanation especially appeals to academics who tolerate unresolved contradictions in art or life no better than the most diehard Hegelian; one does Delany no favor by adopting it. In the first place, *Dhalgren*, in spite of its overt modernism evident from the homage to James Joyce's *Finnegans Wake* in the opening and closing lines (which begin and end in mid-sentence), has nothing in common with that deluxe literary commodity, the comfortable Victorian mansion protected by a posthumously modernist façade. In this book Delany stands close to the line of modernist experimentalism associated with Duchamp, Stein, Brecht, and Cage, and his novel functions as a work in progress, not a speciously enclosed verbal fortress. Second, to argue (as does Jean Mark Gawron in a long, thoughtful introduction to the Gregg Press edition of *Dhalgren*)[8] that one can, given sufficiently powerful theoretical tools, read out a coherent meaning from these deliberate inconsistencies amounts to robbing them of their force. Criticism, however well intentioned, that follows this line of reasoning erects a network of defenses to protect us from potential assaults on our own established beliefs.

Let us assume that Delany's paradoxical treatment of the apocalypse theme in *Dhalgren* results neither from carelessness nor artistic willfulness; let us assume that Delany wants to make a logical point: the idea that the end of the world is per se contradictory and logically impossible. Or to put it somewhat differently, one can choose any of the three apocalypses the book offers; but the instant you try to relate it to an event in the real spatiotemporal continuum, the other two will appear to challenge it and thereby render impossible any decision. Apocalyptic discourse moves in a realm of its own that has no relation to human history; it represents in the first place an idea projected onto history. Rather than affirming the possibility of apocalypse, *Dhalgren* exposes its inherent implausibility, and in doing so raises two nontrivial questions: Why should this terminally violent event exercise such a fascination? And why should it in particular continue to haunt the pages of science fiction? To formulate a provisional answer to both of these queries entails a brief detour through the backroads of eschatology.

Outside religious circles, the branch of theology that deals with "'the last things' strictly so called—the idea of judgment and retribution, or of a Day of Judgment, Millennial ideas, the catastrophic end of the world and its renewal, and how the dead are related to that end of all things"[9] has not enjoyed wide popularity. Luther still believed in an imminent Last Judgment, but Calvin postponed the event to the indefinite future. With the rise of the natural sciences, the idea was increasingly relegated to the basement of speculative theology. The article on eschatology in Hastings's *Encyclopaedia of Religion and Ethics* judiciously concludes that "the tendency now is more and more to seek the more spiritual concept of judgment, and for men to concern themselves less and less with the close of the world-order as an event to which has been attached, more or less mechanically, the idea of Last Judgment."[10]

Although apocalypticism played a significant role in the poetics of English romanticism, as Harold Bloom has rightly emphasized, one would search in vain for apocalyptic themes in the realistic novel. Talk of the day of wrath, except coming from a religious fanatic or a lunatic, would have been as out of place in the world of Richardson, Austen, or Dickens as the sight of a turd on Miss Woodhouse's parlor carpet. Nevertheless, in the period between the two world wars, the apocalyptic light once more cast its crepuscular glow over a number of important literary works—among them Robert Musil's *Der Mann ohne Eigenschaften* (1930–43) and Elias Canetti's *Die Blendung* (1935), both of which depicted the collapse of traditional European culture. And it even found its way into such American novels as Djuna Barnes's *Nightwood* (1937) and Nathanael West's *Day of the Locust* (1939). Yet when all these forebodings proved to have been well founded, the fulfillment of such prophecies left little room for artistic commentary. How could the disintegration of the Austro-Hungarian Empire supply a paradigm for the fate of European Jewry? And how could the latter, as Brecht admitted, ever serve as the subject of a work of art? As Mary McCarthy, summarizing the inability of realistic fiction to portray the post-Auschwitz, post-Hiroshima world, remarked: "We know that the real world exists, but we can no longer imagine it."[11]

At this point enter science fiction, no stranger to the apocalyptic themes from the time of Mary Shelley's *The Last Man* (1826) down to the present. Curiously, however, in contrast to its usual pattern of rationally explaining traditional myths, science fiction in this case has tended to remain within the limits of eschatological speculation. According to the latter, the end of the world occurs as punishment for man's sins; preceded by a period of travail and persecution such as that set forth in the Book of Revelation, the Last Judgment marks the end of human history, after which the righteous will live in Paradise with God and the unrighteous will suffer eternal torment. Thus Edgar Allan Poe in "The Colloquy of Monos and Una" depicts a final catastrophe brought on by man's thirst for knowledge and exacerbated by popular agitation and industrialism. An explicitly religious work such as Walter Miller, Jr.'s, *A Canticle for Leibowitz* (1960) blames a future nuclear holocaust on the fall from grace, while even more sophisticated productions such as Doris Lessing's *The Four-Gated City* (1969) or Thomas Pynchon's *Gravity's Rainbow* (1973) fall back on the idea of an original state of nature which human civilization—and technology in particular—has violated and for which act we must atone.

One of the best known science fiction apocalypses, that which Wells presents at the end of *The Time Machine* (1895), aptly points up the difficulties science fiction seems to encounter in dealing with this theme. Carried to the end of time, the protagonist sees first an eclipse of cosmic proportions, after which "the pale stars alone were visible. All else was rayless obscurity." In this obscurity he makes out an undifferentiated blob of living matter "hopping fitfully about. Then I felt I was fainting."[12] Doubtless Wells's intention was to present a completely natural event divested of religious associations. Yet, immediately following the story of the Eloi and the Morlocks, the episode takes on the significance of an act of punishment entailed by humankind's descent into weakness—a possibility that John Campbell explicitly developed some years later in his story "Twilight"; on the other hand, retroactively, the vision conjures up the prospect of a biological fatality presiding over the destiny of the race, with the Eloi marking just another step in the inevitable progress of decay. In spite of Wells's intention, his naturalistic apocalypse merges natural and social categories, and both fall prey to the irresistible spell of eschatology.

What all apocalyptic speculations, in or outside science fiction, share in common—as the foregoing sketch should make clear—is a large dose of paranoia, of collective rather than individual origin. Even if one does not trace the genesis of society, as did Hobbes, back to the subjugation of the weaker by the stronger, an incredible quantity of aggression has to be forfeited before any social organism can come into existence. Part of this energy accrues to the collectivity in its subordination of the individual to its own aims—hence the violence Kid or any other person experiences when he or she attempts to break this bond. Another part, however, is directed outside: toward the conquest of the natural environment—anthropomorphically viewed as the enemy—and toward human strangers, reduced to the status of dangerous beasts. Awareness that what has been attacked might likewise attack leads to the fear that the violence one has directed without could return upon its sender like a boomerang. Eschatology, in a second stage of reflection, attempts to parry the ever-present threat of reprisal by transfiguring the initial act of aggression and remolding it into the promise of future reward. Yes, it admits, we have all sinned, but by enduring the punishments God has waiting at the end of time we will all share in bliss. Moreover, the "narcissistic wound" that eschatology inflicts on the individual with its doctrine of original sin is more than compensated for by election: as the main actors in this cosmic drama, the community of believers occupies the foreground on the world historical stage.

Eschatology ill disguises its intrinsic paranoid features: megalomania, fear of persecution, and readiness for aggression toward outsiders. At the same time, it by no means escapes its sociocultural causes, which it mystifies by transporting them outside time: on one end, into a prelapsarian era of perfection and wholeness from which we have fallen, and, on the other, into an eternal reign of happiness for the faithful and damnation for the reprobate. In the most interesting works of science fictional eschatology, the text allows these elements to stand forth clearly without being able to exorcise them, and one might well doubt whether it is possible to do so at all. To the extent that it had any meaning, eschatology belonged to the period before myth and religion gave way to science; keeping it artificially alive whether as a means of scaring people into good behavior or for purely speculative ends necessarily leads to ideological compromise.

After this digression, we find ourselves back with Delany, who, as we have seen, depicts the apocalypse as an impossibility. And in fact, appearances to the contrary, I do not think that the apocalypse, though it supplies one of the themes for *Dhalgren*, in any sense constitutes Delany's main concern. This idea served him as an extreme case of the way we use representations to defend ourselves from what we fear—and representation, not apocalypse, stands at the center of *Dhalgren*. From George reenacting a primitive myth to the Scorpions literally embodying a biblical plague; from Tak adoring the images of George to Calkins, playing the role of philosopher king, representation obsesses the inhabitants of Bellona. Representation, and not production, one might add. When Kid visits the deserted warehouse in which Tak shows him the props used by the Scorpions, he immediately perceives the signs—the representation—of a conspiracy. Doesn't the warehouse belong to the mysterious Mateland Systems Engineering firm that Arthur Richards works for? Yet wouldn't it make more sense to reason that where there is a product there must be a producer?

But this fascination with representation, which deconstruction promotes to the status of a metaphysical dogma, in fact indexes, for the characters in the novel and for us, an important socioeconomic fact. With the continuing stagnation of productive forces in the capitalist economy, with the saturation of markets and the overproduction of goods that cannot be sold for a profit, increasingly large amounts of money go into advertising and the media, which become industries and not just vehicles for selling goods. Pushed beyond a certain point, the advertisement—the representation—takes the place of the commodity, and the latter itself becomes an advertisement, blurring whatever difference might remain between use and exchange value. In an essay on Antonin Artaud, Jacques Derrida states that "because it has always already begun, representation has no end."[13] Sadly, the most ready illustration one could find of this today is not the theater of cruelty but MTV.

An act of true cognition means in the first place freeing oneself of the power of ideological representation. Delany has no illusions about the difficulties of accomplishing this task; the characters in *Dhalgren*, unable to do so, return to Bellona to perform their private apocalyptic drama over and over again. At the same time, invisible to them, the productive forces that make their lives possible continue to move about them, to determine their existences down to the last detail. Unwilling to make the sacrifice necessary to see these forces and gain control over them, the characters prefer to impose upon them the archaic drama of apocalypse.

Postscript

Some time after I had originally composed this essay, Susan Sontag denounced the spurious allure of contemporary apocalypticism at the conclusion of her essay *AIDS and Its Metaphors*. Since she articulates, in language far more eloquent than my own, some of the points I have attempted to make in my discussion of *Dhalgren*, I can find no better way of concluding than by citing a passage from her work:

> AIDS may be extending the propensity for becoming inured to vistas of global annihilation which the stocking and brandishing of nuclear arms has already promoted. With the inflation of apocalyptic rhetoric has come the increasing unreality of the apocalypse. A permanent modern scenario: apocalypse looms . . . and it doesn't occur. And it still looms. . . . Apocalypse is now a long-running serial: not "Apocalypse Now" but "Apocalypse From Now On." Apocalypse has become an event that is happening and not happening.[14]

Notes

1. Seth McEvoy, *Samuel R. Delany* (New York: Frederick Ungar, 1984), p. 105.
2. Darko Suvin, *Metamorphoses of Science Fiction: On the Poetics and History of a Literary Genre* (New Haven: Yale University Press, 1979), pp. 7–8.
3. Samuel R. Delany, *Dhalgren* (Boston: Gregg Press, 1974), pp. 15–16.
4. Samuel R. Delany, *Triton: An Ambiguous Heterotopia* (New York: Bantam Books, 1976), p. 333.
5. I am indebted, especially in later sections of this essay, to the brilliant exposition of paradox by Gilles Deleuze in *Logique du sens* (Paris: Minuit, 1969). As Deleuze writes, in words that one could also apply to *Dhalgren*, "Paradoxes are only pastimes when one considers them as stimuli to thinking, not when one considers them as 'the Passion of thinking,' discovering what can

only be thought, what can only be spoken—which is as well the ineffable and unthinkable" (p. 92). This and all other translations are my own.
6. Delany, *Dhalgren*, p. 92.
7. In effect, this violation of logic results from a confusion of two time scales, *Chronos* and *Aion*: "While *Chronos* expresses the action of bodies and the creation of physical qualities, *Aion* is the locus of intangible events and of attributes distinct from qualities" (Deleuze, *Logique*, p. 193). The possible physical destruction of the universe belongs to the first of these scales; the apocalypse, an ideal theological event, only to the second.
8. Jean Mark Gawron, Introduction to *Dhalgren* (Boston: Gregg Press, 1977), pp. v–xliii.
9. J. A. MacCulloch, "Eschatology," in *Encyclopaedia of Religion and Ethics*, ed. James Hastings (New York: Scribners, 1951), 5:373.
10. Ibid., p. 391.
11. Mary McCarthy, "Fact in Fiction," in *On the Contrary* (New York: Harcourt, Brace, 1961), p. 265.
12. H. G. Wells, *The Time Machine*, in *The Complete Science Fiction Treasury of H. G. Wells* (1934; reprint, New York: Avenel), p. 63.
13. Jacques Derrida, "La clôture de la représentation," in *L'écriture et la différence* (Paris: Seuil, 1967), p. 367. Translation my own.
14. Susan Sontag, *AIDS and Its Metaphors* (New York: Farrar, Straus and Giroux, 1989), pp. 87–88.

Chapter 12

Demonic Therapy: Reading the Holy Word in the Mushroom Cloud

Scott Dalrymple

> The shape is there, and most of us come to realize what it is sooner or later: it is the shape of a body under a sheet. All our fears add up to one great fear, all our fears are part of that great fear—an arm, a leg, a finger, an ear. We're afraid of the body under the sheet. It's our body. And the great appeal of horror fiction through the ages is that it serves as a rehearsal for our own deaths.
> —Stephen King, *Night Shift*

Death has always been the obsession of humankind. It represents both an end to worldly life and the quintessential unknown. When people have chosen to deal with the prospect of death, they have generally turned to organized religion, which most often rationalizes what comes after death as the reward or punishment for a life well or badly led. In the past, death could be taken in stride because people believed in individual immortality. When people died they reaped their deserved reward, and the world continued as it had done before. Even for people without religious faith, some vestiges of hope could be seen in the continued existence of the human race as a whole, or at least in the survival of nature. In our age, however, for the first time in history, the consoling thought that life will continue beyond our own deaths has been threatened, if not obliterated. In the nuclear age we are not at all certain that the world will continue after a nuclear holocaust.

A major shift has occurred. Our world differs fundamentally from that of any other age. "For the first time in six centuries (since the great European plagues) a generation has been born and raised in a thanatological context, concerned with the imminent death of the person, the death of humanity, the death of the universe, and, by extension, the death of God."[1] The problems we face now are much more deadly for the planet as a whole than the Black Death ever was. For the first time in history, the possibility of a violent and inescapable death is actually a fact of life for everyone and almost everything on the planet. The threat of thermonuclear warfare actually broadens our concept of death; accordingly, even children, who were once spared most of the anxiety about human mortality, must learn to deal with death.[2]

Nuclear anxiety has become more than an isolated phenomenon. It is no longer a term reserved for psychologists—it now has a place in our everyday language and culture. For the secular part of our society, those who find little comfort in religion, there seem to be only two choices: apathy or despair. In 1961, Hans Morgenthau wrote that

a secular age, which has lost faith in individual immortality in another world and is aware of the impending doom of the world through which it tries to perpetuate itself here and now, is left without a remedy. Once it has become aware of its condition, it must despair. It is the saving grace of our age that it has not yet become aware of its condition.[3]

Now, more than thirty years after this statement was made, we are perhaps becoming more aware of our condition.

We are now facing fundamental changes that trigger a questioning of previously unquestioned beliefs. One of these inescapable changes is that humans can now join God in his ability to destroy the world and all in it. When God is no longer alone, or necessary, in his apocalyptic capacity, then he is no longer alone as a god. Nuclear destruction has, in a sense, become our new evil god. In our world, concepts of death have become dehumanized and depersonalized because this new god is inhuman and impersonal. There seems no comfortable way to deal with death now.

When crimes are of a certain magnitude and character, they nullify our power to respond to them adequately because they smash the human context in which human losses normally acquire their meaning for us. When an entire community or an entire people is destroyed, most of those who would mourn the victims, or bring the perpetrators to justice, or forgive them, or simply remember what occurred, are themselves destroyed. When that community is all mankind, the loss of the human context is total.[4]

We are forced by the thought of nuclear destruction to remember it in advance; there will be no literature, no humans, no memory to do so after the fact. This necessarily alters our formerly romantic visions of the apocalypse: "In any event, the image of the wrathful God, before whom you quake and tremble and who is yet also the loving father who will forgive and rescue you, has lost much of the hold it had on the hearts of our forefathers. Modern stories assume the end of the world to be decreed by much, much lesser powers."[5] The images of puritan Jonathan Edwards's "Sinners in the Hands of an Angry God" are no longer more frightening than reality—such fire-and-brimstone sermons and passages from the Bible are no longer much comfort against the real fears felt by the children of the nuclear age.

Perhaps one of the reasons for our new awareness of and discomfort with death is an increased importance of visualization in our culture. This century has seen television propel previously intangible and unbelievable horrors right into our living rooms. From the atrocities of Dachau and Auschwitz to Vietnam and starving children in Ethiopia, things that were once the stuff of grim fantasy have been thrust upon us as harsh reality in documentaries and newscasts. Probably the most potent and frightening of all visual death images is that of the ominous, towering mushroom cloud. Eyewitnesses of Hiroshima and Nagasaki tell very real stories of the living dead crawling in the streets of the ruined cities, an all-too-horrible fiction come to life. The nuclear mushroom cloud, the symbol of this terror, has now attained almost mythic status; it is visualized not only in stock newsreel footage but in popular music videos and even in commercials. Robert Jay Lifton has called such "imagery of extinction" a "major rift in our psychic tissues," and he feels that in order to cope we are now searching for an increased awareness of death which is "long overdue."[6] We have been repressing death awareness for too long, and now, when the prospect of death seems at its most final and imminent, we must uncover our fears and deal with them on a conscious level.

Because we don't know how to deal with a dehumanized concept of death such as that of nuclear extinction, we try to twist the cause of our anxiety into something familiar; we become confused and anxious, and we "try very hard to make new problems look like old ones and to cope with them in old ways."[7] Doing so unconsciously makes the problems somewhat easier to handle. I suggest that one way in which we try to transform our new fears into old fears, a strange new therapy in the nuclear age, is our societal immersion in the horror genre.

To understand the problem of nuclear anxiety and its relationship to horror more thoroughly, let us examine a work by the most successful of modern horror novelists, Stephen King. In King's *The Dead Zone*, Johnny Smith, whose name suggests Everyman, has awakened from a coma after more than four years to find that he has a disturbing power. Now, when he touches certain people or their belongings, he receives images of their futures. The central conflict of the novel arrives when Johnny shakes the hand of Greg Stillson, a seemingly small-time political candidate. Johnny foresees that Stillson, appropriately named "dead child," will become president—and that he will lead the United States into a full-scale nuclear war. The possibility of this future is too terrifying for Johnny to accept, and, driven by fear, he decides that he must risk his own life and assassinate Stillson. The vision of the world being destroyed by thermonuclear weapons is the most horrific thing Johnny can imagine. It becomes his obsession. He has psychically experienced the rape and murder of a small girl and has seen her killer bent over a toilet with his throat slashed, but this more anonymous, faraway threat of nuclear war affects him as nothing else can. Johnny becomes a scared, self-proclaimed martyr bent on becoming the savior of the nuclear age. The old ethics question "Would you assassinate Hitler in 1938?" has now assumed an even more terrible significance.

In *The Dead Zone*, Johnny seems alone in his nuclear anxiety. None of the other characters can see his awful vision, and accordingly they go about their lives with relatively little thought of destruction or apocalypse. Nuclear anxiety is certainly present in everyone to some extent. Occasional evidence of it pops out, as when Chuck jokes in a letter to Johnny that he thinks one of his old teachers "would really have been more happy making doomsday weapons and blowing up the world,"[8] but the anxiety is dealt with and covered up by psychological mechanisms, such as Chuck's joking attitude. But Johnny Smith is a member of the first generation to grow up in the face of the nuclear threat, and he reacts to it in a different way. He struggles to do something drastic to remove one cause of his anxiety. He becomes the spokesman and hero for those who are concerned about the planet, those who cannot avoid the issue or dismiss the nuclear threat as someone else's problem.

One other character displays a kind of anxiety about the end of the world, however: Johnny's mother, Vera, whose name suggests the older "truth." Her anxiety is much different from Johnny's, but it is important to analyze it. Vera Smith represents that facet of society which turns enthusiastically toward religion in order to cope with life. The only apocalypse she imagines is the Last Judgment, the religious apocalypse that the Jews and Christians were looking for thousands of years before the reality of thermonuclear weapons. In her formative years God was considered the only ultimate destructive force, and she has turned to religion to deal with her fears. Although she now lives in the nuclear age, she nevertheless selectively blocks out information she doesn't want to hear.[9] She accepts that we are in danger but contends that nuclear weapons are not what we should fear. Instead, we should fear the wrath of God in a sinner's world where New York is Sodom and Los Angeles is Gomorrah (124). She is a fanatic who truly feels that the holocaust is coming, but she still hopes, because she believes in God and thinks she will be saved. Therefore, although she is anxious about what she feels to be certain coming destruction, she does not fear death as such.

But Johnny is not allowed this luxury. He grew up in a different world. He seems to be an agnostic, making his vision of the postatomic mushroom end of the world a more final and terrifying one. He and his generation have grown up in a more absurd, existential world where the end of humankind may be triggered not by an angry God but by an unknown terrorist firing a single missile at Washington or Moscow, starting an exchange for a reason the world may never have the chance to learn. Mushroom clouds will sprout all over the planet, and it is likely that no one will be left to ask why.

Johnny Smith finds his mother's God impotent and the inaction of his fellow humans an unacceptable solution. The Bible, for some the joyous and fearful Word of God, has lost its ability to instill fear in him. King could have been writing about Johnny when he said in his book *Danse Macabre* that "a ghost in the turret room of a Scottish castle just cannot compete with thousand-megaton warheads, CBW [chemical biological warfare] bugs, or nuclear power plants that have apparently been put together from Aurora model kits by ten-year-olds with poor eye-hand coordination."[10] If horrifying warheads and agents of chemical biological warfare are truly the products of clumsy, naïve ten-year-old mentalities, then we no longer have to look far away to a religious source of fear. Like the ghost in a Scottish castle, the God who caused it to rain torrentially and leveled two small cities like Sodom and Gomorrah just does not seem as real or frightening to Johnny as nuclear arsenals which can at any moment wipe out virtually all life as we know it. It does not require much stretching of the imagination to see how nuclear weapons, in their apocalyptic capacity, have replaced God as a source of fear. What terrifies Johnny is not the coming of the Last Judgment heralded by Vera but humankind's own destructive capability.

Yet the need for a text that rationalizes and gives perspective to fear and anxiety, both for Johnny and for us, still remains. Our new destructive god, however, is not fully served by the old Bible; the creation of a stranger, more pertinent holy text is demanded. We must be terrified by the word of this new god for it to be effective, but at the same time we need to be soothed by what it says. Johnny finds no such bible. Instead, he becomes the Christlike sacrificial savior of his world when he is killed while causing Stillson's downfall. And in his death Johnny is a savior not only for his fictional world but for ours as well. We may not have to fall victims to our anxiety, because in a sense he has died for us. What King is showing is that we should kill future Hitlers, regardless of personal loss.

In other words, as *The Dead Zone* suggests, the entire horror genre has become a helpful therapy for dealing with life in the nuclear age. Horror fiction performs an important therapeutic function by removing our unhealthy repression of death imagery. While Vera Smith was growing up, a child could reach adulthood without ever actually seeing anyone die a truly violent, horrifying death.[11] But in our society it is almost impossible that an American child would not view or read about many violent deaths. In a world in which annihilation did not seem as real or close, it was not necessary to expose ourselves to such an open, violent fascination with death. Now death "appears to be discussed more openly than at any time since the Black Death."[12]

In addition to its function of uncovering the repression of death imagery in our culture, the horror genre performs a role not unlike that of a religious text. Many people are certainly frightened by it, just as many are frightened by the word of God. Indeed, fear seems to be a necessary component of religion. And even though a ghost in a Scottish castle or Jack with a roque mallet in King's *The Shining* (or an ax in the movie version) are not all-encompassing fears like nuclear anxiety, they still scare us in some ways. We *are* still afraid of dying, no matter what form it takes, and horror fiction still scares us on an almost instinctive level. Like a bible, horror gives us something to feel in awe of—but here it actually helps us more than a bible. Instead of only feeling helpless in the face of an awe-inspiring power (as we do with God), horror allows us to become, temporarily, the masters of our fears; we can put down the book or look away from the film and thereby be in control, a luxury not permitted by omnipresent sources of fear such as God or a nuclear catastrophe.

Even though when we watch or read horror fiction we usually are not dealing with something from everyday life, horror makes our new fears more manageable. It is true that most situations in horror fiction—like falling victim to psychic abilities or vampires or demons, or being arbitrarily axed by a psychopathic serial killer—lack a banal context and usually have little to remind us of our everyday lives. But at the same time these things are dehumanized and depersonalized, they are usually somewhat familiar to us. The strange visualizations conjured up by novelists incorporate real, intrinsically human horrors. We know that fears of psychic abilities or magic, of monsters, and of other human beings have been with our culture for as long as we can remember, and we know that when we make these very real fears into imaginary ones they become safer and easier to control. But more important, by rekindling these old fears we are trying to cope with the new fears, the totally dehumanized fears of the nuclear age, which make us so "confused and anxious." Stephen King's killer dog, Cujo, is not exactly soothing, but we are more capable of dealing with this familiar fear (who has not been afraid of a dog?) than with intangible, and entirely alien, nuclear weapons.

Because visualization of death and horror can be so powerfully portrayed through television, it is not likely that our society is going to make itself less aware of the violence in its midst, so it may seem strange that we are so hungrily reaching out for fictional death—and we *are* reaching out for it, as evidenced by the amazing popularity of horror. Why should we need death in our fiction when there seems to be enough of it in the news? A reason for this hunger, and the true value of the genre, can be found in the very fact that it *is* fiction, that it is a harmless arena where we can wrestle with our fears and attempt to come to terms with them without actually being hurt. Horror permits us to explore frightening, and even traumatic, feelings in the relative safety of our imaginations.

Moreover, horror attracts us because it usually allows us to see people fighting against their fears. Rarely, if ever, do we find characters passively accepting death. The characters *act* against their fears, using any means possible to destroy the horror, and—contrary to much of what we see in the news—sometimes they win. This is where horror fiction becomes so different from reality. Readers in the nuclear age often do not feel that they have such power to act against their nuclear anxiety. Therefore horror is not simply a rehash of the day's most violent stories or superstitions (something we definitely would have little use for); it is a powerful vehicle of hope and empowerment. Johnny Smith and most of the successful protagonists of horror become necessary outlets for our wish to remove our fears, and they become role models who actually do make the decision to kill the Hitlers of the world.

Horror prepares us to face our fears by reminding us that death may be just around the corner. We realize as we watch *Halloween* that we are not the ones being killed—this time. We will live on after this film or this book, but we will be slightly more aware that violent death is out there waiting for us in the shadows; and because we are aware we will be slightly more prepared. In our age it isn't unhealthy or paranoid to admit the reality of a horrible death. Parents may cringe because their children think it's "cool" when a person's throat is slashed or when a severed head sits in the refrigerator in *Friday the 13th*, but we must remember that for these children death may very well come in the form of a violent killer who gives no explanations. Such visions open discussion and thought about death. We can tell ourselves that it is only fiction, that the blood is fake and the bullets are blanks, but the very fact that we have thought about it at all is a form of self-administered therapy. Horror fiction lets us take our fears of death and dying "and turn them into tools—to dismantle themselves."[13] Johnny Smith's story is a small chapter in our new bible. It scares us, but at the same time it makes death, and the looming outbreak of the mushroom cloud, slightly easier to deal with by allowing us to experience them by proxy.

Horror in all forms is immensely popular today. Horror novels constantly top the best-seller list, and Stephen King reigns as the best-selling author in the United States. Likewise, Hollywood is producing more and more horror films. The proliferation and phenomenal success of this genre is more than an arbitrary fluctuation of the marketplace. Horror is filling a deep psychological need for the generation that grew up in the dreadful shadow of the mushroom.

Most works of horror do not, as *The Dead Zone* does, deal overtly with the nuclear threat. But subliminally they do; for they deal with sudden, irrational, irrevocable death. And that is what we think of instantly when we see the mushroom cloud, as instantly as when we see the skull and crossbones on a poison label. But my argument is that the cloud, unlike the skull, has become a holy icon as well: a symbol of death that at the same time offers the means of hoping to overcome that death. In past ages when only God had the power to destroy the world, his holy books, in which that destruction is prophesied, were the only means of curbing that fear. Today, horror fiction is secular writ for an age in which we, the people who write such fiction, have usurped God's power to destroy. There are still, certainly, many Vera Smiths, for whom the Judeo-Christian holy books suffice. But for those of us who have grown up in the shadow of the cloud, in the shadow of a weapon that lies beyond God's good judgment, any text that can help us control our fears, even a simple horror novel, has taken on the aura of something holy.

Notes

1. Edwin S. Shneidman, *Deaths of a Man* (New York: Quadrangle, 1973), p. 189.
2. Jerome D. Frank, "Nuclear Death: An Unprecedented Challenge to Psychiatry and Religion," *American Journal of Psychiatry* 141 (November 1984): 1344.
3. Hans Morgenthau, "Death in the Nuclear Age," *Commentary* 32 (1961): 234.
4. Jonathan Schell, *The Fate of the Earth* (New York: Alfred A. Knopf, 1982), pp. 145–46.
5. Robert Plank, "The Lone Survivor," in *The End of the World*, ed. Eric S. Rabkin et al. (Carbondale: Southern Illinois University Press, 1983), p. 29.
6. Robert Jay Lifton, *The Future of Immortality* (New York: Basic Books, 1987), pp. 229–33.
7. Jerome D. Frank, *Sanity and Survival in the Nuclear Age: Psychological Aspects of War and Peace* (New York: Random House, 1982), p. 13.
8. Stephen King, *The Dead Zone* (New York: Penguin New American Library, 1980), p. 348. All subsequent references are cited by page number within the text.
9. Jerome D. Frank, in his helpful book *Sanity and Survival in the Nuclear Age*, categorizes this type of behavior as a type of defensive avoidance (p. 30). There are many manifestations of this behavior; most rely on either blocking out disturbing information or denying the magnitude of the threat. Belief in religion does not necessarily mean that someone is avoiding the nuclear threat—on the contrary, many people turn to religion precisely because of nuclear anxiety—but in an extreme, fanatical case such as that of Vera Smith, religion is being used as a replacement for reality. Apathy, along with de-

fensive avoidance, is a common psychological mechanism for coping with nuclear anxiety (pp. 32–33). Here a person accepts the reality of the nuclear threat but accepts as well the consequences of that threat. Apathetic people often turn feelings of helplessness into total inaction and fatalism.

10. Stephen King, *Danse Macabre* (New York: Everest House, 1981), p. 213.
11. Certainly death has been a part of life for any person living in any time (indeed perhaps more previously than today because of recent medical advances and the like), but *violent* death is probably not as much a part of everyday life for Vera Smith as it is for her son. Wars have always been the major exception, of course, but the percentage of a population that could have been killed in any war is tiny compared with our situation; all of us are targets for violent death. Whether our age is more violent than others, our exposure to the possibility (and likelihood) of violent death, and certainly to the visualization of death, is incredibly high.
12. Shneidman, *Deaths of a Man*, p. 179.
13. King, *Danse Macabre*, p. 26.

Chapter 13

The Hidden Agenda

Martha A. Bartter

Many SF stories depicting nuclear war have been published in the United States since H. G. Wells named the "atomic bomb" in 1914.[1] In virtually all such stories the plot is organized by an *agenda*—the reason the author chooses to tell a particular story.[2] Fiction presents two things: organized Gestalten, with which the reader transacts through the act of reading, and a tacit justification for the ways in which these Gestalten are organized.[3] The author presents a viewpoint on some psychological, political, or historical topic, vividly conveying this information through the actions of characters in a recognizable setting. Authors who choose nuclear war as their organizing Gestalt usually have agendas that concern the interplay of history and human nature, and they usually put special emphasis on defining the results of "natural" human aggression.

Nuclear agendas fall, roughly, into six categories:

1. *Awful warnings.* The position here is relatively mild: nuclear war is terrible but not inevitable. The author helps the reader imagine just how terrible it is, but always in hopes of averting catastrophe in the future. Some examples of this category are "The Final War," by Carl Spohr (1932); "Thunder and Roses," by Theodore Sturgeon (1947); and *Warday*, by Whitley Strieber and James Kunetka (1984).

2. *Really awful warnings.* The position here is sterner: nuclear war can and will kill off human life, and ultimately all life on Earth, unless we heed the warning and change our path at once. Examples include: "The

World Gone Mad," by Nat Schachner (1935); *Level 7*, by Mordecai Roshwald (1959); *The Last Day*, by Helen Clarkson (1959); and *The Fate of the Earth*, by Jonathan Schell (1982).

3. *Be prepared.* These stories are stern about the consequences of nuclear war and locate the cause of the conflagration in the unavoidable political conflict between the United States and the Soviet Union. They assure us, however, that we can either deflect or survive the attack if we develop adequate weapons systems or civil defense measures. Examples are "The Power Planet," by Murray Leinster (1931); *Tomorrow!* by Philip Wylie (1954); *Alas, Babylon*, by Pat Frank (1959); and *Pulling Through*, by Dean Ing (1983).[4]

Most of the works in these three categories have open and obvious agendas. Other stories, however, have, to one degree or another, covert or "hidden" agendas. These we sense through disparities, or even contradictions, between their stated "message" and the unstated impetus of certain textual strategies. There are several categories of hidden agendas in nuclear holocaust fiction:

4. *Conquest.* The underlying assumption is that political conflict will lead to invasion and conquest of the United States by Russia.[5] Good Americans must be prepared to resist this invasion if they are to survive. Examples are *The Conquered Place*, by Robert Shafer (1954); *Not This August*, by C. M. Kornbluth (1955); and *Vandenberg*, by Oliver Lange (1972).

5. *Beginning over.* These stories are in a sense corollaries to those in category 4. Here, following the nuclear holocaust, we are taken on a journey or quest in order to survey the extent of the damage inflicted on the country and its people. We experience the primitive, and yet romantic, existence these survivors lead, and we glimpse the direction of the new beginning. Examples: "After Armageddon," by Francis Flagg (1932); "The Place of the Gods," by Stephen Vincent Benét (1937); *Ravage*, by René Barjavel (1944); *Fahrenheit 451*, by Ray Bradbury (1951); *The Long Tomorrow*, by Leigh Brackett (1955); *A Canticle for Leibowitz*, by Walter M. Miller, Jr. (1959); *Davy*, by Edgar Pangborn (1964); *Heiro's Journey*, by Sterling Lanier (1973); and *Emergence*, by David Palmer (1984).

The stories in category 5 contain a necessarily hidden agenda, a message not only implied in the text but implied often in contradiction to the explicit statement of a new beginning. This agenda sees that the way to save humanity is in fact to allow the bomb to get rid of its "bad seeds" (or just its "bad cities").[6] In order to re-create a healthy civilization, humankind must be "purified" through the winnowing reversion to medievalism, or even to hunter-gatherer tribalism. We can attribute the popularity of these stories to the fact that their hidden agenda refutes the pessimists whose "really awful warnings" predict the end of the world. But, as we see, their hidden agenda exacts a terrible price for this new beginning.

6. *End of the world.* With the exception of Leigh Brackett's *The Long Tomorrow*, all the stories mentioned in category 5 were written by men. The "new beginning" would seem to be a male agenda. In category 6, however, we have works that also depict the aftermath of nuclear war, or of some devastating disease representing war. But these stories have a significantly different slant. They focus on fundamentally life-denying aspects of aggression, such as disruptions of the reproductive process, the separation of the sexes, or the enslavement of one sex to another.[7] And they are almost always written by women. Examples: "The Hole in the Moon," by Margaret St. Clair (1952); *Where Late the Sweet Birds Sang*, by Kate Wilhelm (1974); *Walk to the End of the World* and *Motherlines*, by Suzy McKee Charnas (1974, 1978); and *The Shore of Women*, by Pamela Sargent (1986).

In this essay I focus on this last, "female," form of the hidden agenda. The purpose of these stories is not to make us acquiesce in the status quo of a primitive and still patriarchal culture. Their agenda is a protest against the male rituals of winnowing the bad seed. And they do this by showing that this same male-dominated human race is prepared and willing to commit species suicide in the name of defending its prerogatives. These stories largely focus on genetic or reproductive "experiments" that in reality are euphemisms for genocide. And they suggest that, even by tacitly complying with tales of "regeneration" and new beginnings such as *Fahrenheit 451*, we are just as guilty of genocide as those who, for reasons of good "conscience," chose not to act against tyrants like Hitler. In this context, a recent novel, though little known, deserves to be discussed in detail, for it raises the question of this patriarchal hidden agenda—and of all hidden agendas—with great acuity: M. J. Engh's *Arslan* (1976).[8]

Arslan at first appears to be just another category 4 or category 5 story. In it the United States is conquered by a foreign power using the threat of nuclear destruction. As in Kornbluth's *Not This August* and Shafer's *The Conquered Place*, *Arslan* shows Americans dealing with victorious invaders. *Arslan* resembles a category 5 story in its presentation of the problems such a postwar society must deal with: lack of technological support, disrupted communications, isolation, limited supplies, hunger, and disease. Like Brackett's *The Long Tomorrow*, *Arslan* shows a population returned to pioneer-type farm life. Like Frank's *Alas, Babylon*, it shows the fortunes of a favored group. Though many people are killed, more are kept hostage as they are forced to billet soldiers in their homes. And though all are forced to obey capricious, restrictive orders, they seem to suffer a very decent, almost polite war. As a semirural area under Arslan's personal protection, the people of Kraftsville, Illinois, have it easy. They should have little difficulty "beginning over."

But *Arslan* really belongs in group 6, though it is unusual in several ways. For one thing, it has a peculiar shape: the climax of the action occurs in the first thirty pages. The rest of the book depicts about fifteen years of falling action, dedicated not (as one might expect) to explaining and exculpating the initial act but to showing with increasing clarity how desperately wrong it actually was. For another, Engh exposes the hidden agenda instead of reflecting it metaphorically. Arslan openly admits his plan. He intends to save the "web of life"—now "strained and twisted and torn"—from man, "a mistake of evolution" (82). "This is my hope, sir: once destroyed, civilization will not rise again" (83). But his agenda remains hidden because viewpoint characters cannot credit or actually perceive it. This inability of intelligent people to perceive the hidden agenda forms the overt agenda of the book.

Arslan is narrated by two viewpoint characters: Franklin Bond, a forty-two-year-old school principal who becomes Arslan's local administrator and thirteen-year-old Hunt Morgan, who is forced to become the conqueror's homosexual favorite. Their use of the past tense makes the book sound like reminiscence, but neither narrator employs the standard clues of new understanding (e.g., "if I had only known" or "I found out later"). Despite his victimization and his mixed love and hate for Arslan, Hunt seems an acute observer, less interested in gathering information than is Bond, but more willing to act and more reliable emotionally. While Hunt seems anxious to make himself understood to some unknown audience, Bond seems to be speaking to himself, still trying (and still failing) to create knowledge—meaning he can act from—out of the information he assembles.

Bond fails to "read" the situation, to convert information to knowledge. In the act of reading, a reader, by transacting with a text, constructs meaning from it. "Constructing meaning" may be described as the creation of a Gestalt, a pattern of events that the reader can put himself into and understand. "Transacting" changes both the actor and the thing acted upon; in this case, reader and text.[9] The reader emerges changed from the encounter; and so does the text, *for that reader for that time*. One can never reread "the same" text, or "not know" what one has discovered from the reading. But if the patterns available to the reader significantly violate (or fail to connect with) the patterns built into the text, then the reader fails to complete the Gestalt and will either construct a "meaning" demonstrably false to the text[10] or complain of "not understanding" it.

The viewpoint characters in *Arslan* try—and significantly fail—to create a pattern within which to understand Arslan's agenda, and from which to decide what their role can and should be in an Arslan-dominated world. Bond has sufficient information to disclose Arslan's hidden agenda at several points in the text. He even spells it out at least once to Arslan; at least once Arslan explains it to Bond and Hunt (83–84). The question then becomes how and why do they fail to complete the Gestalt, to organize information into patterns from which to act? The outcome of this discontinuity between information and knowledge—the details and the pattern—is precisely the end of the world.

Arslan opens in a world so afraid of nuclear holocaust that a twenty-five-year-old modern Alexander, armed with charisma and a vision, can literally take over the world using little more than audacity and nuclear blackmail. Arslan moves from a foreign name in the news to the commander of all U.S. armed forces so fast that all information is out of date; as Bond complains, "all the rules had been changed when we weren't looking" (3). The United States government has abdicated to Arslan (28) and the country is under martial law as the story opens.

Arslan's first act after roaring into Kraftsville at the head of his army is to hold schoolchildren hostage for their parents' good behavior; his second, to hold a feast in the middle school in the course of which he selects the youngest female teacher for his future sexual pleasure and casually sends the coach out to be killed. He then publicly rapes two eighth-graders, a girl and a boy. Bond, bound and gagged, is a "guest" at this event. He witnesses the appalling spectacle with forced calm; he reports himself more upset by the singing of the Turkestani soldiers—"As noise, it was acceptable. As music, it was desecration" (15)—than by the murder and rapes. His flattened affect chills the reader.

The next morning, Arslan sends the high school children off to parts unknown (we assume the girls will serve in brothels and the boys in a "U.S." army in some other country) and puts Bond in charge of the district. When the two men are alone together in Arslan's Land Rover, Arslan hands Bond his loaded pistol. Bond, who describes himself at that moment as aching "to get my hands on his neck or my foot in his face" asks Arslan, "Are you daring me to attack you?" and Arslan softly answers "Yes, sir" (22). Bond correctly interprets this act as tacitly suicidal (31), even though Arslan has threatened that if anything happens to him, his men will "exterminate the entire population of the district, beginning with Kraftsville, which will be surrounded and burned to the ground" (22–23).

Arslan has told Bond that his first job is to convince people that Arslan is more dangerous dead than alive. Astutely, Bond asks, "Do we have anything to gain by *not* killing you?" In response, "[Arslan] smiled sweetly—sweetly is the word: 'That, of course, you cannot know with certainty. But it is a chance, and you cannot afford to lose any chance. . . . there are plans to be fulfilled before I die'" (23). Arslan's plan will "make the world a good place in which to live" by solving problems of "hunger and crowding" (26). He will not redistribute food; instead he will "redistribute people" (27) and "destroy civilization" (26). Bond feels intellectually insulted by Arslan's "outmoded Middle-Eastern strain of agrarian socialism" (26), but he does not ask—here or later—the most important question: Who will live in this "good place"?

The question becomes even more important as we learn the ramifications of Arslan's "Plan One": he intends "that every community should be self-sufficient. It should produce everything it consumes, and contain no more people than it can support in comfort" (27). If this wreaks hardship on rural Kraft County, the reader can imagine what must be going on in cities like Chicago, but Bond does not report such hardship. Bond thinks of his people as already damaged or dead; he aims the gun as Arslan watches, but he goes on wavering between doubt and conviction, goes on asking questions and getting apparently straight answers, and finally—as the climax of the action—decides that he cannot "decide, on the shabbiest sort of data, which of two intolerable directions the world should take" (29). Tacitly denying that he acts by not acting, Bond throws away the gun, and with it his only chance of stopping Arslan before Arslan can put his hidden agenda into operation.

When Bond finally leads the Kraft County Resistance (KCR) against Arslan, he does so too cautiously and much too late, after Arslan tells him that "Plan One was obsolete before it could be applied" (112). The sterilizing virus came from China within a month of Arslan's arrival in Kraftsville and was used at once; like Russia and Western Europe, "North America is totally sterile" now (113). Bond hopes to accomplish a coup d'etat by capturing Arslan, on the theory that few of Arslan's officers and men "would go along with [Plan Two] at all if they realized what they were doing" (114), but this plan is interrupted by the murder of Rusudan, Arslan's wife, and the KCR settles for symbolic action: secretly decorating the graves of the men killed by Arslan for the murder. After some delay, Bond reschedules his coup. Prematurely initiated by Arslan, the great putsch fizzles, though Bond does achieve one anticlimactic success: he keeps his house from burning down. Arslan leaves Kraftsville for seven years, during which he completes Plan Two, sterilizing all human females with the possible exception of some in the jungles of South America; he then abdicates his leadership role, eliminates usurping successors, and retires to Kraftsville to watch the world end.

When Bond calls Arslan "a barbarian Hitler" (26) in the Land Rover, he apparently means this only as an epithet, not a recognition. He significantly fails to connect Arslan's career with Hitler's or to examine historical congruences. Arslan's meteoric rise parallels Hitler's in the 1930s, and his initial actions—political blackmail, followed by usurpation of legal governments and occupation of territory—are also similar. Unlike Bond, Arslan knows how Hitler operated (25). As he later tells Bond, he chooses a sterilization program, despite the "possibility of undiscovered pockets of survivors" (84), because killing people has certain disadvantages: "death is irreversible, sir, and it is recognizable" (85). His intent is both "to save mankind much suffering" and "to save the world from mankind" (84). Bond has not yet heard this declaration as he holds the gun on Arslan, but he has evidence—armed conquest, child rape, and casual murder—that Arslan's words do not match his deeds, that his arguments are specious and his plans deadly. He should guess that these plans can be stopped only by stopping Arslan. But Bond fails to create the pattern, and failing, ignorantly repeats the solution tried by leaders of Jewish ghettoes under Hitler.

By collaborating with the Germans, those leaders kept a diminishing number of their people alive, but only at the cost of selecting members of the community to be shipped off, ostensibly as slave labor but actually to die. Refusing to perceive that anyone, even Hitler, could plan genocide (despite the evidence), most of them counseled moderation, patience, self-sacrifice, and a low profile—time-honored tactics that have allowed the Jews to survive other perils. They bought temporary survival by refusing the violence that might have made a significant difference for others, though at the immediate sacrifice of their lives. The eventual cost was almost a whole people.

We may contrast Bond to Dietrich Bonhoeffer, a German pacifist minister who informed himself about Hitler and believed he meant what he said. This recognition presented Bonhoeffer with equally intolerable choices. If he continued safely to preach Christian love while Jews were being killed, he remained a pacifist but colluded in their deaths. If he acted against Hitler, he had to condone violence or perhaps participate in it himself. Either choice violated his conscience. He chose to act.[11]

Bond thinks of himself as a humanist; to him human life is of paramount importance. Like the Jewish leaders, however, he behaves like an academic. He assesses the situation intellectually, repressing his emotions in favor of analysis, demanding more and better information while withholding meaningful action. Arslan recognizes that Bond is emotionally incapable of grasping the ramifications of the real plan; he assesses Bond as clever, persuasive, and excellent at short-term planning, the perfect Arslan-in-little to manage Kraft County as Arslan's eventual retirement home.

Bond and Arslan are linked in many ways, psychological and metaphorical.[12] On the first night, Arslan selects for his attention the same people, for the same reasons, whom Bond has chosen: the teacher for her youth and vulnerability, the coach for his easy popularity and fundamental untrustworthiness, the children as his "best eighth-graders." The case of the coach is particularly illuminating. While Bond notices that Perry Carpenter is "scared rotten" and "willing to sell the school or the whole country, whichever was in demand, to whoever held the gun" but argues that "I couldn't blame him, any more or less than I blamed myself for having a bad stomach," Arslan simply says, "You are not worth keeping alive" (14) and has Perry killed.

Arslan plays both a suicidal and a murderous role. He has the excuse of a miserable childhood.[13] He has identified with his father's terrible judgment—that he is only worth killing—and has projected this judgment on the rest of humanity.[14] If people are evil, then generation is evil; preventing generation relieves his guilt or renders him no longer guilty. Arslan seeks to annihilate fertility, the natural female principle, by perverting sexuality and by sterilizing women in the name of protecting and preserving "Mother" Earth. He justifies this to himself by claiming that just as war is natural to man, and thus inevitable, so "it is natural to man to build a civilization, and it is natural to civilization to destroy itself and to wreck the world" (81).

This justification seems as falsely logical as his program to save humankind by saving the world from humankind (84).

Like Arslan, Bond demonstrates the dissociative Gestalt.[15] Having classified part of himself as alien and hostile, he spends his energy blocking the natural expression of these characteristics. Arslan denies his fundamental self-worth; Bond denies his emotions. When Arslan tells Bond that he has been chosen to administer the district because he shows no fear, Bond clutches at the explanation. He has done such a thorough job of repressing his normal reactions that he is virtually unaware of his justifiable terror. He denies feelings that he should turn outward and act upon, instead turning them inward and experiencing them only as the physical pain of his spastic pylorus. Bond's unusually flattened affect is only one symptom of this; his inability to act without absolute certainty and to comprehend what he himself has just clearly explained are also signs of his dissociation.

Other men in the story seem equally dissociated. With conscious generosity, Bond offers Hunt sanctuary but withholds his trust; he later accuses Hunt of killing Rusudan because she was a rival for Arslan's affection. Hunt's father disowns him for homosexuality ("The only thing I asked for was that he wouldn't *volunteer* himself to that greasy devil. For God's sake, Franklin, what do you expect me to do—encourage him?" [71–72]), a clear case of "blame the victim." The men who seduce and kill Rusudan, the only woman in the whole world known to be fertile, act against their own best interests, as do the men who form the rape gang that tries to force other women to re-create the conditions they believe allowed a girl to get pregnant. The men are shown not only as violating (or accepting the violation of) the female role in reproduction, but also as denying or perverting their male role.

Significantly, the women play no important role. Though Bond calls his wife trustworthy and stable, he treats her more like a convenience than a lover; after her death he admits to missing her housewifely activities, not her advice. Rusudan, despite her passion, is unintelligible; the weeping of the young teacher wordlessly represents the vast number of sexual slaves. Jean Morgan, Hunt's mother, deprived of her son and future generations, teaches the remaining children to sing. This is permitted as a triviality in their new world, though it reflects one of the few creative efforts to maintain time binding.[16] But even Jean is dominated and silenced by her husband, whose rejection of Hunt damages them all. The most convincing evidence of the tacit denial of value and voice to the women comes near the end of the book, when a girl who becomes pregnant kills herself and her child; the men comment that "she wasn't what you'd call a decent girl" (267) and use her pregnancy to justify gang rape. This evidence of the deadly nature of Bond's society provides another reason why Arslan finds his conquest so easy.

Bond may declare that he sold his soul to prevent violence (136), but he can never permit himself to realize the consequences of his failure to kill Arslan. Even when Arslan retires to Kraftsville, Bond fails to take in the magnitude of the disaster. It is Hunt, doubly damaged by Arslan, who most clearly expresses his awareness of the human tragedy. Watching Arslan's son, Sanjar, with the young men of Kraftsville, he notes that they "would be forever the babies of their families; old men in the young wilderness, they would wither unmatured" (279). When Sanjar leads many of these young men northward in a futile search for fertile mates, Arslan reacts with typical indirection. Invoking the charisma that made him a great leader, he commands the village to provide a feast—"The Feast of Sanjar!" (295). Bonfires blaze and fatted hogs are slaughtered to celebrate the young men's departure. But like Arslan's other deeds, this too follows the hidden agenda: the feast depletes the stores painfully saved against the winter. If Sanjar returns, there may be few alive to welcome him. Bond, still denying the hidden agenda, will grimly restore his community to what health it can muster, but Arslan's presence promises a continued reminder of their inevitable death.

The metaphors that Engh uses to delineate the destruction of the human species are impressive. Despite his charisma, Arslan's actions are life denying: the taking of hostages, murder, and rape, especially homosexual rape, are overt acts, while the destruction of communication, society, and education—the destruction of time binding—dehumanizes the survivors. Even when he marries and sires a child, Arslan's use of sex, as well as his long-range plan of sterilization, expresses his repudiation of life.

Bond, like Arslan, suppresses his fertility. The early death of his only child metaphorically indicates this; so does his tacit refusal to treat women as contributors to Kraftsville's community. He apparently fears their "emotionality": he tries to ignore the young teacher's hysterical weeping before she is sent away, and he feels uneasy around Rusudan, who alternates between violent outbursts of anger and equally violent outbursts of affection. Bond's flattened affect is another sign of his life-denying suppression of normal emotion.

Bond also fails to communicate Arslan's plan in ways that might make long-term survival more possible. When the local doctor confirms that sterilization has occurred (111), neither he nor Bond requests special care for fertile women. This results in the murder of Rusudan[17] and the senseless suicide of the pregnant teenager. After the putsch fails and Arslan leaves, Bond never communicates Plan Two to "Arslan's officers and men," though he often deals with the occupation troops.

Bond has plenty of information, but he renders himself incapable of using it effectively by two assumptions: first, that hope and his faith in a vague "Christianity"[18] can mitigate evil (51); and, second, that he is fully self-aware and capable of achieving perfect understanding. Engh does a remarkable job of showing, through Bond's own words, how Bond gathers information, draws a verifiably correct conclusion, and then immediately ignores or fails to act on it, and how completely unaware of his failure he remains. Bond never compares his ideas with anyone else's. Though Bond's wife must keep house for Arslan, he never compares her information with his own; though he collects information from Hunt, he never consults him; the same holds true for his Kraft County Resistance group. Bond can act only from certainty. Testing his pattern against the patterns drawn by others might endanger that certainty.

Arslan looks like a conqueror, but he conquers only to carry Hitler's agenda to its logical end, the annihilation of the human species. Instead of committing genocide on one group designated as scapegoats to enable conquest of the world by another group, he makes scapegoats of everyone and commits total genocide. In creating *Arslan*, Engh thus joined other writers of group 6 works, like St. Clair, Charnas, Wilhelm, and Tiptree, who rehearse the agenda of self-destruction. They give the lie to our claim that we prepare for nuclear war only so we won't have to wage it.

Group 6 writers reject the popular love-hate relationship with the dramatic immolation of humanity that undoes in one nuclear fireball what it took so long to build up. They claim that we, like Bond, collect information but refuse knowledge, drawing only the inferences we wish to see. They claim that we, like Bond, fail to look at the pattern we are making, a life-denying, even life-destroying pattern. Simply to die lacking issue, to wither slowly, denies humanity a romantic ending.[19] But it is the end that Engh shows, very persuasively, in *Arslan*. It is an end made possible because, blinded by fear of his own anger, immobilized by assumptions about "how things are" and "how people behave," Franklin Bond fails again and again either to recognize Arslan's pattern or to act on any recognition.

Like Bonhoeffer, Bond wants desperately to save his people. Unlike Bonhoeffer, he limits "his" people to those he knows. He "saves" them safely, by keeping Arslan alive; but to save Arslan is to condemn humanity to extinction. Early in their acquaintance, Arslan asks Bond "how people forget. By what mechanism do your minds shut out parts of themselves?" and claims "I, I do not forget" (85). Arslan is, of course, both right and wrong, about Bond and about himself. Neither man allows himself to engage in the self-altering transacting that creates knowledge. Bond is not forgetting; he is significantly failing to create a pattern within which to know the information he has received, a Gestalt from which to act. The problem here is not Bond's ignorance; it is not *knowing* that he does not know. We share his problem.

Our culture fails to learn from the works in categories 1 and 2 because information does no good unless we create knowledge from it, a pattern to live from. That we do not shows that we also live with repression and denial, a flattened affect; the horrors of history that Arslan recites to Bond (80–81) are forgotten and the dangers of the present are ignored. If Bond represents us in our self-serving shortsightedness, and Hunt the children whose future our actions destroy, Arslan represents the culture as a whole, acting out its dissociation to its own destruction. The horror of the book comes from the recognition that Arslan's agenda is made possible almost as much by the tacit collaboration of the conquered as by his own actions. *Arslan* is not an awful warning; it is a diagnosis.

When we pretend to absolute certainty, refusing to alter our pictures of how things work, when we fail to transact with our information so as to create knowledge we can share and test with others, when we live out the dissociative Gestalt, we create patterns of self-destruction. As *Arslan* graphically demonstrates, any civilization that lives this way pays more attention to eliminating itself (whether through starvation, pollution, or war) than to living. It will wind up with precisely the end result it has worked for: terminal sterility.

> This is the way the world ends
> Not with a bang but a whimper.

Notes

1. *The World Set Free* (1914). For a further listing of stories depicting nuclear war, see Paul Brians, *Nuclear Holocausts: Atomic War in Science Fiction* (Kent, Ohio: Kent State University Press, 1987).
2. *Agenda* should not be confused with authorial *intention*. Agenda refers to the way in which the author presents the topic that forms the basis of the text to the reader, rather than to the way in which the author intends the text to be interpreted by the reader.
3. A "Gestalt [is] a figure of focal interest to the organism, bounded by a ground or context more or less empty of interest" (C. A. Hilgartner and John F. Randolph, "Psychologics: An Axiomatic System Describing Human Behavior," *Journal of Theoretical Biology* 23 [1969]: 296). A completed Gestalt forms a pattern from which one can act and functions as an expectation in the next relevant situation. A Gestalt without a figure "represents an 'unfinished situation' that clamors for attention and interferes with the formation of any novel, vital Gestalt. Instead of growth and development we then find stagnation and regression" (Frederick S. Perls, Ralph Hefferline, and Paul Goodman. *Gestalt Therapy: Excitement and Growth in the Human Personality* [New York: Julian, 1951], p. ix).
4. David Brin's *The Postman* (1985) forms a significant exception to this agenda; here, the survivalists actually do more damage than the (brief) nuclear war.
5. If any story describes the invasion and conquest of Russia by America, I have not seen it.
6. See my "Nuclear War as Urban Renewal," *Science-Fiction Studies* 39 (1986): 148–58.
7. These stories often experiment with asexual reproduction, cloning, or parthenogenesis, usually to show its limitations. In *Where Late the Sweet Birds Sang* and *Motherlines*, Wilhelm and Charnas give the same message: preventing normal species diversity leads to a lack of species vigor. Stories like "When It Changed," by Joanna Russ, and *A Door into Ocean*, by Joan Slonczewski, reverse this message; since males are the aggressors, these authors seem convinced that salvation of the human race requires their elimination—provided women can arrange egg-egg reproduction.
8. M. J. Engh, *Arslan* (New York: Warner, 1976). *Arslan*'s publishing history is unusual. The paperback edition vanished virtually unnoticed in 1976; Arbor House reprinted the book in hardcover in 1987. All page numbers in the text refer to the Arbor House edition.
9. For a fuller description of the construct of transacting, see John Dewey and

Arthur F. Bentley, *Knowing and the Known* (Boston: Beacon Press, 1960). See also Hilgartner and Randolph, "The Structure of Empathy," *Journal of Theoretical Biology* 24 (1969): 1–29.

10. The reading is "false to the text" when a reader imposes a pattern on the text that no (or few) other readers find there, or makes an unsatisfying Gestalt with no figure, or imposes a pattern only by eliminating important sections of the text from consideration.

11. The underground group Bonhoeffer joined was successful in getting selected Jews out of Germany but failed in their plot to assassinate Hitler. He was hanged mere weeks before the Allies took Berlin.

12. Bond and Hunt Morgan are also linked. Both have been seduced by the charismatic Arslan, Hunt by force, and Bond, more subtly, by his own short-term, self-serving logic. Hunt is the first of the young victims of Arslan's hidden agenda: victimized sexually and psychologically, disowned by his family, forever prevented from natural reproduction, Hunt, unlike the others of his generation, is fully aware of the hidden agenda and sufficiently educated (by Arslan!) to know what has been lost.

13. Engh has noted that "*after* I had Arslan's character and history well in mind, I started reading up on dictators ancient and modern, in search of parallels—and found nothing I considered significantly close until I came upon Kemal Ataturk" (correspondence with the author, April 5, 1988). Ataturk overthrew the Turkish sultanate, drove the Greeks from Asia Minor, and then used his power to modernize and Westernize the Turkish state as a nominal republic, though it was actually a moderate dictatorship. I see Arslan's father as more closely resembling Ataturk than does Arslan.

14. "A projection is a trait, attitude, feeling, or bit of behavior which actually belongs to your own personality but is not experienced as such; instead, it is attributed to objects or persons in the environment and then experienced as directed *toward* you by them instead of the other way around" (Perls, Hefferline, and Goodman, *Gestalt Therapy*, p. 211; for a fuller explanation of psychological projecting, see chap. 8, pp. 211–24).

15. "The dissociative Gestalt comprises the conclusion that our [human] organism cannot, by means of his fundamental affirmations [process of pursuing normal goals], achieve the focal condition [goal] of his own preservation-and-growth, and that he will continue to achieve the focal condition of his own bare survival if and only if he maintains a stable state of self-paralysis, viz., if he manages in each encounter to interrupt his own fundamental affirmations" (68). This Gestalt includes offering excellent "reasons" for such self-paralyzing

behavior (Hilgartner and Randolph, "The Structure of 'Impaired' Behavior," unpublished manuscript).
16. Alfred Korzybski, *Manhood of Humanity*, 2d ed. (Lakeville Conn.: International Non-Aristotelian Library, 1980). By accumulating, contributing to, and handing down human knowledge, humans "bind time": they develop and continue culture so that no human need "reinvent the wheel." Time binding, as heritage, as responsibility, and as opportunity, serves as the defining mark of humanity. By failing to eliminate verifiable errors from the time-binding heritage, the people in Engh's book give themselves no alternative but to follow suicidal patterns.
17. Significantly, this is the only action in the book reported by both Bond and Hunt Morgan. In the contrast of their viewpoints we see both the complexity of Arslan's personality and the tragedy of the sterilization program.
18. Interestingly, the doctor's faith in now-destroyed medical technology to reverse the sterilization forms a perfect analogy to Bond's Christianity: faith without works. Bond is acutely aware of the impossibility that the "physiologists and geneticists and virologists and biochemists and plain old general practitioners all over the civilized world working on a hundred different approaches" to the problem "right now," as the doctor believes (113–14), will succeed, but does not see the analogy.
19. Arslan refers to the control of the screwworm fly in Florida through the release of sterile male flies (84–85); cf. Alice Sheldon's story "The Screwfly Solution" (as Raccoona Sheldon, *Analog*, June 1977), in which aliens use a similar program to remove inconvenient humans from a planet they want for themselves. The difference is that Arslan has no one in mind to succeed humanity. "The Last Flight of Dr. Ain," also by Sheldon (as James Tiptree, Jr., in *Warm Worlds and Otherwise* [New York: Ballantine Books, 1975], pp. 61–68), has the same outcome with a very different emotional tone. Like Arslan, Ain saves the world from humanity. But he does not hypocritically claim to make the world "a better place to live" when no humans will be doing the living. His love affair with Earth is consummated in his death and the survival of other species. Ain loves. Arslan only hates.

Chapter 14

Third World Fantasies

George Slusser

> Everybody knows this is nowhere.
> —Neil Young, "After the Gold Rush"

The essential conflict today—heralded in fiction and nonfiction alike—is between the so-called First and Third worlds, "our" world and "theirs." If we believe Pascal Bruckner in his recent book *The Tears of the White Man: Compassion as Contempt*, the only fantasy here is the one that pretends such a conflict is not real. The sentimental fantasies of Western liberals are unmasked as a device of *Realpolitik*. Turning things around, the aggressive responses of the Third World are called fantasies only because those who have them lack the power to realize them. Thus William Beer, in the introduction to Bruckner's book, sees a Frantz Fanon writing "fantasies of violence as a means of self-purification."[1] But what, then, is "Third World fantasy"? It would necessarily have to be a fantasy of conflict. Yet are these not mutually exclusive terms?

Conflict implies territories, contested borders. It demands location. And to locate is to ground, to realize, and thus to abolish fantasy, a mode whose very existence requires it be nonbounded, unlocateable. *Third World*, however, is a strange term of location. For us, Bruckner surmises, Third World derives from *tiers état*. If, however, to eighteenth-century Frenchmen there was a second state, where is it here? The mediator and potential interlocutor is missing. "They" are the aliens we fight but do not communicate with. We impose the structure of rank, place them third down the line, away from the source. They in turn apply the standard of weight or mass. By these terms, a third world is three times more substantial, a peasant village is three times more rooted than some abstract global village. But again, what lies between these two extremes? What can mediate between them?

What tantalizes, then, in the term *Third World* is its threeness, suggesting a secret sharer that inhabits our binary structures of represented conflict. We think of an early Third World conflict, that of Shakespeare's *Tempest*. The above-mentioned elements are all there. Caliban, running with Stephano and Trinculo, seeks the material advantage of being three to one. But Prospero triumphs because he is first on his ontologically rigged scale of being. In this binary struggle fantasy is grounded. Be it black or white magic, the sole purpose of each is to dominate the other.

There is a third element in the equation, however—Ariel, the spirit Prospero uses but in the end must free. And in freeing him Prospero loses the power to project his "insubstantial pageant" of sights and sounds. Ariel is pure medium, something we cannot possess but only use:

> These our actors
> (As I foretold you) were all spirits, and
> Are melted into air, into thin air,
> And like the baseless fabric of this vision . . .
> Leave not a rack behind.
> (IV.i.148–56)

Ariel, then, is fantasy as available and usable medium, and what he mediates are not words but vision and song—forms that are temporally airborne, not spatially located.

We sense here the beginnings of our current fascination with graphocentrism. And Prospero's epilogue bears this out. With Ariel gone, Prospero's charms are "all overthrown," and he must fall back on his own strength. He seeks, first of all, to reinscribe himself in the old either-or logic of conflict: take me from the bare island, give me my dukedom. To do this he appeals to his subscribers, the audience, whose applause will now provide the wind to fill the "sails" left slack by Ariel's departure. What Prospero calls "freedom," then, is a return to the text, the social contract, whose exoneration he begs, through prayer or scripture, for having "enforced" his spirits to dominate Caliban's island. Clearly, this inscribed world, with its polarized antagonisms of "I" and "they," its first- and third-person narrators who ignore the middle "phonic" ground of possible dialogue, is the text as place of combat, of binary struggle.

At this level combat is more than a theme of literature and art. It has become their very structure, one perpetuated by spatial properties, or should we say by a desire for spatiality that seeks to justify its existence by imposing metaphors on physical reality, such as placement or "rank," on one hand, and material substance or "weight," on the other. But by the same token fantasy is also more than a theme. It is now free to operate as a structure as well, but one in contrast governed by spatiotemporal properties—acceleration as the time rate of change of velocity, but with respect less to mass than to direction.

Third World combats, as we learned from both Prospero and Bruckner, are built into the structure of the texts that inscribe and locate them. But not so Third World fantasies. The fantasy model is not binary in the same manner, for it allows the contestants of the text a way out, a way to become sharers of a common medium, and in doing so to turn their attention away from each other toward gradual mastery of that medium. I contend that Ariel, long the prisoner of texts, has at least been potentially freed in today's more insubstantial media—film and broadcasting—and not by Prospero's dispensation alone. For Caliban too has now learned to use him. I will examine a series of films and songs about Third World conflicts produced by both of the contestants. Here it is no longer First looking at Third, or Third looking at First, but both looking first and foremost at the medium they share; and both seeking to master it as the means not of defeating the other but of liberating art from the logic of the battleground.

I wish to look at two thematically combative forms of artistic expression, the kung fu film and the reggae song of protest, and to hold them up to the mirror of a fight film like *Rocky IV*. The first two, when seen from inside our cultural boundaries, can claim to be "authentic" Third World productions. *Rocky* cannot. But in terms of their awareness of the mediating structure they all share, what is the difference between them? Each of these films and songs is *about* combat between two worlds. And though they were produced by people from both worlds, these people now share a common technology. It is this shared technology that becomes their Third World fantasy. And as this sharing happens, fantasy is returned to its original meaning and function.

The verb *phantazein*, in its pre-Platonic sense (or before a hierarchical relationship is decreed between "appearance" and "reality"), simply means "to cause something to appear," "to body forth," in visible or audible form, what we today who are used to science fiction and fantasy call a "world." Originally, fantasy was not a genre—a kind of thing or state of being—but a medium. It is made a state only by relating it to another state, to reality. This locates it, gives it territoriality, makes it a potential combatant. The original nature of fantasy, however, is to be neutral and yet *disponible*, incorporeal yet incorporating. Fantasy in this sense seems perfectly adapted to today's information age with its fascination for mediation instead of substantiation. We store images and sounds electronically on film and cassettes and CDs, and call them forth at will. By virtue of a process that obviates the need for a reality in terms of material location, however, these "appearances" take on an existence of their own. For the photographic (and by extension film) image, André Bazin makes it clear that "in spite of any objections our critical spirit may offer, we are forced to accept as real the existence of the object reproduced, actually re-presented, set before us . . . in time and space. Photography enjoys a certain advantage in virtue of this transference of reality from the thing to its reproduction."[2] The advantage of the sort of image described here, mediatory instead of imitative, is precisely its freedom from material fixity, its speed and range in bodying forth a world.

An antimimetic current as old as Heraclitus is surfacing today thanks to new technologies of mediation. So-called popular films and songs, unlike more experimental works that subsist by maintaining this separation between form and content, are not afraid to effect Bazin's transfer of reality from thing to medium. Nor to do so in the case of the theme of conflict itself.

Mimesis in this larger sense could be called a logocentric vision. Through a tyranny of the referent it prevents us from presenting, and allows us only to re-present. Its referent is simply the beginning in the word, and this is opposed to a secondary existence in image and sound. Plato may distinguish between living and dead discourse—logocentric and graphocentric—but both share an origin in the word. And this word in its "living" form purports to offer the real or ideal, as opposed to the deceptive spectacle of the cave. It is this mimetic cultural "text" that would inscribe fantasy as distorted image of the real. And inscribe kung fu films and reggae songs in an analogous dichotomy between "serious" and "popular" forms; the latter all ephemeral sights and sounds, the former rooted in the traditional and substantive combats of "plot" or the inner struggles of "character." The works I discuss, however, precisely *because* they are fantasies, can speak of conflict and at the same time avoid being governed by a text of conflict. The structure underlying their thematics of conflict is instead the logic of networking, of information distribution. This is a totalizing rather than a divisive process, one in which combatants on the level of theme become, at the same time, on this deeper level co-users of the same medium.

For Jacques Derrida to want to separate the dis- in dissemination means that he, like other so-called deconstructionists, considers writing more an end than a means, a place rather than a way or path. Writing, for Derrida, is the making of traces that endlessly defer, in a textual web that endlessly divides. In creating such patterns of sequency, writing becomes a means of producing space. The media I am considering, however, film and broadcasting, are those that, in the words of political scientist Serge Moscovici, "produce time."[3] Underlying the hegemony of written space for Derrida is an assumption that time is irreversible, that it is composed of a sequence of unique and unrepeatable events. In this sense each new occurrence logically demands a "next." Yet each such begetting must, in its "nextness," necessarily refer back to a former happening, thus inscribing a structure that is fixed or located at the same time that it is endlessly expanding. The media Moscovici considers, however, aim at "introducing reversibility in irreversible time." And they do so by seeking to become radially, universally, accessible, by striving for the simultaneity of emission and reception that defines the "media event." Such an event, in terms of material or textual space, has no precise or necessary locus and leaves no trace beyond its instant of dissemination.

Derrida's use of the word *text* in its original sense of a "weave of words" seeks to ground, or locate, the medium of discourse by attributing to it the qualities of writing and print. And even critics ostensibly more concerned with that production of time which is political and social statement seem, despite their stated intentions, to need a *space* of interpretation as well. Fredric Jameson, in the final pages of *The Political Unconscious*, calls this concept of the text "essentially antiempirical." It is suspect, and yet interpretation must somehow have recourse to it. Jameson still talks of the "text" of the state, and this remains for him a "space of class struggle."[4] It is implied here that, seen as subtext, struggle is most easily studied or interpreted when confined to a space, and that the most convenient space is a text, conceived as a holding vessel rather than a conveying medium. The logic of time production, however, dictates that we consider our Third World subtext and text—the struggle and the medium that depicts that struggle—as really antiempirical. These texts do not locate—a space or territory of class struggle is too easily colonized, as past experience shows—they dislocate. They network their way free of the webs of critical discourse by which the intellectual academy would trap them. Their struggle is measured not by boundaries but by velocity of connections, by the ratio of distance to time that abolishes the tacit colonialism of Derrida's text, even of Jameson's space of class struggle.

A space of class struggle is what we had, perhaps, when Prospero fought with Caliban for proprietary control of the island. But where is that same space in a film like Wes Craven's *The Serpent and the Rainbow* (1988)? The text on which this film is based, Harvard researcher Wade Davis's account of partaking in voodoo rites in Haiti in order to learn the formula for a zombifying drug and bring it back to a Western pharmaceutical firm, remains a story of territorial violation, a variant on Prospero and Caliban. Transposed into the medium of film, however, the story seems to generate very different structures. The filmed sights and sounds of this island are so immediately captivating that they literally draw, on the level of story and on that of the viewer, our solid world into its imagistic "confines." Discussing the making of his film, Craven tells how several members of his crew were physically possessed, how they fell into a catatonic state upon coming to the island of Haiti, and how they became normal again upon leaving.[5] But for the viewer there is no such separation of worlds, and no easy return home. Possession by the film's electronic "island" is a total and unifying experience, one whose earth and sky are not bounded but simulated by the title's serpent and rainbow. These simulacra operate here as presences that, unlike conventional symbols, inhabit only and yet completely the time of the images, thus have no territorial referent outside, or before, them. The spatiality of the biological process itself, as we conceive it in metaphors such as the "journey" from birth to death, is abolished totally in images like that of the live burial. Here we experience a wholly cinematic "resurrection"; out of a completely black screen comes first the sound of fists beating on wood, and then (a seemingly endless time later) light. And in like manner the historical process itself dissolves into screen immediacy as the fall of Duvalier's regime is made to coincide with the protagonist's victory over dark forces. The latter scene is a crowning instance of the logic of medium suspending the logic of text. For the space of history is here compressed into the time of a media event, both literal and figurative, and the potential complexities of a combative text—the struggle between our science and their magic—dissolves into the industrial light and magic of a Spielberg-like apotheosis as spectacle. What we have finally is not a clash of cultures but a play of complementaries—black and white magic.

For Third World cultures that occupy large, diverse territories, things may seem to be moving, in terms of historical sequence, impossibly slowly. But the cultures I am talking about are island cultures. Islands are satellites. And it is precisely because they are satellites in the older territorial sense—the small surface that reflects a larger landbound culture—that they are disposed to act as what we call a satellite today: not so much a microcosm as a mediacosm, a world whose sole function is to receive and broadcast information. The island's lack of space and territory allows it to function not in the past or in the future, but in the present of the mediatory act itself. In this present the slow process of spatialized time is converted, in the creation of radically accelerated and mobile forms like the film or song, into instances (in fact, islands) of temporalized space. The territorial claims of tradition or genre are suspended in the near simultaneity of the "hit" film or song experience—an event simultaneously totalizing and evanescent, conserved on reels and cassettes but not *located* there in any material sense. In kung fu films and reggae songs, how can we "ground" the place of the fight when the logic of these media, developed to the maximum by the island cultures using them, obviates the concept of location altogether?

Where, for instance, do we locate the Shaolin temple, the Third World fantasy that "supports" the kung fu film? There is a historical Shaolin monastery, in fact a succession of monasteries, as one can see in the elaborate "genealogy" published in the special issue of *Cahiers du cinéma* (September 1984) devoted to the Hong Kong movie industry.[6] Shaolin, apparently, dates from the sixth century. It was burned twice in the eighteenth century; its surviving masters each time continued resistance to the Manchus, until one of the "ten tigers of Guandong," a certain Huang Fei-Hong, made the move from political struggle to cinema, not only becoming the subject of eighty-two martial arts films but actually engendering sons who, trained as martial artists, became actors and finally the directors of the films that celebrated their father. The shift here, from life to film legend, marks another displacement—that from mainland monastery to island studio, from Mandarin culture to popular Cantonese film.

But the real mediator of the kung fu fantasy is not a Shaolin monk, real or celluloid, but the total film presence of Bruce Lee. Born in San Francisco to a Chinese actor and educated at the University of Washington in Western philosophy, Bruce straddled two worlds. He became a media event, however, because of the success he achieved in superimposing these worlds, materially so rife with conflict, in a single unified film experience. Before his film kung fu could become the act that produced time out of the traditional space of political and cultural conflict, he had to effect a "revolution" in martial arts cinema. This he did by embracing techniques of informational immediacy analogous to those used in the musical comedy[7]—or rather by commanding them into existence by his simple presence on the screen. In his first film, *Fists of Fury*, the camera, as if hypnotized by Bruce's moves, turns away from the trick shots and crude special effects of earlier Hong Kong films and adopts instead the stable visual field characteristic of the musical. Filling this cinematic space is no longer an actor but the personal style of a specific fighter. In the musical, character and plot fall away and we find ourselves watching Fred Astaire or Gene Kelly. Here, all pretense at history and story falls away as Bruce moves, and those moves are instantly disseminated, in a now-transparent medium in which nothing is asked to fall between the simultaneity of the act and its viewing shadow.

Bruce Lee made four and a half films. His presence became increasingly dominant, until he found himself, in the fourth film (*Return of the Dragon*), on both ends of the camera, directing the shots that recorded his moves. The theme of these films, on the level of situation and story, is increasingly Third World struggle against the technologically superior oppressor—European, American, or Japanese. The deeper theme of these films, however, conveyed not by the logic of story but by the medium itself, by the immediacy of gesture and image, is that of translation, the step-by-step matching of an oppressive technology of space (history and story) with an alternate technology in the realm of cinematic time. In history, Bruce's world, which he claims to be a world without guns and knives, has irreversibly succumbed to the guns of the superpower oppressor. In film, however, as Bruce used it, lies the power to reverse the irreversible—a power unleashed as the screen presence of Bruce condenses, and finally abolishes, the space of conflict. In this condensing is manifested the technology of the medium itself, a technology of time that does not defeat so much as it displaces the oppressive technology of space, matter, and territorial conflict.

In the final scene of *The Chinese Connection*, Bruce leaps into the guns of the oppressor. Held in mid-leap in a freeze frame, he enters a world of time in which the sequential nature of events, the guns still going off as he hovers in the air, no longer concerns him. Throughout the story there are gates Bruce cannot pass, like the one marked with the sign "No Chinese or dogs allowed." Denied a place in their world, he takes his final leap at another gate and enters his own world, passing from the stated tyranny of three dimensions into the screen controlled by a fourth, where the image can be held until we turn it off, or until the reel, at twenty-four frames per second, runs out.

Territorial conflict, the story of this film, is a fact of space, of the historical evolution (a spatially evocative term, "to unroll") of a technology that establishes, in its logic of causal sequences, rankings and walls and exclusions. But if at the end of the film the walls of territory dissolve, this vanishing point is prepared for throughout by a series of transfers, places in the "action" where material process instantly dissolves into temporal presence—change suddenly held before us as immediacy, frames frozen in defiance of the resolution of a plot line. *The Chinese Connection* begins not with the burning of Shaolin but with Bruce falling on Teacher's fresh gravesite and digging like an enraged dog. Contact with the ground or an animal is a means, in conventional kung fu films, of tracing techniques of fighting to their source. Chang Cheh's *Five Masters of Death* shows fighters sifting the ashes of Shaolin to find implements that enable them to bring to life in movements on the screen styles like "the stork," originally derived from the imitation of animal fighting techniques. Other films reconstruct this imitation process. In a typical scenario, a young boy, beaten by bullies, watches an animal combat, say, between a cobra and a mongoose. From this he derives his personal fighting style, which he then adapts to a series of training machines—sophisticated contraptions of pulleys and counterweights—that in turn imitate the moves of the animal adversary.

Already, in the *Five Masters* scenario, we experience a compression of history and space, as if the entire thirty-six rooms of Shaolin were brought to life in a single instance. With Bruce Lee, however, the process is much more radical. There is no Shaolin, nothing but a cinematic grave upon which Bruce, in the absence of all teachers, furiously digs. And not simply *like* a dog, for in his movements he *becomes* a dog, instantly assimilating the spatial source in the flash of his imaged movements. The film is a series of such moments—call them lightning apprehensions, instants when technologies of combat spring full-blown from immediately engaged situations, much like dancing styles in a Stanley Donen musical. Reluctant to fight, Bruce is battered until, probing his wounds with his finger and tasting his own blood, he leaps without transition into deadly combat, uttering cat cries and instantly extending the fighting radius of the naked animal with simple machines rendered sophisticated by their use: poles, darts, and those twirling nunchakus Stuart Kaminsky compares to Fred Astaire's canes.[8] In these moments an entire technological evolution is foreshortened into a burst of pure kinetic light and sound.

What the image expresses here, producing time at the expense of all spatial constraints, is less the triumph of time than the equivalency of time. As the film ends, the space of the text remains superimposed upon Bruce; but it cannot defeat him because it is unable to hold sway over him in his alternate, and now equivalent, world of temporal production. His image remains on the screen as the sound of the shots fades and as the credits roll over him, naming the cast of characters that recapitulate a plot in which his death is inscribed. Even the signature "the end" does not obliterate the image, but coexists with it until both pass as time and the reel run out. In this emblematic frame, Bruce operates as a Third World version of $E = mc^2$; with his speed-of-light kick (reputed to be so fast he appeared not to move) he converts the mass of history, narrative, and text into the pure radiant energy of the image.

The whole question of unequal struggle between matter and energy, or between material reality and insubstantial fantasy or text and image, is relegated, by Bruce's presence, to a prerelativistic frame of reference. In the end, the screen kung fu fighter achieved parity with, and independence from, the logocentric technology that sought to contain him. Bruce took on an existence outside his film stories and even outside their replay in his own films. He escaped, in fact, the material limits of his own death. The "Bruce" who returned to the screen after that death is not a real personality but a carefully imitated visual style. From the different spellings of the actors' last names—Le, Li—we see logos seeking to inscribe and limit the image. But these written discriminations are not pronounceable. In this case to share a spoken name is to create a screen presence that seeks to dissolve the hegemony of the written word. This is made clear in a scene from the omnibus film *Bruce and the Shaolin Kung Fu*. In a training session, a Korean Tae Kwan Do master takes a brush and dabs characters on a canvas. As he does this, Bruce Le (as the name is spelled in the credits) moves his arms and legs to embrace the curves of the brush stroke, and in doing so literally releases the kinetics of the image from all spatial location in a text.

The Rastafarian movement followed an analogous direction away from groundings in "solid" historical tradition toward the status of media event—passing from the slow history of black political and cultural resistance to colonialist oppression to the rapid dissemination of a style and a hit music. What was originally a pan-African movement has become the "culture" of an island—Jamaica. Political figures like Marcus Garvey gave way to religious fantasies such as the enshrinement of Haile Selassie, Ras Tafari, emperor of Ethiopia, as the living God. And the instant revelations of religion have yielded in turn to even more instantaneous phenomena. The Guyanian writer Eusi Kwayana describes Rasta as the movement of a society increasingly led to *acceptance* of cultural mobility and rootlessness. As he puts it, those who do not accept the religious ideas accept the dress; those who do not accept the dress accept the language; and "those who do not accept the language, with the movement's redefinition of the order of things, accept the music."[9]

Dress is an important element of the kung fu fantasy. In *Return of the Dragon*, Bruce Lee steps from a plane in Rome wearing peasant blue and soft kung fu shoes; he stands out iconically against Western clothes and cars. As style, he inverts the material order of things, offering simple constancy as alternative to the First World's continual change of fashion. Rasta dress, however, does more. It assimilates and compresses a long (and continuing) process of evolutionary struggle into a "statement" that is both singular and cumulative—a genuinely synchronic act. Rastamen wear their hair in "dreadlocks" and cover these with knitted "tams." The one evokes the African warrior past, the other the garb of the European colonialist oppressor, the Scottish planters who gave their names to so many Caribbean slaves. But they also wear, as Freddy Macgregor puts it in his song "Joggin'," "the track shoes and the big bobby sox." In this song, Rastamen practice for "the run for creation" by jogging down Kingston's Trafalgar Road. But the shoes they are wearing are Adidas and Pumas. The brand names of the latest American fad resonate through a song that is all about Armageddon and the fall of the very Babylon that has produced their stylish means of escape. As Rasta dress continues to assimilate First World fads, it is itself increasingly disseminated as a style through the medium of an equally First World tourist industry, which allows Rastamen to be seen in the streets and public places of the capitals of Europe and Asia.

If you cannot accept the dress, Kwayana says, you accept the language. And this, what he calls the movement's means of redefining the order of things, makes statements that are even more instantaneously synthesizing in nature. Terms from a broad and varied warrior past—Ashanti, Nyabinghi, Uhuru, Buffalo Soldiers—are compressed in ritual incantations. And First World words are continuously assimilated. Native *ganja* becomes *sinsemilla,* a new American graft on the ancestral weed. Ital food—that is, native-grown food as opposed to the oppressor's market economy soda pop and corn flakes—is praised by Peter Tosh in his hymn to natural Rasta,

Third World Fantasies 181

"Mystic Man," but at the same time supplemented in a more recent song by "vitamins A and C and D for a healthy body." Keeping fit for Armageddon means incorporating the latest health food fads as well.

I speak of incorporating, but where is the body of this movement outside its style and its language? Indeed, in that same language Rasta calls its redefinitions of the order of things, which are essentially acts of eluding material location, "versions." Steel Pulse's "version on the King James Version" simply declares that in Africa was found the Garden of Eden.[10] The "roots" of an entire race (and if we believe Eden is the universal source, of the human species itself) are placed, within the ephemeral confines of a song, in a country of the mind which derives its power, paradoxically, from its fantastic mobility, its rootlessness. Reggae music is the ultimate "location" of Rasta. But like the kung fu film, it is not a place so much as a process of dissemination. And again, this process is a technology shared with the First World, the thematic adversary that Rasta, on the level of style and words, continues to attack. Rasta meeting places become "sound systems," giant decks of amplifiers and speakers intended to broadcast the music. The "rocker" beat they blast is not produced on native drums but on synthesizers. This in turn is fed back through the system as "dub": wordless, electronically replicated versions of songs in which only the rhythm remains, a rhythm that can serve as ground bass for the continuously topical rappings of "toasting dj's." In this process, new and old, tradition and change, are fused into the self-re-creating present of the media event. An entire resistance movement not only distills itself into a single media personality—in this case Bruce's counterpart, Bob Marley—but becomes no more substantial than an aggregate of the single instances of his hit songs. And each of these grants electronic universality to what otherwise would remain mired in the plodding sequence of history.

Kung fu and reggae, Bruce Lee and Bob Marley, generate fantasy constructs that seek to operate outside spatial constraints, in both the territorial sense and the "textual" sense. These fantasies might be better understood if they were not themselves subject to constraints in the form of critical interpretations that rely on the concept of grounding or material base. It is in the logocentric world that fantasy is said to exist in relation to reality. For when all is said and done, a text remains a territory, and maps to it are supposed to be accurate. The written word is a final vestige of spatial territoriality. As such it remains, insofar as it is a medium, a means of maintaining, on the plane of story or on the "structural" plane of the text, the hegemony of a first, or "real," world. A world locatable here, as opposed to some world located "out there," called "third world" perhaps because there is no "second" world posited to mediate it. Embedded in the term *Third World* is the assumption that all connection is simply absent. This is a strategy of territorial protection that lies behind the Derridean sense of the "lost" primitivist origin and the deferred apocalypse alike.

The media of temporal production—moving pictures and broadcasting—offer a second world, but it is a world without territories or territorial aspirations, where no permanence of the local habitation and name is assured. The implications of such a world seem radical even to Moscovici, who sees these media creating a "temporal imperialism" that merely displaces the old spatial hegemony. Still a bit of a Marxist perhaps, he regrets the *manque de devenir* they engender—the compression of historical spacetime into moments of instant apprehension and gratification that render us idle consumers rather than active participants in the process of making our world. In these films and songs, however, we are immediately there and intimately at home. And as a result, all boundaries have dissolved, even those of the conflict that originally produced the song or film and remains (a ghost) in its lyrics or story. Kung fu films and reggae music, while speaking against the oppressor, actually share a world with him, that of temporal production. As a result, we see, increasingly in our First World films and songs today, a softening of paranoia, once carefully guarded borders becoming more and more porous. Ninja assassins are reborn in the bodies of female aerobic instructors; Chinese-American busboys say, "They Call Me Bruce." And the white savage, Crocodile Dundee, goes to New York, leaving us to wonder where the Third World is: in the souls of aborigines wearing Eton jackets in the outback or in the wild yet charming streets of the United States? Without clear borders, we cannot locate sides or take them.

The changing focus of American films reveals—along the traditional axis of civilization and barbarism—a blurring of the idea of territoriality, and with it the sense of clear adversarial struggle. Howard Hawks's original *Scarface* (1936), for example, is a straightforward tale of Third World incursion and First World expulsion, in which Sicilian lawlessness is excised by a society fully conscious of its operational parameters and which openly articulates its exclusionary ethic in a town meeting setting. Brian DePalma's 1983 remake offers a protagonist who is much more viciously "Third World"—a Cuban criminal even Castro didn't want. But DePalma has him operate in an America that no longer has the old moral and operational boundaries, and where First World bankers, politicians, and police not only vie with but outdo the traditional Third World in lawlessness and violence.

We might think of Vietnam as the event that blurred boundaries. But as late as Michael Cimino's Vietnam film *The Deer Hunter* (1978) there is still a here and a there. The ponderous rhythm of the film contrasts ceremonies and rituals safely transplanted from Europe to an Appalachian mining town—including the stylized deer hunt itself—with chaotic scenes of Third World horror. The same men who obeyed the law of the hunt suddenly find themselves thrashing in a cage immersed in rice paddy water and forced to play Russian roulette for the frantic gaming of Vietnamese soldiers. The return home, in this film, is return to a safe, if less substantial, haven—to a sanctuary made of empty rites that temporarily protect us from the forces of disorder we have disturbed.

In the 1986 film *Band of the Hand*, however, Third World chaos runs amok in our own streets. Sanctuary is no longer possible; indeed, a major scene involves the assault and burning of a "safe house" for juveniles trying to reform. It is a world without clear territories, a world of open streets and circulating hit-and-run attacks. The "hero" who acts in it must, equally, be without territorial inhibitions. In this case it is a Seminole Indian who won a Congressional Medal of Honor in Vietnam, a native American "match" for the Third World native, and a person at home in worlds both with and without guns and knives. More significantly, he is a hero who functions by being *absent*. He is killed in the raid on the safe house. And it is his disembodied spirit that unites a band of potential First and Third World opponents into a unit as organically united, and prone to immediate coordinated action, as the fingers on a same hand.

Hollywood's paradigmatic Third World fantasy, however, is *Rocky IV*, a film in which expectational boundaries are crossed and recrossed until they fade in the culminating unity of pure media event. In earlier Rocky films, the protagonist both fought against and trained with black boxer Apollo Creed. In all cases, though, the final fight was still waged according to First World expectations. As the Italian Stallion battled Mr. T, a Third World arena was carved out against the First World managers and promoters of the boxing sport. Now, however, Apollo has ostentatiously crossed over. He descends into a Las Vegas ring from a levitating dance floor replete with garish chorus line. He is wearing an Uncle Sam hat and star-spangled mantle—now he is America's establishment champion prepared to do battle with a Soviet counterpart. But the Russian—traditionally the brutish third worlder of the 1950s Red scare films—has also crossed over. We do not see heavy peasant features, but a sleek android trained by state-of-the-art technology, thoroughly a product of what we assume to be First World superiority. The Russian is a high-tech killing machine. When he dispatches Apollo, Rocky, who has drifted across boundaries, away from his working-class roots and into middle-class complacency, must seek to recover those roots. But their "location" has increasingly become spatial dislocation, relocation in the temporally determined realm of fantasy. After going to the USSR to train, Rocky finds himself in a country house that he must convert into a natural gymnasium. In an ever-accelerating (and dislocating) rhythm, the camera cuts back and forth between the streamlined machines and computer terminals guiding the Russian's training and Rocky lifting peasant carts out of the mud, chinning himself on wooden beams, outrunning the Mercedes of his KGB tail. Embracing the land and its people, he has taken on the style of *their* legendary folk hero, Ilya Mourometz.

Rocky IV follows the same trajectory as the kung fu film. Here too a fighter, humiliated by a more advanced technology of combat, returns to natural "roots" and from them evolves an alternate technology of the fight that leads him to undertake, and win, a final contest that becomes an event of almost transcendental magnitude. Story concerns, such as the antagonism of First and Third World, are neutralized by the rhythm of equivalency created by ever-accelerated cross-cutting. The space of combat is so compressed into instants of time, and viewers are made so aware of the temporal nature of the "terrain," that we are freed to experience the immediacy of the culminating spectacle as a unifying act.

In *Return of the Dragon*, Bruce Lee fights the ultimate combat against Colt, an American heavy in the pay of the Mafia. This, thematically, is a clear First/Third World opposition. But, visually, what we experience is quite different. The setting is the Coliseum, where slaves did not fight masters but among themselves, as gladiators, professional fighters. As Colt steps forward wearing kimono and black belt, he becomes Chuck Norris, karate champion. In like manner his opponent sheds his peasant shirt and, flexing his muscles, emerges from his "character" to be Bruce Lee. Two top martial artists, and two distinct styles and "philosophies" of combat, now face each other. The screen fight to the death has become a tournament waged according to an international code of conduct. The same happens as Rocky and his opponent step into the ring. Rocky's passage from the "ground up," through a series of everyday moves, to become an accomplished boxer could be that of anybody, indeed that of actor Stallone himself. It is by means of this process that Stallone, in a sense, frees himself from his character. And this in turn, as Stallone steps into the ring to face an actor who himself is obviously a professional fighter, frees the film from the nemesis of its story line, which is the necessary conflict of nations and worlds. The Third World fantasy has resolved into something like a televised media event, whose outcome now exists only in the instant of its production.

The word *televised* is significant here, for in the final scenes of *Return of the Dragon* and *Rocky IV* the logic of film has actually given way to that of the broadcast. What this means, in Marshall McLuhan's terms, is that we have passed from a "hot" to a "cool" medium. A hot medium, as McLuhan explains it, "is one that extends one single sense in 'high definition.' "[11] By "high definition" he means focusing rather than disseminating data, and thus forcing single entities, in linear fashion, into situations of opposition and conflict. In this way film, as a hot medium, is seen as engaging its images in the conflictual patterns of a story line or a thematic opposition. The broad electronic dissemination of television, however (cinema remains a more private medium, one we must consciously choose to see, and pay for), invites the viewer to take a participatory, rather than a partisan, stand toward its images. If fantasy is indeed defined as causing something to appear, then television seems its prime medium, for it allows us actually to participate in bodying forth a vision. And in the case of the televised fight, to ensure through our participation that the vision bodied forth is one of unity rather than contention. The crowd that booed Rocky's entrance to the Soviet arena was still a film crowd, part of the conflictual logic of a "plot." But after the absorbing spectacle of the fight—the camera taking us blow by blow through fifteen rounds—when Stallone finally fells his opponent, this same crowd is on its feet cheering, just like a television audience. Each member has been made an intimate participant, a connoisseur of technique rather than an adept at ideology. With this shift of focus from the *what* to the *how* of the fight comes a unity of vision that can legitimately be crowned by the film's final sermon—Stallone now exhorting us in his own voice to create one world and one love. What would not happen either ringside in the Soviet Union or in the logic of film conflict happens here with the detachment of a televised event.

This final fight scene is no longer locatable in the space of nations or in that of material process itself. Unlocatable, it becomes pure event, the past participle freed of the burden of pastness by being returned to the potential dynamism of the infinitive—to come out, to appear, to be the product of fantasy, and in being such embrace a present that implies a future (*e- venire*). We cannot simply dismiss a fantasy like Rocky's fight by saying that because it has no local habitation or roots in a past, it is powerless to act upon material space. It would be more intelligent to ask how temporal production relates to spatial production. For by saying that fantasy produces time, we are challenging the spacebound distinction between container and content, material world and the production of material things. And the challenge offers a pair of temporal alternatives: the medium or vehicle, and the production of instances. These instances, as events, are temporal vectors, originating in the single moment but carrying, in their unity, a promise of future totality. Rather than rejecting the Bruce Lee or Sylvester Stallone fights as power fantasies, we must reexamine how fantasy, as instant vectored by an individual rather than a collective entity, exercises power.

Horace Campbell, by the very title of his book *Rasta and Resistance*, seems to look for the power of the movement in the wrong place. "Resistance," as metaphor, locates Rasta in a context of material friction instead of the more natural context of dissemination, of abolition of material or spatial constraints. Campbell deplores Rasta's "millenialist" deification of Haile Selassie. Yet what better way to escape from slow history to totality than this instant of god making? And he condemns the individualist tendencies of reggae, its obsessive use of the "I" pronoun. With statements like "I and I we know," there is no grounding in collective destiny, just as with Selassie there is no grounding in material history. Yet in a book replete with buzzwords like *scientific* and *material*, we find the following, astonishing, caption beneath a photo of Bob Marley in concert: "The power that Bob Marley's music represents has done more to popularize the real issues of [the] African Liberation Movement than several decades of backbreaking work of Pan-Africanists and international revolutionaries."[12]

Two words are important here: *popularize* and *power*. The first refers to the ability both to reach everywhere and to do so at once. And today a collective myth no longer seems able to do so, because it is bound—rendered immobile—by its material context, and ultimately by its text. To Northrop Frye a world of myth is "an abstract or purely literary world of fictional and thematic design, unaffected by canons of plausible adaptation to familiar experience."[13] To make that adaptation, which is movement in time, we need something else, something more mobile because more occasional and individual. That something is a legend. Plastered all over the London transport system in the summer of 1984 were posters of Bob Marley, representing the cover of a retrospective revival record album entitled

Legend. Marley died at age thirty-six in the summer of 1981. But he is revived from his image and music every year in birthday "tributes" like this one. The Marley experience is legendary precisely because it is not rooted in material space but rather (I prefer Emerson's term here) is "centered" in a name the man once wore. But now, the body shed, the name has become a mobile point, ready when summoned to expand, to encompass a circumferential totality. *Legend,* the dictionary tells us, is not only a popular and spontaneous story, it is a dubious story. But it is dubious only in the eyes of history, because it has no base or "text" beyond the dehistoricized individual who regenerates it. If myth is logos, legend is the caption on the picture, the name that identifies Lee or Marley; and that vanishes, ceases to attach, as each is awakened to action.

The second term is *power.* Here, it seems, I am pushing my argument toward Emersonianism, dissolving institutions until they become no more than lengthened shadows of individual men, and making form a function of power and not vice versa. With this, it appears, I seek to despecify my initial Third World fantasies, and in doing so to detach fantasy itself from roots in materially determined conditions of production, to de-ideologize it. And yet Campbell, no matter how hard he tries not to, still sees Marley's music having real *practical* power in the pan-African movement. And this is a power as concentrated as it is instantaneous, for he is comparing two decades of backbreaking labor with the time it takes to sing a song. The cover of a reggae album tells us that "word soun' have power." Gone here is "poetry," for that word denotes a locus of historical forms. Instead there is "word soun'," something no longer carrying the burden of its traditional text, but now free to convey, a vehicle for power. In the same way Bruce's hands change written characters into immediately mediated images.

Words like *tradition* simply assume mass, gravity, the "weight" of material history; against this, fantasy's insubstantial pageant is seen to rise and fade—the intense but ephemeral experience conveyed by the speaker of Keats's "Ode to a Nightingale." Two other short-lived artists, Lee and Marley, have through their electronically mediated "already with thees" challenged the materialist model. But another Third World artist, this time using the First World medium of the science fiction thought experiment, offers an alternate model. This is Samuel R. Delany in his novel *Nova.*

Darko Suvin sees the process of SF, its ability to "estrange" us from cognitive norms, as aimed at creating what he calls the novum, new and "totalizing" worlds, but worlds that at the same time remain grounded in the dialectical possibilities of the historical process. They are alternate realities, not fantasies. The latter, for Suvin, "operate in semantic emptiness spiced with melodramatic sensationalism as a compensatory satisfaction, in a runaway feedback system with corrupt audience taste instead of with cognition of tendencies in the social practice of human relationships."[14]

Bruce Lee and Bob Marley also offer us new worlds for old. And Delany's *Nova* may help us see beyond a priori dismissal, into their nature and potential. The central material reality of this novel, a sun going nova, is a transformation of matter into energy, of spatial location into an act of temporal dissemination. And the central narrative reality is analogous, for protagonist Lorq von Ray carries with him the weight of the quest tradition. And he carries it into the nova. "The matter displacement," we are told, "is all toward the center of the sun. The energy displacement is all outwards."[15] But the matter he is seeking is an element called Illyrion. It is called a "trans-300" element. It follows the series from 100 to 298, elements with a material existence measured in half-lives less than 1/100,000 of a second. This is matter that "doesn't stay around very long," therefore whose condition is totally the production of time.

Yet Illyrion is, because it is trans-300, "superstable" as well. But what can be the nature of this "stability" beyond a seemingly total conversion of material space to time? It is said to be "something else" (Delany is playing on the hip idiom in which this means, in the admirative sense, "*fan*tastic"). The *Webster's* of the time tells us: "It is both psychomorphic and heterotropic." And the speaker concludes: "I suppose that's a fancy way of saying Illyrion is many things to many men" (27). Illyrion (Ilium? delirium? illusion?) becomes in its ambiguity the stability of illusion. It is, as with a Lee film or a Marley song, fantasy *as* stability produced totally out of temporally determined matter, matter volatilized to become pure medium. Such matter can indeed be "psychomorphic." For if it is many things to many people, in this story the important question must become, if there is to be a story: What is it to our captain? This is Lorq's quest: yet not so much for the mythical grail as into the hollow of the grail cup, the "doughnut hole" of the imploding star. This impossible center, where the mass of tradition is no longer locatable, can only be filled by a legend—the private fantasy as the sole "reality" possible.

But as it turns out, the real subject of Delany's novel is not the eternal return—the material base of myth that underlies Lorq's adventure. It is instead the transmissional present. Lorq is accompanied by two sidekicks: the learned Katin and Mouse the space gypsy. Katin is a man who likes moons. He likes them because they are, as with the island worlds of

Jamaica or Hong Kong, reflective satellites for larger, more materially diverse planets and cultures: "The passions that come through the diversity of a complete world, or a whole man, he knew—but did not like" (15). The moon offers "variations of sameness," and this is what historian Katin, the man on the moon, produces: visions that are temporal instants, variations of that sameness which is the reiteration of the act of transmission itself. Katin is constantly recording data, constantly dictating into a machine. But on the last page he is still reluctant to write anything down: "Remember all those writers who died before they finished their Grail recountings?" (215). And if what we hold in our hands is supposed to be Katin's text, it breaks off in midsentence, unfinished too. To write down is to spatialize, to locate and delimit a territory. But Katin unlocates: "A moon, Mouse. To retire to some beautiful rock, my art perfected, to contemplate the flow and shift of the net; that's what I want, Mouse. But the subject won't come!" (155). Katin is a disengaged but available medium: he wants to write, but not about something. That would only be to create a containing structure. Significantly, he wants a *subject,* a vector, someone who acts to use the medium he offers. This subject is Mouse the space gypsy.

The Katin-Mouse nexus, in a real sense, plays a cat-and-mouse game with Marxist materialism. Mouse, unlike the rest of his gypsies, has become a "cyborg stud"; that is, he has had neural sockets implanted that allow him literally to "plug in" to the job he performs. The philosopher behind this invention is Ashton Clark, and he seems to have solved, in one fell swoop, Marx's problem of the alienation of labor. Yet what Ashton Clark (echoing Ashton Clark Smith, the fantasy writer) offers is "trans-300" Marxism at best. For not only is there, in this instant creation of a network of wired workers, suspension of any dialectical process, there is displacement from a spatial or material to a temporal location as well. Indeed, networking leads to the very opposite of cultural stability in the old, material sense. Now jobs and labor are disseminated to the degree that those seeking a "place" are, ironically, the gypsies themselves, the people in our culture most recalcitrant to being fixed. Ashton Smith's world is one of temporal production. In it we can no longer have a material base; rather, we have a central, vectorizing instant.

"They're all just looking for our social traditions in the wrong place. There are cultural traditions that have matured over the centuries, yet now culminate in something vital and solely of today. And you know anyone who embodies that tradition more than anyone I've met?" "The captain?" "You, Mouse" (197). On one level, for Mouse, the dealienating sockets are another version of the slave's chains. But the new links are also nonmaterial. And when plugged into a "place" that is itself a mobile entity, a moon or satellite world, they activate a new field of world creation—the broadcast media event. In Katin's words, Mouse is the "spark among the links that illuminates the breadth of the net." The description of his location in what is an immaterial network could be that of Bruce Lee or Bob Marley vectored—as vital subject—by their island satellites: "You've collected the ornamentations a dozen societies have left us over the ages and made them inchoately yours. You're the product of tensions that clashed in the time of Clark and you resolve them on your syrynx with patterns eminently of the present" (197).

But finally, the "bottom line" question (how easily gravity returns to the discussion) remains: What sort of future can such a present offer? Material history, in the root sense of tradition, must eventually deliver up a place to come—a "reality" that must, in the end, relegate Mouse's syrynx to fantasy, to the sort of airy instability the jazz musician refers to when he calls such music "blowing." Indeed, as my epigraph suggests, after the Marxist-denounced gold rush, everybody knows this is nowhere. But utopia is nowhere also. And we must at least consider that, as with Lee and Marley and Rocky, between nowhere and novum today there lies nova. What else is "reggae sunsplash"? And with the Marley song "Catch a Fire," are we trapping the flame, grounding it, or glorying in the instant of conflagration?

Suvin will not allow fantasy its primal power; its flights and fights are not even illusions, they remain the tools of a corrupt exploitation of the masses. And if SF is tolerated, it is because its novae can be seen to remain alternate *realities* on the same "ontological" level as our empirical (read, material) reality. In other words, Suvin's utopia—nowhere—has to be somewhere. I am arguing, simply, that the technology of time production has changed all this because it allows utopia to be nowhere and still to have the power to combine and unify. The resulting media events are not, as Suvin might have it, the product of a "conspiracy" of one world against another. Instead they return that word to its original sense—a "breathing together" of worlds, worlds accessing each other instantly, creating a field that Marley, Lee, and Stallone share alike.

And speaking of sharing, the most representative SF I know shares with these Third World fantasies a fascination with instant mediation, with the "already with thee" that is the production of time. Suvin may fault Jules Verne for translating quantified time into quantified space. But this is exactly what his own "scientific materialism" seeks to do when faced with my fantasies—their "third" worlds must be reterritorialized in a place of class struggle. Yet I have shown how the worlds of Lee and Marley and Rocky revel in their freedom from territory. Western romantics like E. T. A. Hoffmann dreamed that the elevating power of the image, and especially musical sound, might heal (if only momentarily) the effect of our fall into matter. Today, the broadcast media have made this healing power accessible to everyone on the globe. And SF, despite its surface thematic fascination with strife, may be the literary form that most aspires to that power, the power to "cool down" the hot medium of print, to dematerialize conflict in instant visions of unity. The essential SF title is not Bishop's "No Enemy but Time" but Heinlein's "Time Enough for Love," whose whole purpose is to show that to locate utopia is to produce death. Lazarus Long will not be contained by time; instead he displaces utopia as a series of mediational experiments that operate in time. Love here is not a quality; it is a dynamic vector, and time is its field of production. Our experience of Heinlein's SF, generally, is one of immediate access to worlds. That famous sentence Delany isolated from *Beyond This Horizon*, "the door dilated," is crucial to this experience precisely because, as Delany put it, "the technological discourse that redeems it . . . is not explicit in the text."[16] Heinlein frees us from textual locations, even from the past tense, and historical sense, of narrative itself. He throws us into a world where doors dilate. And when in another novel, *The Star Beast*, we learn in an offhand manner, three quarters of the way into the text, that the president is black, we realize suddenly that all the painful process from here to there, all the ploddings of material history, have been elided. Likewise, Bob Marley gives us in an instant an Africa that must be free, and the silent hands of Bruce Lee's kung fu conjure a world without guns and knives. We cannot discount the logic of fantasy simply because it is not, as Suvin says, rationally directed. For why must reason be bound to the logic of the line? The ancient power of fantasy helps us enter the brave new world of temporal production. At the very least it makes us ask a question. Is there time left for history to take its course?

Notes

1. Pascal Bruckner, *The Tears of the White Man: Compassion as Contempt*, trans. with introduction by William R. Beer (New York: Free Press, 1986), p. x.
2. André Bazin, "The Ontology of the Photographic Image," in *What Is Cinema?*, 2 vols., essays selected and trans. by Hugh Gray (Berkeley: University of California Press, 1967), 1:13–14.
3. Serge Moscovici, "L'Espace, le temps et le social," interview conducted by Emile Noël in *L'Espace et le temps aujourd'hui* (Paris: Editions du Seuil, 1963), p. 264.
4. Fredric Jameson, *The Political Unconscious: Narrative as a Socially Symbolic Act* (Ithaca, N.Y.: Cornell University Press, 1981), p. 297.
5. Remarks made by Wes Craven in a speech at the premiere of his film at UCLA, January 30, 1988. The premiere was in the context of a course on "dark fantasy," *Tales from the Darkside*, taught by George Slusser and Dennis Etchison.
6. *Cahiers du cinéma* (September 1984): 362–63. Especially interesting is the article by Lau Shing-Hon, "La saga du kung-fu" (pp. 45–49), which includes a "centerfold" chart giving the genealogy of the Shaolin temple; and the article by Olivier Assayas, "Chang Cheh, l'ogre de Hong Kong" (pp. 50–52).
7. For further discussion, see Hsiung Ping-Chiao, "Bruce Lee: His Influence on the Evolution of the Kung Fu Genre," *Journal of Popular Film and Television* 9 (Spring 1981): 30–42. Some sense of Bruce Lee's philosophy of combat can be gotten from *The Unbeatable Bruce Lee: A Manual of the Master in Action* (New York: Bunch Books, 1978).
8. Stuart Kaminsky, "Italian Westerns and Kung Fu Films: Genres of Violence," in *Graphic Violence on the Screen*, ed. Thomas R. Atkins (New York: Monarch Press, 1976), p. 129.
9. Eusi Kwayana, preface to *Rasta and Resistance*, by Horace Campbell (Trenton, N.J.: Africa World Press, 1987), p. xii.
10. The recent hypothesis of the "black Eve" claims to locate Eden, if it existed at all, in Africa. See the article in *Schweitzer Illustrierte*, February 8, 1988, pp. 30–35.
11. Marshall McLuhan, *Understanding Media: The Extensions of Man* (New York: Signet, 1964), p. 36.
12. Campbell, *Rasta*, p. 145.
13. Northrop Frye, *Anatomy of Criticism* (New York: Atheneum, 1965), p. 136.
14. Darko Suvin, *Metamorphoses of Science Fiction: On the Poetics and History*

of a Literary Genre (New Haven: Yale University Press, 1979), p. 75. Suvin seems to give spatial location an Edenic, prelapsarian quality: "Thus space was a fully plausible locus for SF only before the capitalist way of life.... An Earthly Paradise or Cockayne tale, a humanist dialogue or satire, all happen in a literary or imaginative space not subject to positivistic plausibility" (p. 73).

15. Samuel R. Delany, *Nova* (New York: Bantam Books, 1969), p. 212.
16. Samuel R. Delany, "Shadows," in *The Jewel-Hinged Jaw: Essays on Science Fiction* (New York: Berkley Windhover Books, 1977), p. 78.

Chapter 15

Solos, Solitons, Info, and Invasion in (and of) Science Fiction Film

Brooks Landon

Because what I'm about to say draws heavily on somewhat breathless literature about state-of-the-art computer animation, I fear I may be guilty of "handwaving," one of the suspect practices Stewart Brand cautions against in *The Media Lab: Inventing the Future at MIT*. Brand explains this as referring "to what a speaker does animatedly with his hands as he moves past provable material into speculation, anticipating and overwhelming objection with manual dexterity—a deprecating 'you know' featuring a well-turned back of the hand, or a two-handed symmetrical sculpting of something as imaginary as it is wonderful" (15). What's more, I'm not yet sure whether the developments in SF film that so fascinate me are in theory wonderful or dreadful. So, regardless of what my hands may do, I offer this essay not in a spirit of futurist ecstasy, nor of Baudrillardian alarm or Krokeresque panic, but just in my own sense that we must recognize a fundamental shift of the territory that underlies several models of conflict invoked by both the semblances and the situation of SF film.

It may be premature to speak of postcyberpunk film. Worse, it may be ridiculous, since it could be pointed out that the *first* cyberpunk film has yet to be made. Cabana Boy Production's *Neuromancer* seems permanently stalled at poolside, and prospects for Leonard Mogel's film of *Burning Chrome* do not seem at all bright. John Shirley's script for

Black Glass may lead to the first completed cyberpunk movie written by a cyberpunk author, but it has not yet done so, nor is the production future clear for Shirley's and Gibson's *Macrochip*. Curiously enough, the corpus of *pre*cyberpunk films may have to serve as the literary movement's filmic analogue, with *Blade Runner, Tron, Escape from New York, Looker,* and *Videodrome* the movies most readily associated with cyberpunk's vision of the technosphere.

Nevertheless, I want to invoke the *idea* of postcyberpunk film as an entry to my thesis that science fiction film is now undergoing a radical reformulation in which the depiction of science fiction narratives is being displaced by science fictional modes of depicting.[1] This reformulation seems to be the inexorable movement toward what has been called digital narrative, a description at once literal and metaphoric.[2] Contextually no more than a footnote to postmodern theory's view of fragmenting culture, this is a process in which science fiction *in* the cinema is yielding to a science fiction *of* the cinema, a process discussed by Vivian Sobchack as the transformation of "the centered subjectivity of *special affect*" into the "decentered subjectification of *special effects*" (282). "The genre has transformed its 'objective' representation of a 'high' technology into the 'subjective' symbolization of a technologized 'high.'" Production technology drives this process, as computer graphics and animation more and more displace what Sobchack terms the "wonderfully functional" depiction of science fictional concepts with the "functionally wonderful" showcasing of digital imaging capabilities (283). But I want to move beyond Sobchack's presentation of this change as one of several characteristics of postfuturist film, on to a broader view implied in the cyberpunk writing of William Gibson, Rudy Rucker, and Bruce Sterling, as well as in the cybercriticism of social theorist Jean Baudrillard. To this broader view, the increasing foregrounding of computer imaging in SF film is part of a societal change in which distinctions between science fiction and cultural reality are growing ever more difficult to maintain.[3] Such distinctions are rapidly becoming impossible to make in film, video, and TV, in which live action and computer-generated scenes are increasingly intermixed. Computer industry predictions of entirely computer-animated full-length feature films are both numerous and persuasive.[4] Nicholas Negroponte, director of MIT's Media Lab, describes the motion picture industry as "the smokestack industry of today's information world,"[5] while Tim Onosko simply says, "The only thing certain about the future of computer filmmaking is that it is inevitable" (274).

The late "Max Headroom" offers an obvious index to the mid-ranges of this process, as it at once depicts a science fictional future society and the technological-filmic future of the computer-generated simulacrum.[6] The adventures of Edison Carter are *set* in the future, while I believe that the semblance of Carter's electronic doppelganger, Max Headroom, *is* the future. Max's character literally prefigures the future of the image in SF film and video while figuratively pointing to the possibility of an interactive medium in which viewers will not just watch but will enter directly into real-time relationships with the computer generating the film or video narrative. For Baudrillard, that time is figuratively here already, diffused through all aspects of culture, a condition he calls "private 'telematics,'" in which "each person sees himself at the control of a hypothetical machine, isolated in a position of perfect and remote sovereignty, at an infinite distance from his universe of origin."[7] For computer animation expert Gary Demos, one of the founders of Digital Effects, such a time remains literally ten to fifteen years in the future, to be marked by the public availability of remote interactive scene simulation over cable TV.[8]

All of which brings me back—almost—to the idea of a postcyberpunk film and takes me forward to its implications for one of SF film's best codified arenas of conflict: the story of an individual pitted against a computer. Following the literary lead of myriad writers, SF film has portrayed this human-computer conflict in many ways. *Alphaville, 2001, The Forbin Project, THX1138, Demon Seed, War Games,* and *Savannah Electric* come immediately to mind, with *Tron* significantly relocating the conflict within the virtual world of cyberspace, and *The Terminator*—following the lead of *Westworld* and *Futureworld*—offering a version in which the computer is represented by robot proxy. Call them all big, bad computer films, the rough analogue to a large body of big, bad and occasionally big, good computer stories in SF literature. (That a number of films in this formula place the computer in charge of national defense or war prevention suggests an intensifying complexity not acknowledged in my "big, bad computer" label, as does the fact that most of these narratives play out along the axes of parent-child relations, but I must leave those angles to others.)

Cyberpunk writing, at least in one of its major strains, offers a significant variation on this older formula, focusing more on symbiosis than on conflict and assuming the near total interface of humanity with the virtual worlds of computer technology. The cyberpunk paradigm recontextualizes the conflict between the individual and the computer into a conflict between simulacra of each, in the process changing our perception of the computer from a personality to *a space*—one in which many personalities may be generated. While such recontextualized conflict remains in theory between individual and computer, its experiential or affective impact undoubtedly has more to do with conflict between two individuals.

My point is that if a wave of cyberpunk films ever does develop, some of them will surely recast this conflict *between* human and computer as a conflict of personalities *within* the computer-generated worlds of cyberspace. WNET's production of *Overdrawn at the Memory Bank* marks a tentative step in this direction, while *Tron* and "Max Headroom" already provide examples of one of the aesthetic dangers of such a schema, with its clear temptation to create what will surely have to be called *cyberopera*. But when battle *with* the computer comes to mean battle *within* the computer, we can suspect that at least part of the mythic battle has been lost before it is joined. Indeed, our growing imagination of virtual worlds within the computer obviously parallels our increasing acceptance of the growing role of computers in our own lives, making battle rhetoric sound ever more antique. One example: despite the disturbing power Harlan Ellison's "I Have No Mouth and I Must Scream" had when I first read it twenty years ago, it just doesn't work for me now other than as Kafkaesque parable.

More important, whether such a wave of cyberpunk filmed narratives ever materializes, what I'm calling postcyberpunk film will soon be here anyway—a technological fait accompli. Developments within the mediascape will inexorably recast this theme of conflict as an implicit technodrama in which computer graphics and animation—the digital narrative of the image—displace and possibly replace conventional narratives such as those depicting the individual pitted against the computer. Put another way, the story of this aspect of SF film is that Lemmy Caution and Dave Bowman may have won their fictional individual battles against specific computer personas, but outside of fiction computer technology has won the war—in part by recasting it as progress. To Abraham Peled's observation in the October 1987 *Scientific American* that "the way computing has permeated the fabric of purposeful intellectual and economic activity has no parallel" (57), I'd append a small footnote that computing and video processing are already not only permeating but also reweaving the fabric of film and broadcast industries. The title of a recent article in *Datamation* says it all: "Cray Conquers H'Wood."

It is this kind of future conflict that fascinates me, reifying and exteriorizing in the production and reception matrix of SF film one of the major themes of conflict long dramatized in individual SF movies. My interest, then, lies in noodling around a very abstract model of conflict, implicit in the Möbius-like relation between an industry and one of its products. The four terms in the title of this essay—solos, solitons, info, and invasion—represent an attempt to posit a semantic matrix which will help me explain my sense of this situation.

Solos we understand. Whether Napoleon or Han, Ellison's Vic or D. F. Jones's Forbin, the individual has been valorized by SF film and literature alike as the primary agent of change, the subject of narrative, the hero with a thousand space helmets. Indeed, as Constance Penley recently observed, most recent science fiction film "limits itself to solutions that are either individualist or bound to a romanticized notion of guerilla-like small-group resistance" (68). Penley's point—that this represents "the true atrophy of the utopian imagination"—is not mine, but her description of the failure to conceive "the kind of collective political strategies necessary to change or ensure" our imagined futures strikes me as quite parallel to my perception of a kind of failure in SF film and SF film criticism alike: we have been able to imagine the conflict between human and computer without being able to recognize that our model of that conflict is already a symptom of nostalgia more than speculation, its fictional narratives drained of plausibility by cultural realities.[9]

In big, bad computer films such as *The Forbin Project*, the solo inevitably creates or runs afoul of a seemingly more powerful electronic sentience, which is, at bottom, just another form of solo with a personality as distinctive as that of its human antagonist. Invariably, computers in SF film are shown to be power mad, dangerously flawed by their total and emotionless reliance on mathematical logic, or both. In the first case, represented by films such as *Demon Seed*, the fear seems to be that computers are all too human, in the second, represented by *War Games*, not human enough. At either extreme, however, the computer is depicted as a discrete persona endowed with volition and pride. Very few commentators missed the fact that HAL is a much more interesting character in *2001* than Dave Bowman, and that HAL's "death" is much more affective than are those of *Discovery*'s human crew. The same could be said of the relation between the supercomputer Colossus and its human designer in *The Forbin Project*. Godard's original title for *Alphaville* was the metonymically charged "Tarzan versus IBM," but the actual conflict in the film, between Lemmy Caution and the computer Alpha 60, is personal more than sociological or technological. Perhaps the most recent big, bad computer film is *Savannah Electric*, a low-budget Canadian film by Perry Mark Stratychuck. The genius of this movie is that its big, bad computer,

The Benefactor, *narrates* the story of a successful solo revolt. In contemplating the implications of such a single rebellion (more bother), however, The Benefactor simply becomes another anthropomorphized individual consciousness—another solo. As Chandra, the computer expert in 2010, sniffed, "Whether we are based on carbon or silicon makes no fundamental difference."

Solitons are not so well known—and not at all in the sense toward which I hope to twist this term. James Gleick has reported that a soliton is a newly perceived "indestructible kind of wave" (17). Describing the soliton as "part wave, part lump, part wrinkle in the fabric of matter and energy," Gleick explains that "a soliton can be a true, single wave—the name's origin is 'solitary wave'—or it can take the shape of some other stable, coherent structure in a complex system. A vortex whirling in place in a draining tub of water behaves like a soliton. The red spot of Jupiter, a permanent giant eddy that sits amid the turbulence of the planet's atmosphere, now appears to be a soliton on a vast scale" (17). Superconductivity theorist Robert Schrieffer describes the soliton as "a wrinkle of the medium itself," which is "self-focusing and it just doesn't dissipate."[10] Or, as Gleick summarizes it, "Solitons have an essential topological character, like a knot or a twist in a ribbon that can move from place to place but cannot be eliminated without untying the ribbon" (17).

It occurs to me that what Fredric Jameson calls the "cultural dominant" of postmodernism can be profitably reconceived as a kind of soliton, a cultural configuration that can be moved around but not eliminated. And so can the part played by computers in the creation of postmodern culture. For my purposes, solitons sound big and tough—the way computers used to sound, and it seems that for the technological wave I want to discuss, the rhetoric of futurism needs a metaphor more complicated and durable than "tsunami." My suggestion is that the solos—both human and electronic—of big, bad computer films represent an endangered paradigm, increasingly marginalized by the soliton of computer animation: as the computer has been increasingly "rehabilitated" within SF film narratives—the most dramatic example being the disparate characterizations of HAL in 2001 and 2010—the very nature of those narratives has been more and more changed by computer technology. HAL, the heavy in 2001, becomes a hero in 2010, and in a perfectly appropriate touch, Video Image, which did the greatly expanded computer graphics for 2010, named its own animation master-control package "HAL." In the narrative of culture, HAL got turned up rather than turned off.

In a sense, that filmic invasion we loved to worry about, whether of body snatchers or of flying saucers, from Mars or by the Daleks, has been ironically actualized in the making of SF film.[11] What turned out to be most invasive was information technology itself, and this too is something cyberpunk writing seems to have understood. Indeed, a great part of cyberpunk's savvy response to the hyperdensity of information in postmodern culture was a recognition of the radical implications of computer technology, a recognition, I suggest, that also entailed the inevitable end of cyberpunk itself as a formal literary genre.[12] As dense and as fast as cyberpunk prose was, it was no match for the computer imaging and video techniques so integral to its vision.

Rudy Rucker has explained the appeal of cyberpunk writing in terms of its informational density and complexity, and I think he's right, but events seem to have extended his logic from within the realm of literature to the status of literature in an increasingly electronic society.[13] Measured in terms of other fiction, perhaps particularly other science fiction, the speed and density (informational complexity) of cyberpunk writing is stunning. But measured against a highly textured film such as *Blade Runner*, even dynamite prose reveals that it cannot compete *in precisely these ways*. Nor does the conventionally cinematographic *Blade Runner* seem so fast and dense when compared with any of a number of computer-animated short features such as *Quest (A Long Ray's Journey into Night)*, by Sciulli, Arvo, and White, or Robert Abel's *Hi Fidelity*.[14] And it is this latter kind of visual complexity that seems more and more privileged in the soliton of postmodernism. Clearly, postmodern culture has begun to value information *as a commodity in its own right,* and nowhere is the commodity of information more apparent than in the phenomenon of computer animation. That a Cray supercomputer at 200 million floating-point instructions per second may take anywhere from three seconds to ten hours to generate one second of animated film, or that a particular animation such as *Quest* "took fifty-thousand hours of computing time to process," seems to be the contemporary info-centered analogue to the old public relations campaigns that announced a film as "two years in the making" or "costing X million dollars." Computer time replaces human time as our standard of measurement because computer time has become more meaningful to us than money. One consequence of this development seems to be that we are evolving a visual aesthetics of informational density that is often quite unrelated to an aesthetics of meaning, part of the move from mimetic and analog to digital models of narrative.

A striking example of the technological displacement of narrative from language to electronic display is the William Barg and Stuart Arbright video *Hip Tech and High Lit*.[15] Initially presented in June 1987 as part of a multimedia performance to an audience including both Sterling and Gibson, this impressive but by no means polished eighteen-minute video represents an obvious transition from cyberpunk writing to the electronic modes of information processing so prominent in the cyberpunk semblance. Largely a found-footage collage of stunning computer graphics, TV news tapes, and original videotape, the production establishes a compelling high-tech semblance without offering any sustained verbal narrative. Although the nonlinear progression of its beautiful and complicated images—some of fractal growth patterns—is further textured by a blend of voiceover readings from Gibson's and Sterling's fiction with electronic music composed by Arbright, this is clearly not a dramatic adaptation of cyberpunk fiction but an appropriately technological invocation of the technosphere so crucial to much of that writing.

Hip Tech and High Lit and a growing number of computer animation demonstrations even less tied to discursive narrative seem to create a sensory environment as compelling and as complicated as any conventional narrative that might be set within it—the *spectacle* of technology displacing stories about the impact of technology. I suspect most of us have seen other obvious examples of this kind of enactment of science fiction: the loping mechanoid tyrannosaurs of *Chromosaurus*; Pixar's *Luxo Jr.*, in which two amazingly realistic-looking extension lamps play a friendly and emotional game of ball; the iridescent aquatic life forms of Yoichiro Kawaguchi's *Growth: Mysterious Galaxy*; or Robert Abel's *High Fidelity* or *Sexy Robot*. And awaiting completion is the potential blowout, the most ambitious computer animation project of all, *The Works*, slowly being developed at the New York Institute of Technology. Tim Onosko explains of this full-length feature film with a cast of photorealistic robots: "'The Works' remains one of the most talked about, yet least-seen pieces of computer animation. . . . The present cast of robots includes the film's most amazing character, a giant automated ant (with an android who 'drives' it like an earth mover), and various worker machines involved in building a world in which computers rule (and from which humans, presumably, have been banished)" (274).

There you have it—full circle! From past depiction of humans fighting against computers and usually winning to the future computer-animated depiction of a world from which humans have been banished.

And my guess is that humans have been banished from this world for the very understandable reason that computer animation is not yet capable of rendering a realistic moving picture of a human face. But even that is changing.

In January 1991 Canadian computer filmmakers Nadia and Daniel Thalmann showed their six-minute *Rendezvous in Montreal*, demonstrating the face-rendering capabilities of a new software package called "The Human Factory."[16] Their film features computer-generated images of Marilyn Monroe and Humphrey Bogart, and marks a clear step forward in the computer animation of realistic human faces. (*Rendezvous in Montreal* also raises the science fictional prospect of new computer-generated films "starring" dead actors.)

Daniel Thalmann predicts that within five years we may see film scenes so realistic that no one will know they were made by computer. James Kristoff, president of Cranston/Csuri Productions—best known for its animation of network TV logos—echoes this belief: "It will get to the point where you won't know if you're looking at a real image or a computer generated image."[17] Predictions such as these, backed by the stunning visual evidence of recent developments in computer animation, confront those of us interested in thinking about SF film with a number of intriguing questions, ultimately having to do with the survival of the SF genre as a film category—and with the very survival of film as a competitive part of the entertainment media.

The technological erosion of the older, solo-centered filmic model of conflict between human and computer gives rise to a Velcrosive tangle of conceptual questions. The discourse of postmodernism has generated several rhetorics for the phenomenon of simulation, but much computer animation works toward the creation of virtual rather than simulated images.[18] Moreover, both kinds of images confront critics of SF film with new questions about supportable distinctions between science fictional and mundane epistemologies, and between science fiction and fantasy—all of which boils down to questioning our definition of the real. "If you don't know it's computer generated," argued Digital Effect's John Whitney, Jr., in a recent TV special, "it will be real to you. And if you do know it's computer generated and it looks as all attributes of reality and you can't look at it enough to find out what's wrong with it—you can't tear it down, you can't find its breakdown point—your reaction to it in that case might even be one of greater excitement." Such an image, pointed out my colleague Cheryl Herr, would be effectively nondeconstructible: deconstructing a virtual image to expose its generating algorithms would be roughly akin to deconstructing an ice cube to get to the water.

What most intrigues me about the soliton of computer imaging is that it may eventually resolve one of the central conflicts (not quite armed, but often heated) in the discussion of SF film: the competing claims about the virtues and shortcomings of writing and film as SF media. The complaint that the glitzy tail of special effects has more and more come to wag the shaggy dog of SF film seems justifiable to me, but *transitional*, as technology has already begun to carry special effects beyond *trickery* and into *discovery*. Moreover, developments in computer imaging seem likely to offer a true synthesis for the long-standing conflict between the quite different epistemologies of SF film and SF writing. Among other things, the common criticism that filmmakers don't know anything about science or science fiction begins to crumble when computer "filmmakers" are people like JPL's James F. Blinn, Ohio State's Charles Csuri, or PIXAR's Loren Carpenter.

Those familiar and somewhat petrified complaints have long bogged down the rigorous criticism of SF film and actually obscure our understanding of the genre. Here, one of Brand's *Media Lab* aphorisms really stays with me: "Once a new technology rolls over you, if you're not part of the steamroller, you're part of the road" (9). Solitons, steamrollers, what have you—it seems clear to me that the job of SF film criticism in the next few years is to be *on* rather than *under* that steamroller.

Notes

I express my great appreciation to the Center for Advanced Studies, University of Iowa, for providing the environment in which this paper could be wrestled into existence and the services which made that wrestling a scholar's delight.

1. From the chiasmic structure of this sentence to its self-reflexive thesis, my debt to Garrett Stewart's "The 'Videology' of Science Fiction" must be clear. However, my belief is that the phenomenon so brilliantly limned by Stewart— that "science fiction in the cinema often turns out to be, turns round to be, the

fictional or fictive science of the cinema itself" (159)—may now be seen as a stage in the development of film technology as well as a theme in SF film. My concern is with the next stage in that development.

2. I am indebted to Steve Jones, Department of Journalism, University of Wisconsin, Eau Claire, for this term. His paper, "Cohesive but Not Coherent: Music Videos, Narrative and Culture," presented at the 1988 Popular Culture Association (PCA) Conference, schematizes narrative as mimetic, analog, and digital, specifying that in digital narrative, a nonlinear "mosaic of fragments," "information is presented in discrete steps, bearing no resemblance to what it communicates." Jones applies this term specifically to television narratives, primarily music videos, but I feel it captures a larger postmodern trajectory across the range of media.

3. Of course, Sobchack does extend the implications of this appropriating of technology to the future of SF film, tying it to her argument that "recent SF films have been in the process of celebrating their own generic destruction" (304). Baudrillard's concern goes further still, suggesting that the concept of media has itself disappeared: "There is no longer any medium in the literal sense; it is now intangible, diffuse and diffracted in the real, and it can no longer even be said that the latter is distorted by it" (*Simulations*, 54).

4. Sherry McKenna, Digital Effect's executive producer, flatly calls digital imaging "the future of filmmaking" ("Cray," 27), but her possibly biased view is supported by virtually everyone who writes about computer animation. A. K. Dewdney also envisioned that future in his "Computer Recreations" in the December 1986 *Scientific American*, as did Ivars Peterson in a *Science News* article in May 1987.

5. Brand, *Media Lab*, p. 5.

6. The fact that Max was a simulacrum of a virtual image which actor Matt Frewer made up and videotaped to appear to be a computer-generated talking head complicates my point here. The technology for generating a Max-like talking head has been demonstrated by the New York Institute of Technology Computer Graphics Laboratory's figure, "User Friendly," but the technology would have been both too expensive and too time-intensive for the ABC series. Arthur Kroker presents the idea of Max Headroom as a sign of apocalypse rather than of the future, the emblem of "Panic TV":

This is Max Headroom as a harbinger of the post-bourgeois individual of estheticized liberalism who actually vanishes into the simulacra of the information system, whose face can be digitalized and fractalized by computer imaging because Max is living out a panic conspiracy in TV as the real world, and whose moods are perfectly postmodern because they alternate between kitsch and dread, between the ecstasy of catastrophe and the terror of the simulacra. Max Headroom, then, is the first citizen of the end of the world. (*Invaders*, 18–19)

7. Baudrillard, "Ecstasy," p. 128.
8. Demos describes one possible configuration for such a system:

> The real-time simulation channel would be a direct feed from a supercomputer like the Cray-1 running twenty-four hours a day and available on a subscription basis. So you just tune in and connect your home computer to the central computer by phone modem and you become a part of the movie. The Image Utility presents the generic possibilities and you make variations based on your own personality and abilities. You control things, create a custom movie that will never be seen by anyone else. (Goodman, 180)

> Brand details a number of MIT Media Lab projects already pursuing this interactive goal, and also reports Negroponte's belief that in twenty years TVs will not be linked to computers by cable but will have "50 megabytes of random-access memory and run at 40 to MIPS," basically *making them equivalent to today's Cray computers*" (78).

9. Big, bad computer films also reveal another nostalgic simplification of conflict models common to much SF film and literature alike: the longing for "decisive" battles. Herman Rapaport has detailed the way in which Vietnam exposed the theoretical weakness of American military strategy which insisted on this model, arguing in effect that North Vietnamese strategy rendered it obsolete. SF narratives are driven by imperatives quite different from those guiding the conceptualization of "real" warfare, but the longing for "showdowns" in SF conflict models may also represent a paradigm in need of updating.
10. Gleick, "Indestructible Wave," p. 17.
11. The perfect emblem for this process is *Earth versus the Flying Saucers*, a music video made by San Francisco's legendary underground rock group the Residents. The two-and-a-half-minute video appropriates footage from the better-known 1956 film of that title, then digitizes it, colorizes it, and adds computer-animated background designs and a minimalist soundtrack. The result is a manically compressed version of the original film, stripped of all but the roughest visual story line but packed with new and interesting kinds of information.
12. In "Bet on It: Cyber/video/punk/performance," *Mississippi Review* 16 (Sum-

mer 1988): 245–51, I try to explain this passing as healthy evolution rather than apocalypse, a sign of the movement's conceptual integrity.
13. Rucker's "What Is Cyberpunk" offers the best quick introduction to the movement that I've come across.
14. Videotapes, such as "Computer Magic," that showcase computer animation potential are the best way to experience the field in a hurry, but a couple of hours watching network TV and commercials will provide a pretty good index to current capability.
15. Bruce Sterling told me about this tape, and Bill Barg and Stuart Arbright generously sent me a copy of it.
16. Reported by Richard Reynolds on National Public Radio, January 11, 1988. The Thalmanns had previously worked with the MIRA system of figure animation at the University of Montreal.
17. Kristoff's remarks are taken from a 1987 PBS special on computer animation.
18. I am indebted to Judith Kerman for focusing my interest in the status of virtual space on computer graphics. Her paper "Toward a Phenomenology of the Virtual" and the accompanying videotape presentation at the 1988 PCA Conference helped me assemble a number of disparate concerns. Arthur Kroker claims that computer animation has "rendered obsolescent" Baudrillard's focus in *Simulations* "by the actual transformation of the simulacrum with its hyperreality effects into its opposite: a *virtual* technology mediated with designer bodies processed through computerized imaging-systems" (*Postmodern Scene*, 15).

Works Consulted

Baudrillard, Jean. "The Ecstasy of Communication." In *The Anti-Aesthetic: Essays on Postmodern Culture*, ed. Hal Foster. Port Townsend, Wash.: Bay Press, 1983, pp. 126–34.

———. *Simulations*. New York: Semiotext(e), 1983.

———. "The Year 2000 Has Already Happened." In *Body Invaders: Panic Sex in America*, ed. Arthur Kroker and Marilouise Kroker. New York: St. Martin's Press, 1987, pp. 35–44.

Brand, Stewart. *The Media Lab: Inventing the Future at MIT*. New York: Viking Press, 1987.

Carpenter, Loren. "Faster Rendering Drives Higher Quality." *Computer Graphics World* (July 1987): 27–28.

Dewdney, A. K. "Computer Recreations." *Scientific American* 255 (December 1986): 14–20.
Emmett, Arlelle. "Universal Studios' Computer Graphics." *Computer Graphics World* (February 1986): 26–32.
Falk, Lorne, and Barbara Fischer, eds. *The Event Horizon: Essays on Hope, Sexuality, Social Space & Media(tion) in Art*. Toronto: Coach House, 1987.
Gleick, James. *Chaos: Making a New Science*. New York: Viking Press, 1987.
———. "Indestructible Wave May Hold Key to Superconductors." *New York Times*, December 15, 1987.
Goodman, Cynthia. *Digital Visions: Computers and Art*. New York: Harry N. Abrams, 1987.
Hayles, N. Katherine. *Chaos Bound: Orderly Disorder in Contemporary Literature and Science*. Ithaca, N.Y.: Cornell University Press, forthcoming.
Horgan, John. "Faces, Couches, Cats . . ." *Scientific American* 257 (November 1987): 34–38.
Jankel, Annabel, and Rocky Morton. *Creative Computer Graphics*. New York: Cambridge University Press, 1984.
Jones, Steve. "Cohesive but Not Coherent: Music Videos, Narrative and Culture." Paper presented at the 1988 Popular Culture Association Conference.
Kerman, Judith B. "Notes Toward a Phenomenology of the Virtual: Perceptual Aspects of SF Computer Entities. Paper presented at the 1988 Popular Culture Association Conference.
Kroker, Arthur, and David Cook, eds. *The Postmodern Scene: Excremental Culture and Hyper-Aesthetics*. New York: St. Martin's Press, 1986.
Kroker, Arthur, and Marilouise Kroker, eds. *Body Invaders: Panic Sex in America*. New York: St. Martin's Press, 1987.
Landon, Brooks. "Cyberpunk: Future So Bright They Gotta Wear Shades." *Cinefantastique* 18 (December 1987): 27–31.
———. "Max Headroom." *Cinefantastique* 18 (December 1987): 29, 58.
"Micro-based Graphics System Stars in 2010." *Design News*, February 18, 1985.
Miller, Gavin, and David Ross. "Animation Focus." *Computer Graphics World* (July 1987): 59–60.
Myers, Edith. "Cray Conquers H'Wood." *Datamation* 30 (July 1, 1984): 24–32.
———. "Oscar Computes." *Datamation* 32 (April 15, 1986): 68–72.
Onosko, Tim. "Mathemagicians: Computer Moviemakers of the 1980s and Beyond." In *Omni's Screen Flights/Screen Fantasies: The Future According to Science Fiction Cinema*, ed. Danny Peary. Garden City, N.Y.: Dolphin, 1984, pp. 268–77.

Peled, Abraham. "The Next Computer Revolution." *Scientific American* 257 (October 1987): 57–64.
Penley, Constance. "Time Travel, Primal Scene, and the Critical Dystopia." *Camera Obscura* 15 (Fall 1986): 67–84.
Peterson, Ivars. "Packing It In: Fractals Play an Important Role in Image Compression." *Science News* 131 (May 2, 1987): 283–85.
Rapaport, Herman. "Vietnam: The Thousand Plateaus." In *The 60s Without Apology*, ed. Sohnya Sayres. Minneapolis: University of Minnesota Press, 1984, pp. 137–47.
Sobchack, Vivian. *Screening Space: The American Science Fiction Film.* 2d ed. New York: Ungar, 1987.
Stewart, Garrett. "The 'Videology' of Science Fiction." In *Shadows of the Magic Lamp*, ed. George Slusser and Eric S. Rabkin. Carbondale: Southern Illinois University Press, 1985, pp. 159–207.
Tyler, W. Mike. "3-D Images for the Film Industry." *Computer Graphics World* (July 1984): 63–64.

Contributors

ROSEMARIE ARBUR is a professor of English at Lehigh University. She has written extensively on women authors and women characters in science fiction and fantasy.

MARTHA A. BARTTER teaches English at Ohio State University at Marion.

REGINALD BRETNOR is a science-fiction writer and editor; he has also published articles on military matters and is the author of *Decisive Warfare: A Study in Military Theory* (Stackpole, 1969).

DAVID CLAYTON is a visiting assistant professor in comparative literature at the University of California, Riverside.

SCOTT DALRYMPLE earned his M.A. in English and his M.B.A. from the University of Buffalo. He is now a market research analyst at National Fuel Gas Corporation.

LAURENCE DAVIES is a research associate professor of comparative literature at Dartmouth College. He is coauthor of *Cunninghame Graham: A Critical Biography* and coeditor of *The Collected Letters of Joseph Conrad*.

PETER FITTING is an associate professor of French at the University of Toronto. He has a longtime interest in science fiction and film.

JOE HALDEMAN is a science-fiction writer who has won five Hugo and Nebula awards, including the 1991 award for the novella *The Hemingway Hoax*. He divides his time between Florida and Massachusetts, where he and his wife, Gay, teach at MIT.

BROOKS LANDON is a professor of English at the University of Iowa.

LOUIS PEDROTTI is an emeritus professor of Russian at the University of California, Riverside. He has just completed a translation of Osip Senkovsky's *Fantastic Journeys of Baron Brambeus*.

ERIC S. RABKIN is a professor of English at the University of Michigan and has published widely on science fiction and fantasy.

Contributors

PAULA REA RADISICH is an associate professor of art history at Whittier College. She has published numerous articles on eighteenth-century art and is working on a book about the work of Hubert Robert.

GEORGE SLUSSER is a professor of comparative literature at the University of California, Riverside, and director of the Eaton Program.

ARTHUR CAMPBELL TURNER is a professor of political science at the University of California, Riverside, the campus he helped found. He has published extensively on international relations and on the Middle East.

GARY WESTFAHL has published articles on science fiction in *Extrapolation, Foundation,* the *Los Angeles Times, Monad, Science Fiction Eye,* and *Science Fiction Studies.*

Index

Abel, Robert, 200, 201; *Hi Fidelity*, 200; *Sexy Robot*, 201
Aelita (A. Tolstoy), 56
"After Armageddon" (Flagg), 156
Alas, Babylon (Frank), 156, 158
Aldiss, Brian, 18, 42; *Galactic Empires*, 18
Alien (Scott), 3
Aliens, 128
All My Sins Remembered (Haldeman), 102
Alphaville (Godard), 196, 198
America Fallen (Walker), 65
Anderson, Poul, 29; *High Crusade*, 29
Andromeda: A Space Age Tale (Efremov), 56
"And Then There Were None" (Russell), 35
Angel of the Revolution, The (Griffith), 64, 67
"Animal Origin of Sea Sand, The" (Senkovsky), 51
Ant Farm, 129; *Cadillac Ranch*, 129
Anthony, Susan B., 84
Anticipations (Wells), 75
Arbright, Stuart, 201; *Hip Tech and High Lit*, 201
Arithmetic (Senkovsky), 51
Arslan (Engh), 9, 157–59, 165–67
Asimov, Isaac, 22, 134; *Gods Themselves, The*, 22
Astaire, Fred, 177, 178

Austen, Jane, 139
Autocracy of Mr. Parham: His Remarkable Adventures in the Changing World, The (Wells), 76

Babel-17 (Delany), 133
Ballard, J. G., 122, 130, 131; *Burning World*, 122; *Drought, The*, 122; *Drowned World, The*, 122; *Empire of the Sun*, 130
Band of the Hand, The, 183
Barg, William, 201; *Hip Tech and High Lit*, 201
Barjavel, René, 156; *Ravage*, 156
Barnes, Djuna, 140; *Nightwood*, 140
Barthes, Roland, 124; *Critical Essays*, 124
Baruch, Bernard, 13
Barzini, Luigi, 63
Basic Instinct (Verhoeven), 128
Battle of Dorking, The (Chesney), 60
Battle Truck, 115
Baudrillard, Jean, 204
Bear, Greg, 22; *Blood Music*, 22
Beast from 20,000 Fathoms, The (Honda), 122
Beer, William, 170
Benét, Stephen Vincent, 156; "Place of the Gods, The," 156
Benford, Gregory, 55; *Heart of the Comet*, 55
Bennett, Arnold, 70

Berlin Diaries, 1940–1945
    (Vassiltchikov), 78
Beyond This Horizon (Heinlein), 191
Beyond Thunderdome (Miller), 114,
    116, 121, 124–26, 128
Biggle, Lloyd, 18; *Monument*, 18
Binet, Louis, 105–8; "Elephant Man,"
    105; *La Découverte australe*,
    105, 106
Biskind, Peter, 128
Black Glass (Shirley), 195
Blackwood's Magazine, 62
Blade Runner (Scott), 195, 200
Blinn, James F., 203
Blood Music (Bear), 22
Bogart, Humphrey, 202
Bonhoeffer, Dietrich, 162
Borden, Lizzie, 127; *Born in
    Flames*, 127
Born in Flames (Borden), 127
Bourjaily, Vance, 102; *Confessions of a
    Spent Youth*, 102
Boy and His Dog, A, 117, 130
Brackett, Leigh, 156, 157; *Long
    Tomorrow, The*, 156, 157
Bradbury, Ray, 2, 156; *Fahrenheit 451*,
    156, 157; *Martian Chronicles*, 2
Bradley, Marion Zimmer, 84
Brambeus, Baron, 6, 9, 49, 51, 52,
    54, 55
Brand, Stewart, 194, 203; *Media Lab:
    Inventing the Future at MIT,
    The*, 194
Brecht, Bertold, 138
Brians, Paul, 117; *Nuclear Holocausts:
    Atomic War in Fiction,
    1895–1984*, 117
Brin, David, 1, 8, 22, 55, 167; *Heart of
    the Comet*, 55; *Postman, The*, 167;
    Startide Rising, 18
Bronson, Charles, 125
Brothers, The (Wells), 77

Brothers Karamazov, The
    (Dostoevsky), 56
Bruce and the Shaolin Kung Fu, 179
Bruckner, Pascal, 170; *Tears of the
    White Man: Compassion as
    Contempt, The*, 170
Brynner, Yul, 130
Buddenbrooks (Mann), 73
Bug Jack Barron (Spinrad), 44, 45
Bulgakov, Mikhail, 56; *Fatal Eggs,
    The*, 56
Bulgarin, Faddey, 55
Burning World (Ballard), 122
Burroughs, Edgar Rice, 18, 117;
    Princess of Mars, A, 18

Cadillac Ranch (Ant Farm), 129
Cage, John, 138
Cahiers du cinéma, 176
Callenbach, Ernest, 131; *Ecotopia*, 131
Calvary and Last Judgment Diptych
    (H. & J. Van Eyck), 111
Cameron, James, 114; *Terminator,
    The*, 8, 114, 120, 122–124, 126, 196
Campbell, Horace, 186, 187; *Rasta and
    Resistance*, 186
Campbell, John W., Jr., 40–42,
    134, 141
Canetti, Elias, 140; *Die Blendung*, 140
Canticle for Leibowitz, A (Miller),
    140, 156
Capek, Karel, 56; *War with the Newts,
    The*, 56
Card, Orson Scott, 4, 19, 20, 23;
    Ender's Game, 19, 23
Carpenter, Loren, 203
Chandler, Raymond, 44
Charnas, Suzy McKee, 157, 165, 167;
    Motherlines, 157, 167; *Walk to the
    End of the World*, 157
Cheh, Chang, 178
Chernyshevsky, Nikolai, 50

Chesney, George Tomkyns, 60, 65; *Battle of Dorking, The*, 60
"Chic Bleak in Fantasy Fiction" (Franklin), 121
Childers, Erskine, 72; *Riddle of the Sands, The*, 72
Chinese Connection, The, 177, 178
Christine (King), 130
Christopher, John, 128; *Death of Grass, The*, 128
Cimino, Michael, 183; *Deer Hunter, The*, 183
City of Man, The (Wagar), 70
Clarke, Arthur C., 115; *2001: A Space Odyssey*, 115, 133, 196, 198, 199; *2010*, 199
Clarke, I. F., 60, 61
Clarkson, Helen, 156; *Last Day, The*, 156
Clement, Hal, 41
Close Encounters of the Third Kind, 115
"Cohesive but Not Coherent: Music Videos, Narrative and Culture" (Jones), 204
"Colloquy of Monos and Una, The" (Poe), 140
Coming Race, The (Lytton), 17
Common Sense of World Peace, The (Wells), 72
Conduct of War, The (Fuller), 33
Confessions of a Spent Youth (Bourjaily), 102
Connecticut Yankee in King Arthur's Court, A (Twain), 16
Conquered Place, The (Shafer), 156, 157
Convoy, 115
Crane, Stephen, 13, 15, 63; *Red Badge of Courage, The*, 13
Craven, Wes, 175; *Serpent and the Rainbow, The*, 175

Critical Essays (Barthes), 124
Csuri, Charles, 203
Cyrano de Bergerac (Rostand), 55

Damnation Alley, 115, 117, 130
Danse Macabre (King), 149
Davis, Richard Harding, 63
Davy (Pangborn), 156
Day After, The, 117
Day of the Locust, The (Nathanael West), 140
Dead Zone, The (King), 8, 148, 150, 152
Death of Grass, The (Christopher), 128
Death Race, 115
de Bloch, Jean, 72; *La Guerre*, 72
Deer Hunter, The (Cimino), 183
Defoe, Daniel, 66; *Journal of the Plague Year*, 66
Delany, Samuel R., 8, 9, 132, 134–37, 187, 188, 191; *Babel-17*, 133; *Dhalgren*, 8, 132–39, 142, 143; *Heavenly Breakfast*, 134; *Nova*, 133, 134, 187, 188; *Triton*, 136
Deleuze, Gilles, 143, 144; *Logique du sens*, 143, 144
Demon Seed, The, 196, 198
DePalma, Brian, 182; *Scarface*, 182
Der Mann ohne Eigenschaften (Musil), 140
Derrida, Jacques, 142, 174, 175
de Tarde, Gabriel, 67; *Underground Man*, 67
Dewdney, A. K., 204
Dhalgren (Delany), 8, 132–39, 142, 143
Dick, Philip K., 21, 42, 123; "Second Variety," 21; *Time Out of Joint*, 123
Dickens, Charles, 139
Dictionary of Military Terms (Farrow), 31
Die Blendung (Canetti), 140

Disch, Thomas M., 21; *Genocides, The*, 21
Dispossessed, The (Le Guin), 83
Donen, Stanley, 178
Doom of the Great City, The (Hay), 66
Door into Ocean, A (Slonczewski), 6, 82–84, 167
Dostoevsky, Fyodor, 56, 58; *Brothers Karamazov, The*, 56
Douhet, Giulio, 32
Dr. Strangelove (Kubrick), 117
Drake, David, 2, 3
"Dream of Armageddon, A" (Wells), 75
Drought, The (Ballard), 122
Drowned World, The (Ballard), 122
Druillet, Philippe, 7, 103, 104, 109–12; *La Nuit*, 7, 103, 109–11
Druzhinin, Nikolai, 50
Duchamp, Marcel, 138
Duel, 130
"Dukes of Hazard," 115
Dürrenmatt, Friedrich, 68; *Physicists, The*, 68
Dying Earth, The (Vance), 117

Earth versus the Flying Saucers (Residents), 205
Eastwood, Clint, 120, 121, 125
Ecotopia (Callenbach), 131
Edwards, Jonathan, 147; "Sinners in the Hands of an Angry God," 147
Efremov, Ivan, 56; *Andromeda: A Space Age Tale*, 56
"Electrical Sounds" (Senkovsky), 51
"Elephant Man" (Binet), 105
Elgin, Suzette Haden, 6, 88–90; *Judas Rose*, 89; *Native Tongue*, 6, 88, 89
Ellison, Harlan, 197, 198; "I Have No Mouth and I Must Scream," 197
Emergence (Palmer), 156

Empire of the Sun (Ballard), 130
Encyclopaedia of Religion and Ethics (Hastings), 139
Encyclopedia Britannica, 31
Ender's Game (Card), 19, 23
Engh, M. J., 9, 157, 165, 167–69; *Arslan*, 9, 157–59, 165–67
Erlich, Richard D., 130
Escape from New York (Carpenter), 130, 195
Essay On Liberation, An (Marcuse), 118
Experimental Researches (Faraday), 33
Experiment in Autobiography (Wells), 71
Exterminators of the Year 3000, 117

Fahrenheit 451 (Bradbury), 156, 157
Fail-Safe, 117
Fantastic Journeys of Baron Brambeus, The (Senkovsky), 6, 49, 51, 54
Faraday, Michael, 33; *Experimental Researches*, 33
Farewell to Arms, A (Hemingway), 20
Farrar, Dean, 61
Farrow, Edward, 31; *Dictionary of Military Terms*, 31
Fatal Eggs, The (Bulgakov), 56
Fate of the Earth, The (Schell), 156
Female Man (Russ), 84, 86, 90, 127, 131
Feminine Mystique (Friedan), 89
Fiedler, Leslie, 2
"Final War, The" (Spohr), 155
Finnegans Wake (Joyce), 138
Fists of Fury, 177
Five Masters of Death, 178
Flagg, Francis, 156; "After Armageddon," 156
Flesh Gordon, 115
Floor Games (Wells), 72
Forbidden Planet, 117

Index

Forbin Project, The, 196, 198
Forever War, The (Haldeman), 7, 19, 102
Forward, Robert L., 3
Foundations of the Science of War (Fuller), 28
Four-Gated City, The (Lessing), 140
Frank, Jerome D., 153
Frank, Pat, 156; *Alas, Babylon*, 156, 158; *Sanity and Survival in the Nuclear Age*, 153
Frankenstein (Shelley), 3
Franklin, Bruce, 121, 128; "Chic Bleak in Fantasy Fiction," 121
French Connection, The (Friedkin), 115
Freud, Sigmund, 68
Friday the 13th, 152
Friedan, Betty, 89; *Feminine Mystique*, 89
Friedkin, William, 115; *French Connection, The* (Friedkin), 115; *To Live and Die in LA*, 115
Fry, Edward, 35, 36, 43
Frye, Northrup, 130
Fuller, J. F. C., 28, 33; *Conduct of War, The*, 33; *Foundations of the Science of War*, 28; *Reformation of War, The*, 28
Futureworld, 196
Futurological Congress (Lem), 56, 136

Galactic Empires (Aldiss), 18
Galbraith, David, 127
Galsworthy, John, 70
Garnett, Edward, 61
Garvey, Marcus, 179
Gawron, Jean Mark, 138
Gearhart, Sally, 131; *Wanderground*, 131 (n. 16)
"General Deductions on the Essence of Galvanic Currents, of Electrical and Chemical Affinities, Crystallization, Light, Heat, Etc." (Senkovsky), 51
Genocides, The (Disch), 21
Gernsback, Hugo, 5, 40, 42, 43, 93; *Ralph 124C 41+: A Romance of the Year 2660*, 40
Ghandi, Mahatma, 84
Gibson, William, 15, 195; *Macrochip*, 195; *Neuromancer*, 15, 22, 194
Gilgamesh, 2, 3
Gleick, James, 199
Glory Road (Heinlein), 3
Godard, Jean-Luc, 198; *Alphaville*, 196, 198
Gods Themselves, The (Asimov), 22
Godzilla (Honda), 122
Gogol, Nikolay, 50
Goodman, Paul, 167
Gravity's Rainbow (Pynchon), 140
Great War in England in 1897, The (Le Queux), 64
Green, Martin, 129
Green Pastures (Wells), 74
Griffith, George, 64, 67; *Angel of the Revolution, The*, 64, 67; *Outlaws of the Air, The*, 67
Growth: Mysterious Galaxy (Kawaguchi), 201
Gulliver's Travels (Swift), 55

H. G. Wells (Murray), 72
H. G. Wells and Modern Science Fiction (Philmus & Suvin), 72
H. G. Wells and the World State (Wagar), 70
H. G. Wells: Aspects of a Life (Anthony West), 71
H. G. Wells in Love (Wells), 71
H. G. Wells: Journalism and Prophecy (Wagar), 71

H. G. Wells under Revision
(Parrinder), 72
Haggard, H. Rider, 117
Haldeman, Joe, 4, 7, 19; *All My Sins Remembered*, 102; *Forever War, The*, 7, 19, 102; *War Year*, 102; *Worlds and Worlds Apart*, 102
Hall, Peter C., 130
Halloween (Carpenter), 152
Hard to Be a God (A. & B. Strugatsky), 56
Hardy, Phil, 128
Harmsworth, Alfred, 65
Hastings, James, 139; *Encyclopaedia of Religion and Ethics*, 139
Have Space Suit, Will Travel (Heinlein), 3
Hawks, Howard, 182; *Scarface*, 182
Hay, William DeLisle, 66; *Doom of the Great City, The*, 66
Heart of the Comet (Benford & Brin), 55
Heavenly Breakfast (Delany), 134
Hefferline, Ralph, 167
Heinlein, Robert A., 2, 4, 5, 7, 9, 19, 22, 23, 40–42, 64, 133, 134; *Glory Road*, 3; *Have Space Suit, Will Travel*, 3; *Job: A Comedy of Justice*, 42; *Moon Is a Harsh Mistress, The*, 23; "Solution Unsatisfactory," 40, 41; *Starship Troopers*, 2, 7, 19; *Stranger in a Strange Land*, 133
Heiro's Journey (Lanier), 156
Heller, Joseph, 15, 21
Hemingway, Ernest, 20; *Farewell to Arms, A*, 20
Herr, Cheryl, 202
Hi Fidelity (Abel), 200
High Crusade (Anderson), 29
High Fidelity (Sciuli, Arvo & White), 201
Hilgartner, C. A., 167

Hip Tech and High Lit (Arbright & Barg), 201
Hoban, Russell, 117; *Riddley Walker*, 117
Hobbes, Thomas, 12, 13, 19, 141
Hoffmann, E. T. A., 191
Holberg, Ludvig, 55; *Journey of Niels Klim to the World Underground, The*, 55
"Hole in the Moon, The" (M. St. Clair), 157
Holy Terror, The (Wells), 77
Homer, 9; *Iliad, The*, 1, 14
Honda, Inoshiro, 122; *Godzilla*, 122
Hopkins, Gerard Manley, 94
Horace, 12, 186, 187
Hudson, W. H., 61
Human Slaughter-House, The (Lamszus), 59

"I Have No Mouth and I Must Scream" (Ellison), 197
"Imagination of Disaster" (Sontag), 129 (n. 8)
Ing, Dean, 156; *Pulling Through*, 156
In the Days of the Comet (Wells), 6, 55, 74, 75
Invasion of the Body Snatchers, 122
Invincible, The (Lem), 56
Invisible Man, The (Wells), 3
Island of Dr. Moreau, The (Wells), 71
Is War Now Impossible? (Wells), 72

Jameson, Fredric, 129, 174, 175, 199; *Political Unconscious, The*, 174
Jane, Fred T., 64; *Violet Flame*, 64
Job: A Comedy of Justice (Heinlein), 42
"Joggin'" (Macgregor), 180
Jones, D. F., 198
Jones, Grace, 126
Jones, Steve, 204; "Cohesive but Not

Coherent: Music Videos, Narrative and Culture," 204
Journal of the Plague Year (Defoe), 66
Journey of Niels Klim to the World Underground, The (Holberg), 55
Journey to the Center of the Earth, A (Verne), 55
Joyce, James, 138; *Finnegans Wake*, 138
Judas Rose, The (Elgin), 89

Kaminsky, Stuart, 178
Kawaguchi, Yoichiro, 201; *Growth: Mysterious Galaxy*, 201
Kelly, Gene, 177
Kerman, Judith, 206; "Toward a Phenomenology of the Virtual," 206 (n. 18)
Kermode, Frank, 62
Killdozer, 130
King, Martin Luther, Jr., 84
King, Stephen, 8, 16, 84, 130, 145, 148, 150, 151; *Christine*, 130; *Danse Macabre*, 149; *Dead Zone, The*, 8, 148, 150, 152; *Night Shift*, 145; *Shining, The*, 150
Kornbluth, C. M., 156, 157; *Not This August*, 156, 157
Korzybski, Alfred, 169; *Manhood of Humanity*, 169 (n. 16)
Kristoff, James, 202
Kroker, Arthur, 204
Kubrick, Stanley, 115, 133; *Dr. Strangelove*, 117; *Shining, The*, 150
Kunetka, James, 155; *Warday*, 155
Kurosawa, Akira, 130; *Yojimbo*, 130
Kyukhelbeker, Vilgelm, 55

La Découverte australe par un Homme-volant ou le Dédale français: nouvelle très-philosophique (Restif de la Bretonne), 105, 106

"Lady or the Tiger, The" (Stockton), 42
La Guerre (de Bloch), 72
Lamszus, Wilhelm, 59; *Human Slaughter-House, The*, 59
"Land Ironclads, The" (Wells), 75
Lange, Oliver, 156; *Vandenberg*, 156
Lanier, Sterling, 156; *Heiro's Journey*, 156
La Nuit (Druillet), 7, 103, 109–11
Last Day, The (Clarkson), 156
"Last Flight of Dr. Ain, The" (Tiptree), 169 (n. 19)
Last Man, The (Shelley), 140
"Latest Discoveries of Faraday, The" (Senkovsky), 51
le Carré, John, 13
Lee, Bruce, 9, 176, 179, 181, 188, 191
Left Hand of Darkness, The (Le Guin), 18
Le Guin, Ursula K., 18, 83; *Dispossessed, The*, 83; *Left Hand of Darkness, The*, 18
Leinster, Murray, 156; "Power Planet, The," 156
Lem, Stanislaw, 56, 135; *Futurological Congress*, 56, 136; *Invincible, The*, 56; *Solaris*, 56
Leone, Sergio, 130
Le Queux, William, 64, 65; *Great War in England in 1897, The*, 64; *Siege of Portsmouth*, 65
Lermontov, Mikhail, 49
Lessing, Doris, 140; *Four-Gated City, The*, 140
Level 7 (Roshwald), 156
Library for Reading, The (Senkovsky), 50, 51
Lifton, Robert Jay, 147
Little Wars (Wells), 72, 74
Logique du sens (Deleuze), 143 (n. 5), 144 (n. 7)

Long Tomorrow, The (Brackett), 156, 157
Looker (Crichton), 195
Lorenz, Konrad, 18; *On Aggression*, 18
Lucifer's Hammer (Niven & Pournelle), 55
Lytton, Edward Bulwer, 17; *Coming Race, The*, 17

McCarthy, Mary, 140
McCormak, Thelma, 129
McEvoy, Seth, 134
Macgregor, Freddy, 180; "Joggin'," 180
McKenna, Sherry, 204
Mackenzie, Jeanne, 71, 74; *Time Traveller, The*, 71
McKenzie, John, 14
Mackenzie, Norman, 71, 74; *Time Traveller, The*, 71
McLuhan, Marshall, 185
Macrochip (Gibson & Shirley), 195
Mad Max (G. Miller), 114, 116, 124, 128
Making of Americans, The (Stein), 134
Manchester Sunday Chronicle, 61
Manhood of Humanity (Korzybski), 169 (n. 16)
Mann, Thomas, 73; *Buddenbrooks*, 73
Mardi (Melville), 134
Marley, Bob, 181, 186–88, 191
Marquand, J. P., 70
Martian Chronicles (Bradbury), 2
"Max Headroom," 195, 197
Media Lab: Inventing the Future at MIT, The (Brand), 194
Melville, Herman, 134; *Mardi*, 134
Menzies, William, 131
Merritt, A. A., 117
"Meteorites and the Earth's Internal Fire" (Senkovsky), 51
Micromégas (Voltaire), 55

Mikeria, the Nile Lily (Senkovsky), 51
Military Dictionary, 31
Military Encyclopedia, 31
Millennium (Varley), 22
Miller, George, 114, 127; *Beyond Thunderdome*, 114, 116, 121, 124–26, 128; *Mad Max*, 114, 116, 124, 128; *Road Warrior*, 114–17, 120, 122, 128
Miller, Walter M., Jr., 140, 156; *Canticle for Leibowitz, A*, 140, 156
Mogel, Leonard, 194
Monday Begins on Saturday (A. & B. Strugatsky), 56
Monument (Biggle), 18
Moon Is a Harsh Mistress, The (Heinlein), 23
Morgenthau, Hans, 146
Morris, William, 2
Moscovici, Serge, 174
Motherlines (Charnas), 157, 167
Motorization of American Cities, The (D. St. Clair), 129 (n.9)
Murray, Brian, 72; *H. G. Wells*, 72
Musil, Robert, 140; *Der Mann ohne Eigenschaften*, 140

National Enquirer, The, 137
Native Tongue (Elgin), 6, 88, 89
Negroponte, Nicholas, 195
Neuromancer (Gibson), 15, 22, 194
New Barbarians, The, 117
New Machiavelli, The (Wells), 75
Night Shift (King), 145
Nightwood (Barnes), 140
Niven, Larry, 55; *Lucifer's Hammer*, 55
No Blade of Grass, 128
Nordau, Max, 62
Norris, Chuck, 184
Not This August (Kornbluth), 156, 157
Nova (Delany), 133, 134, 187, 188

Nuclear Holocausts: Atomic War in Fiction, 1895–1984 (Brian), 117

Odoevsky, Vladimir, 55, 56; *Year 4338 A.D., The*, 56
Olander, Joseph, 129
On Aggression (Lorenz), 18
Onosko, Tim, 195, 201
On the Beach, 117
Orwell, George, 71
Outlaws of the Air, The (Griffith), 67
Outline of History, The (Wells), 70
Overdrawn at the Memory Bank, 197

Palmer, David, 156; *Emergence*, 156
Pangborn, Edgar, 156; *Davy*, 156
Panic in the Year Zero, 117
Peace of the World, The (Wells), 72
Pedrotti, Louis, 9
Peled, Abraham, 197
Penley, Constance, 198
Perls, Frederick S., 167
Philmus, Robert M., 72; *H. G. Wells and Modern Science Fiction*, 72
Physicists, The (Dürrenmatt), 68
Piercy, Marge, 127, 131; *Woman on the Edge of Time*, 127, 131
Pinter, Harold, 95
"Place of the Gods, The" (Benét), 156
Planet of the Apes, The, 117
Poe, Edgar Allan, 140; "Colloquy of Monos and Una, The," 140
Poetic Journey over the Great, Wide World (Senkovsky), 49
Political Unconscious, The (Jameson), 174
Postman, The (Brin), 167
Pournelle, Jerry, 2, 55; *Lucifer's Hammer*, 55; *There Will Be War*, 2
"Power Planet, The" (Leinster), 156
Princess of Mars, A (Burroughs), 18
Pulling Through (Ing), 156

Pushkin, Aleksandr, 49
Pynchon, Thomas, 140; *Gravity's Rainbow*, 140

Quest (A Long Ray's Journey into Night) (Sciuli, Arvo & White), 200

Rabkin, Eric, 4, 129
Ralph 124C 41+: A Romance of the Year 2660 (Gernsback), 40
Randolph, John F., 167
Rapaport, Herman, 205
Rasta and Resistance (H. Campbell), 186
Ravage (Barjavel), 156
Red Badge of Courage, The (Crane), 13
Reformation of War, The (Fuller), 28
"Remaking of Zero, The" (Wolfe), 128 (n. 6)
Rembrandt, 111; *Three Crosses, The*, 111
Rendezvous in Montreal (D. & N. Thalmann), 202
Residents, the, 205; *Earth versus the Flying Saucers*, 205
Restif de la Bretonne, 105, 106, 108, 109; *La Découverte australe par un Homme-volant ou le Dédale français: nouvelle très-philosophique*, 105, 106
Return of the Dragon, 177, 180, 184, 185
"Revolution" (Beatles), 125
Richardson, Samuel, 139
Riddle of the Sands, The (Childer), 72
Riddley Walker (Hoban), 117
Roadside Picnic (A. & B. Strugatsky), 56
Road Warrior (G. Miller), 114–17, 120, 122, 128
RoboCop (Verhoeven), 114, 124
Rocky IV, 172, 183–85

Roshwald, Mordecai, 156; *Level 7*, 156
Rostand, Edmond, 55; *Cyrano de Bergerac*, 55
Rucker, Rudy, 200, 206
Ruff, Howard, 137
Russ, Joanna, 84, 86, 127, 131, 167; *Female Man*, 84, 86, 90, 127, 131; "When It Changed," 167
Russell, Eric Frank, 35, 98, 117; "And Then There Were None," 35

"S.S., The" (Shiel), 62
St. Clair, David, 129; *Motorization of American Cities, The*, 129 (n. 9)
St. Clair, Margaret, 157, 165; "Hole in the Moon, The," 157
Sakharov, Andrei, 15
Sanity and Survival in the Nuclear Age (Frank), 153
Sargent, Pamela, 82, 157; *Shore of Women, The*, 82, 83, 157
Savannah Electric, 196, 198
Scarface (DePalma), 182
Scarface (Hawks), 182
Schachner, Nat, 156; "World Gone Mad, The," 155
Schell, Jonathan, 156; *Fate of the Earth, The*, 156
Schismatrix (Sterling), 23
Schrieffer, Robert, 199
Schwarzenegger, Arnold, 120
Scientific Journey to Bear Island, The (Senkovsky), 49, 51
Scott, Ridley, 3; *Alien*, 3; *Blade Runner*, 195, 200
"Screwfly Solution, The" (Sheldon), 169 (n. 19)
Second Invasion of the Martians (A. & B. Strugatsky), 56
"Second Variety" (Dick), 21
Selassie, Haile, 180
Senkovsky, Osip, 6, 49–51, 53–56; "Animal Origin of Sea Sand, The,"

51; *Arithmetic*, 51; "Electrical Sounds," 51; *Fantastic Journeys of Baron Brambeus, The*, 6, 49, 51, 54; "General Deductions on the Essence of Galvanic Currents, of Electrical and Chemical Affinities, Crystallization, Light, Heat, Etc.," 51; "Latest Discoveries of Faraday, The," 51; *Library for Reading, The*, 50, 51; "Meteorites and the Earth's Internal Fire," 51; *Mikeria, the Nile Lily*, 51; *Poetic Journey over the Great, Wide World*, 49; *Scientific Journey to Bear Island, The*, 49, 51; *Sentimental Journey to Mount Etna*, 49, 51, 54, 55; "Theory of the Natural Sciences," 51
Serpent and the Rainbow, The (Craven) 175
Sexy Robot (Abel), 201
Shafer, Robert, 156, 157; *Conquered Place, The*, 156, 157
Shakespeare, William, 171; *Tempest*, 171
Shape of Things to Come, The (Wells), 70, 73–77
Shaw, G. B., 70
Shcherbatov, Mikhail, 55
Sheldon, Alice, 86, 87, 89, 90, 165, 169; "Last Flight of Dr. Ain, The," 169 (n. 19); "Screwfly Solution, The," 169 (n. 19); "Women Men Don't See," 86
Shelley, Mary, 140; *Frankenstein*, 3; *Last Man, The*, 140
Shelvocke, George, 107; *Voyage around the World*, 107
Shiel, M. P., 62; "S.S., The," 62
Shining, The (King), 150
Shirley, John, 194, 195; *Black Glass*, 195; *Macrochip*, 195
Shore of Women, The (Sargent), 82, 83, 157
Siege of Portsmouth (Le Queux), 65

"Sinners in the Hands of an Angry God" (Edwards), 147
Sleeper Awakes, The (Wells), 75
Slonczewski, Joan, 6, 83, 84, 167; *Door into Ocean, A*, 6, 82–84, 167
Slusser, George, 57
Smirdin, Alexandr, 50; *The Library for Reading*, 50, 51
Smith, E. E., 4
Smith, George O., 41
Smokey and the Bandit, 115
Snail on a Slope (A. & B. Strugatsky), 56
Sobchack, Vivian, 128, 195, 204
Soddy, Frederick, 76
Solaris (Lem), 56
Sollogub, Vladimir, 55
"Solution Unsatisfactory" (Heinlein), 40, 41
Song of Roland, The, 2
Sontag, Susan, 67, 129; "Imagination of Disaster," 129 (n. 8)
Spielberg, Steven, 130; *Duel*, 130
Spinrad, Norman, 44, 45; *Bug Jack Barron*, 44, 45
Spohr, Carl, 155; "Final War, The," 155
Stanton, Elizabeth Cady, 84
Stapledon, Olaf, 1, 2, 18; *Star Maker*, 1, 18
Star Beast, The, 191
Star Maker (Stapledon), 1, 18
Starship Troopers (Heinlein), 2, 7, 19
Startide Rising (Brin), 18
"Star Trek," 115, 128
Star Wars, 2, 26, 30, 115, 130
Steevens, G. W., 63; *With the Conquering Turk*, 63
Stein, Gertrude, 134, 138; *Making of Americans, The*, 134
Sterling, Bruce, 23; *Schismatrix*, 23
Stewart, Garrett, 203
Stockton, Frank, 42; "Lady or the Tiger, The," 42

Stranger in a Strange Land (Heinlein), 133
Stratychuck, Perry Mark, 198
Strieber, Whitley, 155; *Warday*, 155
Strugatsky, Arkady, and Boris Strugatsky, 56; *Hard to Be a God*, 56; *Monday Begins on Saturday*, 56; *Roadside Picnic*, 56; *Second Invasion of the Martians*, 56; *Snail on a Slope*, 56
Stryker, 117
Sturgeon, Theodore, 155; "Thunder and Roses," 155
Suvin, Darko, 72, 136, 187, 191; *H. G. Wells and Modern Science Fiction*, 72
Swift, Jonathan, 55; *Gulliver's Travels*, 55

Taylor, A. J. P., 73
Tears of the White Man: Compassion as Contempt, The (Bruckner), 170
Tempest, The (Shakespeare), 171
Terminator, The (Cameron), 8, 114, 120, 122–24, 126, 196
Thalmann, Daniel, and Nadia Thalmann, 202; *Rendezvous in Montreal*, 202
"Theory of the Natural Sciences" (Senkovsky), 51
There Will Be War (Pournelle), 2
Things to Come (Wells), 70, 73–77
"Third World" (De Palma), 182
Thoreau, Henry David, 84
Three Crosses, The (Rembrandt), 111
"Thunder and Roses" (Sturgeon), 155
THX 1138 (Lucas), 196
Time Machine, The (Wells), 1, 117, 136, 140
Time Out of Joint (Dick), 123
Time Traveller, The (Mackenzie & Mackenzie), 71
Tiptree, James, Jr. *See* Sheldon, Alice

To Live and Die in LA (Friedkin), 115
Tolstoy, Aleksey, 56; *Aelita*, 56
Tolstoy, Leo, 58; *War and Peace*, 56
Tomorrow (Wylie), 156, 157
Tono-Bungay (Wells), 73
Total Recall (Verhoeven), 127 (n. 1)
"Toward a Phenomenology of the Virtual" (Kerman), 206 (n. 18)
Triton (Delany), 136
Tron, 195, 197
Turner, Frederick Jackson, 22
Turner, Tina, 126
Twain, Mark, 16, 17; *Connecticut Yankee in King Arthur's Court, A*, 16
20,000 Leagues Under the Sea (Verne), 17
2001: A Space Odyssey (Clarke; Kubrick) 115, 133, 196, 198, 199
2010 (Clarke), 199
Tzu, Sun, 27

Ultimate Warrior, The, 117, 130
Underground Man (de Tarde), 67

Vance, Jack, 117; *Dying Earth*, 117
Vandenberg (Lange), 156
Van Eyck, Hubert, and Jan Van Eyck, 111; *Calvary and Last Judgement Diptych*, 111
van Vogt, A. E., 42
Varley, John, 22; *Millennium*, 22
Vassiltchikov, Marie, 78; *Berlin Diaries, 1940-1945*, 78
Verhoeven, Paul, 114, 128; *Basic Instinct*, 128; *RoboCop*, 114, 124; *Total Recall*, 127 (n. 1)
Verne, Jules, 55, 191; *Journey to the Center of the Earth*, 55; *20,000 Leagues under the Sea*, 17
Versins, Pierre, 3
Videodrome (Cronenberg), 195

Violet Flame (Jane), 64
Voltaire, 55; *Micromégas*, 55
von Clausewitz, Carl, 15, 32
Voyage around the World (Shelvocke), 107

Wagar, W. Warren, 62, 70, 71; *City of Man, The*, 70; *H. G. Wells: Journalism and Prophecy*, 71; *H. G. Wells and the World State*, 70
Walker, J. Bernard, 65; *America Fallen*, 65
Walk to the End of the World (Charnas), 157
Wanderground, The (Gearhart), 131 (n. 16)
War and Peace (Tolstoy), 56
War and the Future (Wells), 72
Warday (Kunetka & Strieber), 155
War Game, The (Watkins), 117, 121
War Games, 196, 198
War in the Air, The (Wells), 72, 73, 76, 77
War in the Air and Other War Forebodings, The (Wells), 72
War of the Worlds, The (Wells), 1, 17, 66, 72, 75
War That Will End War, The (Wells), 72
War with the Newts, The (Capek), 56
War Year (Haldeman), 102
Washington and the Hope of Peace (Wells), 72
Watkins, Peter, 121; *The War Game*, 121
We (Zamiatin), 17, 56
Weaver, Sigourney, 126
Wells, H. G., 1, 3, 6, 17, 55, 70-73, 77, 117, 131, 136, 140, 141, 155; *Anticipations*, 75; *Autocracy of Mr. Parham: His Remarkable Adventures in the Changing World*,

The, 76; *Brothers, The*, 77; *Common Sense of World Peace, The*, 72; "Dream of Armageddon, A," 75; *Experiment in Autobiography*, 71; *Floor Games*, 72; *Green Pastures*, 74; *H. G. Wells in Love*, 71; *Holy Terror, The*, 77; *In the Days of the Comet*, 6, 55, 74, 75; *Invisible Man, The*, 3; *Island of Dr. Moreau, The*, 71; *Is War Now Impossible?*, 72; "Land Ironclads, The," 75; *Little Wars*, 72, 74; *New Machiavelli, The*, 75; *Outline of History, The*, 70; *Peace of the World, The*, 72; *Shape of Things to Come, The*, 70, 73–77; *Sleeper Awakes, The*, 75; *Time Machine, The*, 1, 117, 136, 140; *Tono-Bungay*, 73; *War and the Future*, 72; *War in the Air, The*, 72, 73, 76, 77; *War in the Air and Other War Forebodings, The*, 72; *War of the Worlds, The*, 1, 17, 66, 72, 75; *War That Will End War, The*, 72; *Washington and the Hope of Peace*, 72; *What Is Coming? A Forecast of Things after the War*, 72; *When the Sleeper Wakes*, 75; *World Set Free, The*, 73, 74, 76

West, Anthony, 71; *H. G. Wells: Aspects of a Life*, 71

West, Nathanael, 140; *Day of the Locust, The*, 140

West, Rebecca, 71

Westworld, 130, 196

What Is Coming? A Forecast of Things after the War (Wells), 72

"When It Changed," 167

When the Sleeper Wakes (Wells), 75

Where Late the Sweet Birds Sang (Wilhelm), 157, 167

Wilhelm, Kate, 157; *Where Late the Sweet Birds Sang*, 157, 167

Wingrove, David, 128

With the Conquering Turk (Steevens), 63

Wolfe, Gary, 129; "Remaking of Zero, The," 128 (n. 6)

Woman on the Edge of Time (Piercy), 127, 131

"Women Men Don't See" (Sheldon), 86

Woolf, Virginia, 71

Works, The, 201

"World Gone Mad, The" (Schachner), 155

Worlds and Worlds Apart (Haldeman), 102

World Set Free, The (Wells), 73, 74, 76

Wylie, Philip, 156; *Tomorrow*, 156, 157

Year 4338 A.D., The (Odoevsky), 56

Yojimbo (Kurosawa), 130

Zamiatin, Yevgeny, 17, 56; *We*, 17, 56